RURAL PLANNING PROBLEMS

edited by
GORDON E.CHERRY

Contributors
Gordon E. Cherry
Michael C. Dunn
Andrew W. Gilg
Ian Martin
David G. Robinson
Alan W. Rogers
Judy White

BARNES & NOBLE

BOOKS

10 East 53d St., New York 10022
(a division of Harper & Row Publishers, Inc.)

Acknowledgements

The publishers thank Jim Doveton, John Foster and Cliff Tandy for lending their photographs for the cover; and Jim Doveton and Ted Hillman for their photographs for the text.

First published by
Leonard Hill
a division of International Textbook Company Limited
450 Edgware Road, London W2 1EG
a member of the Blackie Group

© International Textbook Company Limited 1976

First published 1976

Published in the U.S.A. 1977 by
HARPER & ROW PUBLISHERS, INC.
BARNES & NOBLE IMPORT DIVISION

ISBN 0 06 491115 2

Library of Congress Catalog Number
76 19861

Printed in Great Britain

CONTENTS

BIOGRAPHICAL NOTES

GORDON E. CHERRY is Professor of Urban and Regional Planning at the Centre for Urban and Regional Studies (where he is Deputy Director) at the University of Birmingham. He is a London geographer, a professional town planner and chartered surveyor. Before joining Birmingham in 1968 his career was with local planning authorities, and latterly he was Research Officer at Newcastle upon Tyne. His publications include *Town Planning in its Social Context*, 1970, *Social Research Techniques for Planners*, 1970 (with T.L. Burton), *Urban Change and Planning*, 1972, *The Evolution of British Town Planning*, 1974, *Urban Planning Problems* (ed.), 1974, and *National Parks and Recreation in the Countryside*, 1975. He has been engaged in a number of planning studies concerned with social problems and is especially interested in aspects of planning history. He is a member of the Council of the Royal Town Planning Institute.

MICHAEL C. DUNN has a degree in geography from the University of Birmingham. He is a research fellow at the Centre for Urban and Regional Studies, University of Birmingham, and has been associated with research into various aspects of rural planning, including countryside recreation, the social impact of Green Belt policy, and practical application of landscape evaluation techniques. Currently he is engaged on research (with Alan Rogers and Marilyn Rawson, of the Countryside Planning Unit at Wye College) on housing and population movement in English rural areas, a major joint study funded by the Social Science Research Council. His publications include a C.U.R.S. Occasional Paper, *Countryside Recreation Planning: Problems and Prospects in the West Midlands* (with Judy White).

ANDREW W. GILG, a geographer, graduated from Edinburgh University in 1969, when he was awarded the Silver Medal of the Royal Scottish Geographical Society. Between 1969 and 1970 he was employed in the Ministry of Housing and Local Government's Regional Planning Office in Bristol as a Research Officer, working on the economic, social and physical aspects of the South West Economic Planning Region. Since 1970 he has been a Lecturer in Geography at the University of Exeter. His main research interests lie in the field of countryside planning, particularly in the areas of landscape evaluation and village planning. With Dr. Mark Blacksell of the same Department, he has also been researching into aspects of development control. Andrew Gilg has published a number of articles and commentaries in the geography and planning fields. His book *Countryside Planning* will be published during the winter of 1976-77.

IAN MARTIN took a degree in Social Anthropology at L.S.E. He worked abroad, in Sweden and in British Antarctica, before joining Derbyshire as a Planning Assistant in 1963. After obtaining a Diploma in Town Planning, he worked for Liverpool C.B. on policy and research into social planning. Later, he moved to Denbighshire, now Clwyd, where he is Assistant County Planning Officer (Research). He has worked for the Royal Town Planning Institute Study Groups on geography and on sociology as Contributory disciplines in planning and was a member of the R.T.P.I./ Association of Community Workers Joint Working Party on Planning and Community Work. He has published several articles on social planning and on tourism.

DAVID G. ROBINSON is Professor of Regional Planning and Director of Courses in the Department of Town and Country Planning at the University of Manchester. He is a professional planner and before joining the University his career was with the former Lancashire and West Riding of Yorkshire county planning authorities. He was a contributor to J. Ashton and W.H. Long (Eds.): *The Remoter Rural Areas of Britain,* Oliver & Boyd, 1972, and is joint author of publications arising from Departmental research projects, notably *Regional Shopping Centres*, Department of Town and Country Planning, University of Manchester, 1964, and *Landscape Evaluation*, Centre for Urban and Regional Research, University of Manchester, 1976. Particularly interested in rural planning, he has been leader of the Royal Town Planning Institute's Planning Policy Group on Rural and Resource Planning and has represented planning interests on the Natural Environment Research Council's Land Use and Terrestrial Life Sciences Grants Committees.

ALAN W. ROGERS is a Lecturer in Environmental Studies at Wye College (University of London), where he works in the Countryside Planning Unit. A geographer from the University of Oxford, his main research interests have concerned the structure of rural settlements, second homes and, latterly, the problems of housing in rural areas. He is the author of *The Urban Countryside* (with Robin H. Best), *Second Homes in England and Wales* (with G.P. Wibberley and C.L. Bielckus) and the editor of *Agricultural Resources* (with Angela Edwards) and has written articles on various problems of land use and rural planning. He is currently engaged on a study of housing and population movement in English rural areas with Michael Dunn at the Centre for Urban and Regional Studies.

JUDY WHITE graduated in Geography at Birmingham University in 1967. This was followed by work as a Research Officer at the National Parks Commission/Countryside Commission, after which she read for a Ph.D. in Recreational Planning at Cambridge University. In 1971-72, she worked for the Ironbridge Gorge Museum Trust before joining the Centre for Urban and Regional Studies at Birmingham as a Senior Research Associate, now Research Fellow. She has been engaged at the Centre in research into countryside recreation planning in the West Midlands and is currently assessing for the Social Science Research Council the problems of priorities in recreation research and its organization. Her publications include a C.U.R.S. Occasional Paper, *Planning: Problems and Prospects in the West Midlands* (with Michael Dunn).

B

Introduction

Gordon E. Cherry

For many years British town planning has not regarded rural problems with an adequate perspective. Long-standing policies have seemed sufficient: the twin objectives of urban containment and countryside protection have been generally well received; moreover, where recreation facilities for the urbanite have been required, then the provisions of the National Parks and Access to Countryside Act, 1949, and its successor the Countryside Act, 1968 (for Scotland, 1967) have seemed reasonable. But these wide policies in their application run hard up against some difficult questions. It is therefore timely to consider the range and nature of rural planning problems today, and how far present day policies are adequate to deal with them.

The fact is that (and there are obvious reasons for this) British town planning throughout the post-war period has concentrated on *urban* questions. Indeed, much of our general thinking has been conditioned by this urban framework. The result has been that urban attitudes, urban approaches to problems and even urban policies have all been at the root of our consideration of rural problems. For too long we have lacked a specifically rural viewpoint and a rural understanding; coherent rural policies have therefore been slow to emerge. In the meantime, sharp rural planning problems have not received the attention they deserve: particularly exposure to conflict situations in which the long-term rural dweller is frequently disadvantaged. The insistent problems of poor housing, lack of regular employment, and limited access to choice and opportunity are not confined to settings of urban deprivation, they have their rural dimension too. *Rural Planning Problems* is a collection of specially commissioned essays which, in attempting to redress this imbalance in town planning attention, comprehensively reviews the range of contemporary problems and their interrelationships.

We ought not to find it necessary to begin with definitions, although the terms 'urban' and 'rural' are far from precise. On the one hand, we can consider economic criteria and think of rural areas as those where agriculture and forestry are the dominant forms of production. Rather more narrowly we might focus on the truly rural areas, and see those in which the village as a distinctive settlement unit is still paramount, with its old physical fabric; but this definition would leave a blurred zone of transition between urban and rural, and this we would have to identify as the urban fringe where suburbanized village processes have taken place. Alternatively, there might be a social definition if we were able to recognize and delineate areas characterized by a 'rural way of life', as distinct from an urban one, but the problems of definition seem insurmountable. Factually, we might simply rely on statistics of land use. In broad terms, 81.5% of the total land area of the U.K. was given over to agriculture in 1965; 7.5% to forestry and 8.5% to urban land, leaving 2.5% unaccounted for ([1]). It is the area covered by the nine-tenths or so of Britain's non-urban land surface with which this book is concerned.

The countryside has a popular image of unchanging tranquility. This is almost part of our difficulty, because we have to learn to appreciate that the countryside is in fact changing rapidly; the myths, impressions and beliefs which have been transmitted to our present generation have now to be systematically explored by careful study in order to expose a contemporary reality. As Anthony Russell has written: "Given only half a chance the Englishman retreats to the refuge of the countryside and the greenwood. The most haunting symbolic figure in our literature is that fusion of Robin Hood and the Green Man, who is part tree, part of the ancient magic, and yet demands justice of the outside civic world" ([2]). We cling to our myths of the unchanging village, its old squirearchy and our nostalgic, romantic regard for a country way of life. We forget that the housing conditions of the villages were deplorable, that the social structures were oppressive and that agricultural labour was arduous, ill-paid and without security. But none the less it is fair to

2

remark that, even so, for many the countryside has an undoubted attraction. We see in cities commercial offices, factories and teeming populations in anonymous, crowded conditions; in the countryside we have space and see communities where the individual is more readily recognized, and where the means of production are themselves not unattractive—crops, animals and woods. Dr. Johnson remarked that heaven would contain the amenities of the town and the pleasures of the country. Whatever the pleasures were then held to be, we now have to acknowledge that substantial changes have since taken place, both long term structural ones concerned with agriculture and rural society, and shorter, post-war trends which we are just beginning to chart; these changes we need to build into our understanding of the situation to which present day planning has to respond.

Agriculture, for example, now employs only a small proportion of the working population. Not that it ever has been very large over the last century. Even by 1801 agricultural workers were in a minority in this country, and agriculture's share of the work force has fallen from an estimated 20% of the employed population in 1851 to less than 4% today ([3]). Declining numbers (with increased *per capita* production) have been accompanied by a displacement of agricultural activities through other competition: recreation, urban expansion and afforestation ([4]). Losses to urban land have been severe. Conversion to urban use was particularly striking between the two World Wars, and in the 1930s more than 24,000 ha were transferred annually in England and Wales. In the period 1945-65 the average annual rate fell to more than 15,000 ha, though there were yearly variations between 12-18,000 ha, and of course there were large regional differences to record. ([5])

Other changes in the rural scene may be briefly touched upon. Rural areas have been seen largely as locations of primary production; agricultural output remains high but the value of this production has dropped relatively as a share of the gross national product. Meanwhile, food processing and marketing have become increasingly industrialized, and what was a largely rural function, giving rural employment opportunities, has been transferred to urban locations. Today, only very small proportions of village populations in lowland areas will be in any way connected with the land: perhaps 10-20% in any rural area of the Midlands and seldom above 30% in remote East Anglian villages.

A growing number of related social changes suggests how different from the past the present situation really is. While employment needs to continue to be met in the town rather than the country, with the consequence of long-continued exodus of population from rural to urban areas, certain villages now positively attract some city dwellers. These are the commuter settlements in the typical urban fringe situation and the retirement villages in areas of medium to high landscape value. In both cases, conflict over a common resource, housing, is strongly in evidence, particularly where nationalist sentiments are aroused. Further tension stems from the growing urban demand for countryside recreation, and classic polorization of interests occurs. Furthermore, there are differences of view about the balance between economic and environmental factors: how far is economic exploitation of resources legitimate against the conflicting values of environmental conservation? This question itself might be overlain by distinctly different urban/rural attitudes.

All this begins to suggest that the rural planning problem is both broader and rather different from earlier town planning concepts. Rural planning is not just a question of protecting the countryside in visual and developmental terms or of providing facilities for outdoor recreation (although both these aims are of great importance). It is now much more a question of recognizing emergent areas of conflict in values and of taking action to reconcile or otherwise meet that conflict: conflict of urban interests against rural, of one power group against another, of one sectional interest against another, of one value system against another. We are only just beginning to appreciate this new framework for rural planning. Certainly there are singularly few reviews or statements of countryside problems which have much to say about this wider setting; instead they have tended to select and be concerned with particular issues in a rather fragmented way. Compared with urban studies there is little by way of any conceptual framework in which we can place and relate the forces of development and change. The predecessor to this book, *Urban Planning Problems* (1974), had many more targets to aim at.

On the face of it, the post war period began well enough with the Scott Report on Land Utilisation in Rural Areas (1942) and C. S. Orwin's classic review *Country Planning* (1944). But there followed 20 years or more when the broad canvas was forgotten and particular themes held sway. T. Sharp's *The Anatomy of the Village* (1946) was a physical design study which carried little momentum. H. E. Bracey's *Social Provision in Rural Wiltshire* (1952) failed to attract much comparative work of a similar nature. On the other hand, studies of rural depopulation attracted a number of geographers and economic historians. We had from J. Saville in 1957 *Rural Depopulation in England and Wales 1851-1951*, and much later J. W. House's *Rural North East England 1951-61* (1965) was a contemporary study of migration.

Perhaps the most fruitful area turned out to be the sociological investigation of village communities and a clutch appeared between 1954 and 1964, including *Gosforth: the Sociology of an English village* (W.M. Williams, 1954), *Westrigg: the Sociology of a Cheviot Parish* (J. Littlejohn, 1963), *A West Country Village: Ashworthy* (W. M. Williams, 1963), and *Commuters' Village* (Ruth Crichton, 1964). A rather greater emphasis on process of change and conflicts between sectional interests began with R. E. Pahl (*Urbs in Rure: the Metropolitan Fringe in Hertfordshire*, 1965). This was continued by Elizabeth Radford (*The New Villagers: Urban Pressure on Rural Areas in Worcestershire*, 1970) and P. Ambrose in his study of the Sussex village of Ringmer (*The Quiet Revolution*, 1974). There have recently been attempts to bring at least the social aspects of rural planning together, and H. E. Bracey in *People and the Countryside* (1970) offered a broad review. Additionally, two planners, the first for a quarter of a century made contributions: R. J. Green (*Country Planning: the Future of Rural Regions*, 1971) and A. Thorburn (*Planning Villages*, 1971).

Meanwhile, land use aspects emerged as a profitable field of study. *The Changing Use of Land in Britain* (R. H. Best and J. T. Coppock, 1962) was highly relevant to the strong debate at that time about the loss of farmland to urban development and followed on work by G. P. Wibberley (*Agriculture and Urban Growth*, 1959). The recreation scene was explored from the late 1960s onwards largely by geographers, such as J. A. Patmore (*Land and Leisure*, 1970), J. T. Coppock and B. S. Duffield (*Recreation in the Countryside*, 1975) and G. E. Cherry (*National Parks and Recreation in the Countryside*, 1975). In recent years the wider environmental aspects of the countryside have been stressed and at least two popular publications have captured this concern: Robert Arvill's *Man and Environment* (1970) and Nan Fairbrother's *New Lives, New Landscapes* (1970). The technical aspects of conservation are reviewed in *Conservation in Practice* (A. Warren and F. B. Goldsmith, 1974).

This is a highly abbreviated selection of titles, but the total volume is limited and compared with other aspects of planning there have been few developments of depth and lasting significance. On the other hand, there is no denying the general interest that rural themes often engender. For example, 1965 was the Golden Jubilee Year of the Women's Institutes and in that year they were invited to make scrapbooks as records of village life. Paul Jennings in *The Living Village* (1968) brought these records together as a portrait of contemporary village life; subsequently, Ronald Blythe's *Akenfield: Portrait of an English Village* (1969) has been immensely popular. This general interest is perhaps confirmed by a regular output of topographical, 'country life'–type publications. It is against this background that the professional planner and others from a variety of disciplines explore again, for the first time for 30 years, the totality of rural problems and speculate about what planning and management of community affairs can achieve in relation to contemporary questions.

The performance of planning is coming under a new scrutiny in all its fields of operation. Its policies are being questioned against its objectives, implicit and explicit. As far as rural planning is concerned it will be argued in this book that this review is timely and relevant. The term 'town and country planning' was first used in British legislation in the Act of 1932, but the countryside occupies a much earlier place in British planning. Indeed, the diagnosis of, and prescription for, the problems of rural areas entered into Ebenezer Howard's *Garden Cities of Tomorrow* (1902) and its forerunner of 1899, although to be true the examination was largely of urban ills. His proposal, the marriage of town and country life, was one "in which all the advantages of the most energetic and active town life, with all the beauty and delight of the country may be secured in perfect combination". His Garden City was to be designed to incorporate the attractions of the countryside: "fresh air, sunlight, breathing room and playing room" ([6]). With hindsight, we can appreciate today that this was a planning solution which was a form of urban exploitation of the countryside. The insistent rural problems of that time remained: conditions of labour, housing conditions, low wages, irregular employment and lack of security were scarcely resolved.

The rural condition was analyzed again in planning terms in the inter-war period as a result of intense concern about the despoilation of the countryside by pressures of development. Patrick Abercrombie was an eager supporter of the Council for the Preservation (now Protection) of Rural England, formed in 1926, and it is interesting to reflect that his texbook of 1933, *Town and Country Planning*, had no less than one-third of its contents devoted to country planning and preservation. His analysis of the English countryside and his approach to country planning, admirably comprehensive, still makes good reading. Between the Wars, in the words of Raymond Williams, "a traditional and surviving rural England was scribbled over and almost hidden from sight by what is really a suburban and half-educated scrawl" ([7]). Classics such as *England and the Octopus* by Clough Williams-Ellis in 1928, "an angry book, written by an angry young man", as he wrote in a 1975 reprint, described the tentacular spread of urban building in the countryside; it was matched by Thomas Sharp's *Town and Countryside* (1932). They contributed to important developments in planning practice such as in the form of Green Belts, rural zoning and restriction of ribbon development.

Land use planning came into its own in the 1940s, and the Town and Country Planning Act, 1947, provided the basis for post-war land control. The preservation of the countryside and the careful location of rural recreation facilities were the keynotes. In spite of contravensions to the guiding principles of amenity (such as oil development at Milford Haven, nuclear power stations as at Traws-fynedd and an anti-ballistic missile early warning station at Fyling-dales), the consistently applied strategy has been successful accord-ing to the objectives generally specified. Towns have been contained (though with enlarged suburbs), sprawl on a North American scale has been avoided, and recreation facilities in the countryside have been provided. The great land use concern in the 1930s produced the Land Utilization Survey, organized by Dudley Stamp. While this work has continued since the war through the work of Alice Coleman, much of the anxiety about urban absorption has been eased by the planning control measures of the 1947 Act.

But we now appreciate that the social and economic problems of rural Britain cannot be tackled effectively by policies which are overtly land oriented. Neither can they be tackled speedily in a statutory framework which makes policy revision slow and uncer-tain. That was the basis of the Development Plan system, and it has been overtaken through the Town and Country Planning Act, 1968, by the Structure Plan, which at least offers the possibility of continuous monitoring and regular revision not only of land questions but also of their social and economic contexts. But even so, it is remarkable how much of the countryside is still excluded from the statutory planning process. On the old style Development Plans 'white land' formed those areas where existing uses were expected to remain for the most part undisturbed. Many forms of agricultural building are outside planning control, and so too are forestry and agricultural practices in terms of land use. Ploughing, afforestation and hedgerow removal have all been lively topics in their day where a call for measures of public control has been made. But many government or *ad hoc* agencies well outside town planning contribute massively to changes in the appearance of the countryside. The Ministry of Agriculture formerly with its own system of guaranteed farm prices, grants and advisory services, but now much more importantly the European Community with its influences on farm prices, are major determinants of the agricultural geography of Britain. The Forestry Commission has its afforestation programme. The Nature Conservancy has its Nature Reserves. The Water Authorities contribute to ecological planning, though with their schemes for reservoirs in particular confront planning authorities with enormous problems. The Countryside Commissions and the Tourist Boards are perhaps nearer the planning system because of their closer concern with development issues.

It is within this context of the present inadequate state of rural planning in Britain that the substantive Chapters of the book unfold. In Chapter 1 Michael Dunn analyzes recent changes in the demographic structure and distribution of rural population. In particular, he highlights two issues: first, the long-standing problem of population loss and settlement reorganization in remote rural regions and, second, the more recently experienced effects of metropolitan pressures on rural districts adjoining or near to large urban centres. For the planner these are two well known problems: the areas of sustained outward migration with consequent social dislocation and economic collapse, and the villages in the urban fringe where population displacement is taking place as city dwellers seek out rural housing stock and otherwise overwhelm an old village's physical fabric and community structure with new buildings and social groups of a different type.

Ian Martin considers the problems of rural communities in Chapter 2. He begins with a review of recent studies of village communities and usefully reminds us that while the village has often been depicted as a stable community, there has been greater physical mobility than is generally appreciated; migration flows both inward and outward have brought urban influences into village life. He goes on to consider rural social services: first, transport, followed by education, health and a variety of community services and facilities. As a town planner himself in a rural county he looks at the problems concerned with the actual operation of planning in relation to small settlements, expanding settlements and the setting of strategic guidelines. He writes strongly in favour of public participation in helping communities to articulate their needs, preferences and aspirations at the grass roots level.

Chapter 3 is concerned with rural housing. Alan Rogers begins with a historical review, showing the progression of legislation from that which dealt with public health and living conditions to that which has been the concern of town and country planning. Next he describes the nature of the present day housing stock. It is clear that major improvements in rural living have been made since World War II; rural areas are now better equipped from the point of view of household amenities than urban Britain. In turning to the problems of need for, and provision of, dwellings, Rogers deals with the present day problems faced by local authorities; how many houses to build or reserve land for, where and for whom, and in this section there are useful links with Dunn's Chapter on population movement flows.

In Chapter 4 Andrew Gilg discusses the problems of rural employment. Rural areas are faced with enormous difficulties, the principal problem being lack of opportunity for work; falls in population and economic decline are inescapably linked. Prospects for employment vary between different employment categories and Gilg looks at the job situation in agriculture, forestry, fishing, mining, manufacture, service industry, the distributive trades and tourism. He then turns to the evolution of rural employment planning from the 1930s to the present day. Three case studies, Mid-Wales, the Highlands and Islands Development Board, and the North Pennines Rural Development Board, allow him to show in detail how the problems of remote rural areas have been tackled in contrasting circumstances.

Chapter 5 deals with the traditional meat of countryside planning as far as the planner has so far been concerned. David Robinson looks at the changing rural landscape and how the planning control system is tackling the many new problems that are emerging. His central concern is that our approach must be in terms of conservation rather than preservation, and this leads him to focus on the question of landscape management. He rightly points out that we cannot rely on the old, visual appearances of our countryside being preserved through the maintenance of a soundly based agriculture, since traditional practices are changing substantially as a result of technology and other pressures. New approaches to countryside management are required in order to allow for the sensitive evolution of the rural landscape. Within this theme Robinson first reviews recent planning work in the field of landscape evaluation

9

and then looks at the performance of planning control in relation to various aspects of landscape change. Finally, he considers problems specifically concerned with the landscape of farming and forestry.

Judy White considers recreation and tourism in Chapter 6. By way of introduction she briefly reviews the emergent problems concerned with the growth of the use of the countryside for recreation purposes. She then turns to the legislative framework for the provision of recreation and leisure facilities, followed by an examination of the work of the agencies of provision, such as local authorities, and the *ad hoc* bodies. After considering the contribution to be made by new directions of research enquiry she concludes with some suggestions for the improvement of policy and the reconciliation of conflict of interest.

In Chapter 7 I attempt to draw the various strands together. I begin with a historical reminder of the place of the countryside in British planning by looking at the various phases of development which it has experienced over the last two centuries. This enables me to offer a conceptual framework for rural planning at the present day: we should see its problems as being concerned with the progressive substitution of a variety of dominant value systems over others. Planning is concerned with the adjudication of, and reconciliation between, conflict situations: they relate to land use, environmental and economic priorities, community values and competing sectional interest groups of many kinds. I then turn to the performance of rural statutory planning and highlight the main points made in earlier chapters: urban growth and aspects of land management, people's interest in the countryside and their activities, and services for the community. I conclude with some suggestions for the planning system and our present day policies.

Each Chapter is well referenced and has its own recommended reading list. It will be obvious from these sources that this book has a comprehensive framework and enlarges the vision of rural planning for the professional worker. Inter-linkages abound and individual Chapters inevitably reinforce each other. I naturally hope the book will make a useful contribution to the literature before the student of planning and related disciplines. Certainly it should not be regarded as a passing, fashionable view of rural problems, with its emphasis on social questions, but rather one which is comprehensive, of long standing, but which we for too long have ignored.

George Bourne, a pseudonym for George Sturt, wrote his highly readable and influential *Change in the Village* in 1912; it was reprinted on numerous occasions. It was a close scrutiny of a Surrey

Village, and it repays careful attention today. He recognized then that "the old life is being swiftly obliterated. The valley is passing out of the hands of its former inhabitants. They are being crowded into corners, and are becoming as aliens in their own house; they are receding before newcomers with new ideas, and, greatest change of all, they are yielding to the dominion of new ideas themselves". That was in the first Chapter, and he returned to the theme in the last. "I know that the landscape is not peopled by a comfortable folk, whose dear and intimate love of it gave a human interest to every feature of its beauty; I know that those who live there have in fact lost touch with its venerable meanings, while all their existence has turned sordid and anxious and worried; and knowing this I feel a forlorness in country places, as if all their best significance were gone. But, notwithstanding this, I would not go back. I would not lift a finger, or say a word, to restore the past time, for fear lest in doing so I might be retarding a movement which, when I can put this sentiments aside, looks like the prelude to a renaissance of the English country folk" [8].

These observations and sentiments 64 years or so ago have formed part of the agenda for rural planning throughout this century. *Rural Planning Problems* is a book which looks again at these issues, bringing together the questions of land, economic production and social relations.

References

1   EDWARDS, A.M., and WIBBERLEY, G.P., *An Agricultural Land Budget for Britain, 1965-2000*, Studies in Rural Land Use No. 10, Wye College, 1971.It is now possible to give figures for 1971. See BEST, R.H., 'The Changing Land-use Structure of Britain', *Town and County Planning*, 44, 3, March, 1976.
2   RUSSELL, A.J., *The Village in Myth and Reality*, Chester House Publications, 1975.
3   COPPOCK, J.T., *An Agricultural Geography of Great Britain*, Bell, 1971.
4   CHAMPION, A.G., 'Competition for Agricultural Land', in *Agricultural Resources, An Introduction to the Farming Industry of the U.K.*, Angela Edwards and Alan Rogers, (Eds.), Faber & Faber, 1974.
5   WHITBY, M.C., ROBINS, D.L.J., TANSEY, A.W., and WILLIS, K.G., *Rural Resource Development*, Methuen, 1974. (via Edwards and Wibberley).
6   HOWARD, E., *Garden Cities of Tomorrow*, 1902, Faber & Faber, 1946.
7   WILLIAMS, R., *The Country and the City*, Chatto and Windus, 1973.
8   BOURNE, G., *Change in the Village*, Duckworth, 1912.

CHAPTER ONE

Population Change and the Settlement Pattern

Michael C. Dunn

This Chapter is intended to provide an analysis of recent changes in the structure and distribution of the population of rural Britain, with particular emphasis given to the resultant problems of certain specific rural regions, and to the physical, social and economic manifestations of planning responses to such problems.

A summary of past changes in the structure and distribution of population in rural areas is followed by definition of rural population problems, and by detailed examination of two contrasting themes: population loss and settlement reorganization in the more remote rural areas, and the effects of metropolitan pressures in easily accessible rural districts. The discussion is concluded by a summary consideration of emergent rural population problems, and of policies designed to alleviate or eradicate such problems.

An Historical Perspective

The available evidence suggests that out-migration from the countryside during the first half of the nineteenth century was at least balanced by natural increase and limited in-migration, such that the overall rural population increased slowly during this period. The drift to the towns, prompted by the search for higher wages and increased welfare, became of greater significance after

1850, when the problems of labour-intensive enclosure and improvement of agricultural land widened into mechanization and rapidly decreasing demand for agricultural labour.

Ravenstein, writing in 1885, recognized the increasing displacement of population from rural areas to the economically attractive towns and cities, so that although he demonstrated that most population movement took place over short distances, he accepted that 'currents of migration' existed which channelled movement "in the direction of the great centres of commerce and industry which absorb the migrants" (1.1). Ravenstein also detailed the manner in which this process occurred: "The inhabitants of the country surrounding a town of rapid growth, flock into it; the gaps thus left in the rural population are filled up by migrants from more remote districts, until the attractive force of one of our rapidly growing cities makes its influence felt, step by step, to the most remote corner of the kingdom" (1.2). Whilst his 'laws' have in general been verified by more recent research—for example, the 'Mobility and the North' survey in 1967 found that over 40% of all moves took place within fifteen minutes walk of the previous residence (1.3)—this notion of 'migration by stages' has largely been discounted.

Saville suggests that this pattern of steady rural depopulation, largely prompted by contraction in demand for agricultural labour, remained stable until the 1920s, when it was changed by the combination of two factors, one gradual and the other dramatic (1.4). First, the suburbanization of the countryside around towns, originating in the late nineteenth century, but accelerating as a result of greater personal mobility after the first World War, resulted in a blurring of distinctions between town and country, largely due to the growth of an adventitious 'rural' population (itself leading to a concurrent reduction in the value of studies based upon the analysis of 'rural district' population statistics. Second, the economic crisis centred around 1929 transformed certain of the urban regions, which had hitherto consistently attracted in-migrants because of their greater employment opportunities, into depressed areas. The result of the operation of these factors was an apparent slowing of the rate of depopulation of rural areas in the twentieth century—with the proviso that the census returns mask the change in status of peri-urban rural districts, and thereby conceal very considerable population losses in remoter areas.

Certainly, as Saville confirms, the more rural and predominantly agricultural the area, the more likely was a decline in total population, to such an extent that "the proportions of the rural exodus and the absolute decline in many parish populations suggest that the question of the future viability of the smaller villages may be important" (1.5). Vince reached the same conclusion in suggesting that "unless new adventitious population is somehow attracted there seems to be a real danger of a vicious spiral of depopulation in many rural areas" (1.6).

More recently, out-migration from rural areas caused by lack of employment opportunities and so on has been more than balanced by in-migration, either by city-dwellers seeking the benefits of rural life or by urban overspill into peripheral areas designated as rural. The effect, between 1951 and 1961, was that the total population of rural districts in Britain increased from 8.42 million to 10.77 million. That this could occur during a period when many truly rural areas were experiencing severe losses of population illustrates the care required in interpreting census-derived estimates of population change, and to some extent explains the predilection of research workers for small-scale surveys based upon alternative sources of information.

It is not the intention here to describe exhaustively the merits and defects of the alternative population estimates, but it is necessary to consider them briefly before examining contemporary rural population problems.

Contemporary data: problems and possibilities

It is somewhat ironic that the apparently-sophisticated information collecting machine of the population census is of severely limited use in measuring anything other than the mere statistics of population loss and gain in rural areas (1.7), but the fact has to be faced that census data are of little analytical value, and even as population estimates are not ideal. Specific major limitations relate to the consequences of basing census spatial units on administrative areas, which lack three important properties—homogeneous size and composition, stability of boundaries, and comparability with social and economic divisions. Similarly, census data are second-hand, relate to the enumerated rather than the resident population (important where areas contain armed forces' establishments, hospitals and other large institutions subject to rapid and unpredictable change), are published only after a protracted interval, and omit certain basic items of information (1.8).

Nevertheless, a number of studies of rural population change have utilized census data, although such studies have largely been restricted to the description of net movement between relatively large administrative units. Certainly there has been no opportunity to meaningfully disaggregate the data in order to examine local population flows, or to examine change in specific critical sub-groups of the population. Even the inclusion of migration-specific questions in the census from 1961 onwards (on a 10% sample basis), which provided a new impetus to studies at a regional level (1.9), has provided very serious problems of interpretation for rural population studies, for two main reasons. First, bias inherent in the data, which results in the under-representation of very small and very large households, affects migration figures particularly seriously, since single-person households have, *ceteris paribus*, the highest propensity to move (1.10). Second, because the migration questions were asked of only a 10% sample, the data relating to rural areas of sparse population may be subject to considerable error.

The many problems associated with using census data to investigate rural population change may have prompted the comment that there is a "dearth of objective data available at present in Britain in the field of rural migration" (1.11). Whilst it is impracticable to dismiss the census entirely as a source of information, it is apparent that the aggregate data available in the census cannot allow more than broad generalizations of limited value to be made regarding changes in the structure of the population. Further, no information is available concerning the behavioural characteristics of migrants—attitudes, motivations and so on. It is therefore pertinent to consider alternative sources of information, which may well be of more limited scope and content, but which could prove capable of more flexible and ultimately more valuable application.

Three alternative sources immediately present themselves, each having been previously applied to the task: the Annual Mid-Year Population Estimates, derived by the Registrar-General, the electoral registers, and independent social surveys. It is tempting, on the evidence presented by Edwards (1.12), to dismiss the first of these possibilities out of hand on the grounds of sheer inaccuracy; Table 1.1 illustrates this point. The major problem is that of progressive cumulative error, most apparent where population change is considerable, which affects intercensal mid-year estimates. Again, the estimates are available only for relatively large administrative units, namely Districts (formerly Rural Districts). The result has been little

Table 1.1   Population Estimates for Rhondda M.B.

	Mid-year estimate	Total Change	Natural change	Migration balance
1960	105,360	—	—	—
1961	100,600	—4760	177	—4937 (census adjustment)
1962	100,390	—210	300	—510
1970	94,000	—300	—25	—275
1971	88,990	—5010	—12	—4998 (census adjustment)

Source: EDWARDS, J.A., 'Rural migration in England and Wales', *The Planner*, 59, 1973, pp. 450-453.

use of the estimates as a data source (1.13) and an acceptance of their limited value in this respect.

The electoral registers have been used in a number of studies, both as the raw material for estimates of population change and as a sampling frame for questionnaire surveys. The registers, compiled annually for parish units in rural areas, comprise a list of the names and addresses of persons qualified to vote; they have been found to achieve a high level of accuracy (1.14). The technique relies upon the comparison of the names contained in the registers at different dates, and the extraction of lists of those named only on the first register, and those named only on the second. Subject to a number of qualifications, the first such list will comprise out-migrants, the second in-migrants, and the difference between them will represent population change due to migration (total population change is, of course, the difference between the total numbers enumerated on the two registers). The qualifications mentioned are, however, numerous and surmountable only as a result of painstaking research. The first list extracted will contain the names of those deceased during the period studied, and those who have changed their name by marriage but remained within the parish. Analogous adjustments must be made to the second list (1.15). The elimination of these non-migrant elements is possible (in most cases) through documentary sources in the parish, or through interviews during fieldwork, but the major difficulty facing accurate use of the registers is the fact that only the population aged over 18 (over 21 until 1969) is included. The marked disparity in migration behaviour between young independent migrants and those aged over 21 underlines the significance of this problem.

Although the use of electoral registers requires careful and time-consuming research to overcome the deficiencies and restrictions of content mentioned, the registers remain probably the most accurate source of information on population change in rural localities, and their potential value is increased considerably by the fact that they can be used not only to estimate change numerically, but as the basis of a questionnaire survey in the same area. Relatively accurate base data can therefore be supplemented by information concerned with the determinants and characteristics of population change: migrant and non-migrant elements in rural areas can be isolated, and their attitudes, motivations and socio-economic characteristics compared. Inevitably, this type of research has yet to be widely applied, although sample studies have demonstrated its utility (1.16).

This review of sources of information for studies of rural population change has indicated a lack of readily-available detailed information, and has underlined the problems associated with each of the sources. Despite the inherent difficulties of using the electoral registers, it is argued that their potential for yielding data which can be further enhanced by local surveys is likely to provide the information with which to progress beyond head-counting and begin to understand the process of population change. In this respect the census and the mid-year estimates can provide little more than macro-scale background information, so that although this descriptive role is useful in explaining wider patterns of change and movement (as demonstrated later in this chapter), the emphasis must be upon a necessarily more fragmented explanatory approach.

Rural population problems: a synthesis

In attempting to summarize reasons for migration, Bracey notes that 'the availability or variety of employment' was usually the dominant factor, though many of the explanations given by migrants constituted 'social' reasons: better shopping facilities, a wider range of amenities, better transport, superior educational provision, and so on (1.17). Arguably this implied movement towards 'better facilities'—under which heading employment can perhaps be included—over-emphasizes the depopulation aspect of the changing rural population pattern, at the expense of due consideration of the commuter villages, retirement areas and the like, which comprise the other end of the spectrum. The three trends extracted from data covering rural North-East England (1.18) convey a more balanced impression of the situation:

(i)   stable population in the small market towns;

(ii)   rapid increase of population in rural areas in suburban locations;

(iii) a continuing drift of population from more isolated rural areas.

Even this recognition of the two essential mechanisms causing acute problems—metropolitan and other urban pressures, and the forces behind traditional depopulation—is still only a partial analysis, however, sacrificing accurate definition of the problem at a micro-spatial level for broad generalizations of limited applicability. The effects of the popularity of some areas for retirement, or of the spatial concentration of second home ownership and other manifestations of increasing leisure-consciousness, are to considerably distort the overall picture. Accepting this distortion, which is areally restricted by the location of certain atypical conditions (such as attractive landscape or proximity to the coast), it is proposed to concentrate upon an exposition of the characteristics of the two nationally significant tendencies of population in rural areas: rapid increase and consequent social transformation in urban-dominated areas, and continuing population losses, with an inevitable reorganization of the settlement pattern, in more isolated areas.

The traditional problem, and that which has attracted considerable attention and the majority of research, is that of rural depopulation in remoter areas, often dominated by traditional agricultural methods. The incidence of such depopulation is to some extent indicated by census returns, which stress the concentration of high rates of population loss in upland areas which are agriculturally poor and difficult of access—central Wales, parts of the Pennines, Highland Scotland, the Devon/Cornwall border, for example, all of which have consistently lost over 10% of their population in each intercensal period this century. Even when a small increase in population is indicated, however, this is usually attributable to natural increase, which masks a net migration loss.

It cannot be emphasized enough that in many areas, particularly those of marginal farming, the phenomenon is anything but new. Masterman's claim, made in 1909, that "rural England, beyond the radius of certain favoured neighbourhoods . . . is everywhere hastening to decay. No one stays there who can possibly find employment elsewhere" (1.19) may be an overstatement of the extent of the problem, but the examples cited later in this Chapter demonstrate that the problem is real, often acute, and, in the absence of effective rural planning policies, apparently intransigent.

This lack of a cohesive and developed framework for countryside planning is illustrated by the pragmatic response to continuing depopulation: an ill-concealed *laissez-faire* attitude implied by the reduction of service provision in rural areas and by reorganization of the settlement pattern, itself brought about by the concentration of investment in the rural infrastructure in a small number of 'key' settlements. Such an incremental, opportunistic approach to policy development has had little effect on the overall pattern of population losses.

Whilst the bulk of research energy has understandably been directed towards those marginal areas which are characterized by the classic symptoms of rural depopulation and the run-down of an ailing local economy, the seemingly prosperous areas, where local populations are subject to incoming pressures rather than outward attractions, are perhaps deserving of increased attention. The composition of such incoming pressures varies with local circumstances, but two broad complexes may be identified: first, in those areas where metropolitan pressures are strong, the social and economic impact of a significant commuting population is discernible; second, the combination of attractiveness for recreational use and for retired in-migrants in areas of high landscape value accessible to urban populations may produce a vocal and often powerful lobby which is concerned to protect its investment at the expense of less powerful groups in such areas.

The traditional chain reaction of population flows resulting from such urban incursions into rural communities involves the displacement of certain sectors of the established rural-based population and their replacement by (depending on the type of rural area) commuters, second home owners, middle-class retired people, and so on. The planning response has inevitably been one of inaction, with a consequent reliance on the free market system for housing, to the disadvantage of certain established groups in the countryside. Naturally the ramifications of this sequence of events vary from place to place, but their operation is most strikingly apparent in accessible areas of high landscape value, which have had an obvious appeal to an increasingly mobile middle class. Given the financial ability to establish themselves within rural communities, such groups effectively create disadvantage for certain elements of the rural population, namely those who do not possess the resources which are becoming increasingly necessary to sustain their rural existence, but equally do not have the ability to move out to possibly greater opportunities in urban areas. The problem facing young married couples seeking a home in a rural environment is an extreme example of the situation.

The spectrum of rural population change therefore includes both isolated areas of marginal farming which have been subject to continuing population losses for, in many cases, the whole of the twentieth century, and also rural areas assailed by intense and increasing pressure caused by decentralization of adjacent urban concentrations. The former problem may impose on the landscape a pattern of contracting villages and derelict property, channelled and directed by rationalization of service provision, whilst the environmental expression of urban pressures may be the spread of 'conurban' areas of the countryside where housing and socio-economic patterns closely compare with developments in towns (1.20), so that the prediction that in time rural settlements will be indistinguishable from their urban counterparts may yet be proved accurate (1.21). The pattern of problem and response in these two critical rural situations is now considered in turn.

Remoter areas: contracting population and settlement reorganization

The background of continuous and considerable losses of population in the remoter rural regions of Britain has already been summarized; it is necessary now to consider a number of illustrations of this theme in more detail, commencing with studies using census-derived estimates of population change, and continuing with smaller-scale but perhaps more accurate assessments using other data. The *reasons* for migration are then investigated as one point of entry into a discussion of the social, economic and physical *results* of sustained out-migration.

There can be few more obvious starting points for a discussion of the problems of remoter areas than the Highlands and Islands of Scotland, and in particular the Hebrides, which are unlikely to derive much benefit from increased tourism or—except in a few special cases—from North Sea Oil. As Table 1.2 indicates, the population of the Scottish Islands declined from 113,000 in 1951 to just over 93,000 in 1971, a loss of 17.6% in twenty years.

Although the rate of decline lessened in the second half of this period (and mid-year estimates suggest this trend has continued since 1971) this improvement in the situation was largely accounted

Table 1.2   Population Changes in the Scottish Islands, 1951-1971

Islands of:	1951	Change 51-61(%)	1961	Change 61-71(%)	1971
Argyll	8849	—13.5	7745	—3.4	7480
Bute	19283	—25.6	14357	—10.6	12842
Inverness	20429	—8.3	18736	—8.2	17209
Orkney	21255	—11.1	18888	—8.7	17254
Ross & Cromarty	23731	—7.5	22195	—6.6	20739
Zetland	19352	—7.2	17978	—2.3	17567
Total	112962	—11.6	99899	—6.8	93091

Source: CAIRD, J.B., 'Population Problems of the Islands of Scotland with Special Reference to the Uists', Paper presented to IBG Annual Conference, Aberdeen, 1972.

for by population stability in the burghs, and in rural areas depopulation continued. A number of factors might be considered to be contributory causes of this current loss of population, among them declining demand for agricultural labour, sheer isolation in the Outer Hebrides, the failure of attempts to introduce small-scale industrial enterprises, and lack of support for new fishing developments (1.22).

Although an increased commitment on the part of Central Government to development aimed at population retention in the Highlands and Islands has been apparent since the mid-1960s, symbolized by the creation of the Highlands and Islands Development Board, there is a clear indication that net out-migration remains typical, and, significantly, "the age structure of the population has continued to deteriorate" (1.23). This is, perhaps, only to be expected in an area of broken terrain and largely dispersed settlement, and some redistribution of the population and concentration of the settlement pattern may be necessary in order to provide sufficiently large and localized labour catchments for prospective industrial enterprises. But such policies of concentration of investment can needlessly accelerate the pattern of contraction of smaller settlements, already disadvantaged and losing population because of lack of educational facilities, absence of alternatives to agricultural employment (particularly for women), and isolation and lack of facilities in rural settlements other than designated service centres.

The process of depopulation is seen at its most dramatic in such circumstances, but the process is equally present, and the consequences equally apparent, in less remote areas which nevertheless suffer isolation, often from a regional centre with its concomitant social and economic attractions for young rural migrants. Jackson's study of the North Cotswolds (1.24) highlights this problem of severely disadvantaged areas in regions which are otherwise prosperous. Even within her study area the central depopulating zone characterized by high, rolling, sheep-farming country contrasted vividly with the fringe area which was increasingly attractive to commuters from Oxford, Cheltenham and even the West Midland conurbation. Within the central core, however, sustained and substantial population losses by out-migration were evident, and despite problems in interpreting the census data a disproportionate loss of the younger age groups was demonstrated.

Similar trends were apparent in a study of migration in Herefordshire, an area equally conscious of its fringe location in the West Midlands. Table 1.3 demonstrates the extent of and areal variation

Table 1.3 Population Change in Herefordshire Rural Districts

	1951	Change 51-61(%)	1961	Change 61-71(%)	1971	Change 51-71(%)
Bromyard	8903	—4.47	8505	0.68	8563	—3.82
Dore & Bredwardine	8760	—11.43	7759	—6.55	7251	—17.23
Hereford	17489	0.49	17575	9.52	19248	10.06
Kington	4949	—9.96	4456	—11.58	3940	—20.39
Ledbury	12174	—5.58	11495	—2.71	11184	—8.13
Leominster	10506	—8.60	9602	—3.01	9313	—11.36
Ross & Whitchurch	12013	—3.20	11628	—2.22	11370	—5.35
Weobley	6450	—12.62	5636	0.46	5662	—12.22
R.D. total	81244	—5.62	76676	—0.18	76536	—5.79
R.D.s excl. Hereford	63755	—7.30	59101	—3.07	57288	—10.14

Source: DUNN, M.C., 'Patterns of Population Movement in Herefordshire: Implications for Rural Planning', Paper presented to IBG Annual Conference, Birmingham, 1973.

in changes in population, and emphasizes the dichotomy between Hereford rural district, affected by cross-boundary expansion from Hereford city, where a single act of industrial plantation has stimulated a certain amount of regenerative growth, and the truly rural areas, characterized inevitably by consistent and considerable out-migration. The more isolated rural districts in western Herefordshire (Dore and Bredwardine, Kington, and Leominster and Wigmore) are subject to the highest rates of net out-migration (1.25). In fact the population of the truly rural areas of the county declined

23

from 63,750 to 57,300 between 1951 and 1971, as shown in the Table, and when the effect of natural increase is extracted, the estimated total net outward migration becomes 13,400, or about 21% of the 1951 population. It has been suggested that this represents the greatest loss of population by true rural depopulation in England during this period (1.26).

The census data also confirm that the effect of continued out-migration has been the generation of an ageing, male-dominated population, to some extent self-perpetuating as a consequence of the diminuition in the proportion of women of child-bearing age and the associated reduction in the fertility rate. But aggregate census data, as noted in a previous section, allow only broad generalizations to be made regarding structural changes in the population, and reduce consideration of explanations for change to broad-based deduction rather than interpretation of fact. The remedy is supplementation of census material with surveys based on other sources of information, and several cases in which this course of action has been followed are reported on below.

Perhaps the earliest use made of electoral registers as a source of information for rural population change was the study by Dickinson of changes in an area south of York, during the period 1931 to 1954 (1.27). His main objective was that of investigating the reliability of the registers and in particular to determine whether the 'non-migrant' element thrown up during comparison of registers could be taken as constant. He concluded that it could not, but was able to show the extent to which small changes in total population masked very large opposing population movements (thus verifying Ravenstein's law regarding counter-currents of migration, and also underlining one serious limitation of census data), and also to identify the mobile and static elements in the population. Jones, in a study of migration in central Wales (1.28), took the method a little further, and was able to explore the socio-economic and behavioural characteristics of migrants, by interviewing selected members of the communities involved.

Once again the starting point of the study was an attempt to test the validity of Ravenstein's laws of migration, but the methods employed and the treatment of the data allowed disaggregation in terms of age, distance moved, motivation and so on. Jones was able to indicate that out-migration was dominated by younger age-groups (38% were under 25, and a further 24% between 25 and 39), and that long-distance movement away from the study area was equally biased towards the young. The age distribution of in-migrants was significantly different, with a considerable influx of older migrants returning to the area which they had left when they were young, and a much higher proportion of in-migration was of local origin. The net result was a loss of younger people, undermining the 'demographic health' of the area. Motivation was orientated towards education or employment for the young, but with older migrants (46% of those aged 25 to 39, for example) was dominantly local and rural in character, encompassing movement for better housing and, amongst the farming community, from a marginal hill farm to a lowland, more remunerative and often larger farm.

Similar methods were used by Johnston in Nidderdale (1.29), again to examine the relationship between gross and net movement, and the size and composition of the mobile and static elements of the population. He demonstrated the fact that there was no relationship between gross and net population change, so that "the net figures produced by the census cannot be claimed as an accurate index of population change in the area". Residents were classified into three groups according to their length of stay in a specific district:

(i)   permanent residents: listed in the same register for all 11 years of the study period;

(ii) long-stay residents: listed for 4 to 10 years;

(iii) short-stay residents: listed for 3 years or less.

Long-stay residents accounted for 51% of the dale total, permanent residents 30%, and short-stay residents 19%, although it is significant that 51% of those resident in Nidderdale in 1951 had not migrated by 1961. The implication is, therefore, that there is a rapid turnover of the mobile element in the population, and this characteristic, taken together with the prevalence of short-distance migration, provides evidence for a remarkably intricate pattern of small-scale rural spatial interaction.

This impression of overwhelmingly local movement, forming complex and reciprocal flows between adjacent villages, is supported by evidence from field surveys in sixteen parishes in Herefordshire (undertaken in order to enable deeper analysis than that which is possible from the census data summarized above in Table 1.3). This local movement was usually related to housing opportunities, and a significant proportion of such migrants were aged over 45; this group contrasted strikingly with long-distance migration by younger people, usually for employment reasons. There was an overall loss of younger people, and the findings of the Northern Region survey (1.30) that inter-regional migration reaches a peak amongst those aged 20 to 29, and intra-regional migration is most common amongst those aged 30 to 39, were confirmed, except that local migration amongst older age groups and those younger migrants seeking larger or better accommodation (more completely represented than in surveys using administrative areas as the basic unit) modified these conclusions. Additionally, the tendency for the population to become male-dominated, chiefly as a result of lack of employment for women in a rural area and the net out-migration of women upon marriage, was demonstrated.

The inclusion of short-distance movement emphasizes the importance of house availability, and to some extent explains the surprisingly low proportion of migrants motivated by employment opportunities, compared, for example, with House, who found that 72% moved for reasons connected with employment (1.31). Motivations of the Herefordshire migrants are summarized in Table 1.4: net

Table 1.4   Primary reasons for migration in Herefordshire, 1966-1971

	Out-migrants	In-migrants
Employment	32.49	30.77
Housing	28.93	37.81
Marriage	14.22	3.85
Retirement	8.63	10.26
Movement to friends or relatives	11.68	12.82
Other	4.15	4.49

Note: figures are column percentages
Source: as for Table 1.3

outward migration resulting from marriage is re-emphasized, and the net gain of migrants triggered by housing opportunities is an expression of short-distance regrouping of the rural population for larger or better housing, or for council housing. The high percentage of moves attributable to employment reasons in House's sample may be partly due to his threefold division of motivation (the other categories were marriage, which accounted for 25% of moves, and education, 3%) and, perhaps more pertinently, the concentration on out-migration from a depressed area with notably few employment opportunities. Nevertheless, the significance of lack of variety of employment is emphasized, both in terms of continuing contraction in the agricultural labour force, and the dearth of female employment in the countryside.

Furthermore, even amongst *potential* migrants employment was the critical factor given by 36% as the reason they would move; although in percentage terms this was only half as important as for those who had moved, it was still more than twice as significant a causal mechanism as the next most important reasons: better shopping facilities (15%), better social amenities (14%), and improved transport and educational facilities (both 10%). It is also worth stressing the contraction in small rural manufacturing industries. Saville (1.32) gives the example of chair making in the Chiltern Hills, involving 160,000 workers scattered in villages in the 1880s, but concentrated in factories in High Wycombe by the early twentieth century. Equally, there are the difficulties of rural service facilities, afflicted by low turnover and productivity, and also by competition from urban outlets deriving economies of scale (1.33).

Although unemployment problems have been, and may well remain, the primary cause of out-migration in the remoter rural areas, the list of factors considered important by potential migrants from North-East England, summarized above, stresses a further basic factor in rural depopulation, namely the primitive level of social provision in isolated districts. Desire for better shopping and social facilities, improved transport services and so on is the direct and obvious consequence of planned redistribution of facilities in rural areas; the present distribution of services and utilities in many areas is now heavily weighted in favour of market towns and selected larger villages, and the historic exceptions—especially public transport and primary education—have been subject to drastic locational concentration in recent years. One result of such concentration is an acceleration of the rate of out-migration from communities with a low level of provision, especially where the level of provision is reduced. To illustrate this last point, a study of the effects of the concentration of school facilities concluded that the rate of depopulation in a village increased shortly after the closure of the village school (1.34).

There are overwhelming economic arguments against increased provision of basic services in thinly populated rural areas, but it should be recognized that the currently popular alternative of limiting provision of, for example, non-agricultural employment and some social services to a small number of key villages has the inevitable implication that in the smaller villages "the provision of services to the residual population becomes increasingly unsatisfactory and a further cause of rural discontent" (1.35), with the consequence of further losses of population. Little work has yet been reported, however, on assessing the influence of variations in service provision as an aggregate expression of the quality of rural life, or of the degree of development of the social fabric of rural communities, although Mitchell's study in South-West England concluded that the social outlook of four 'fairly distinct types of rural ethos' was as important as physical provision of services (1.36).

The influence of housing conditions in determining the direction of population change has generally been dismissed as relatively unimportant in studies of motivation of migrants, although it has been suggested above that this might be due to the failure to identify local movement (possibly largely home-based) in studies which have used census material, with its coarse mesh of area boundaries. Certainly the provision of council housing only in key villages, a common policy, inevitably encourages short-distance migration across parish—but not local authority—boundaries. The problem of the tied cottage, too, is significant, with farm workers feeling that it is a weapon in the hands of their employer (1.37), and those aged 55 and over apprehensively viewing it with 'an element of fear and insecurity'.

These, then, are the three major 'response' factors, all in some measure attributable to an increasingly noticeable urban/rural dichotomy in living standards, but each finding expression in a very different pattern of movement. There are, of course, other factors associated with the decision to migrate, but it could be argued that these are in some sense derived from the three considered above, or are constrained in type, distance, destination, and so on: movement from a tied cottage upon retirement, movement of retired people to relatives, friends or nursing homes, and migration associated with marriage are all examples of this constrained migration. One method of integrating these varied reasons for movement into a cohesive explanatory framework is to emphasize the relationship between movement, family structure and the stages of the life-cycle, based on the assumption that different stages of the family life-cycle are associated with different family sizes, and consequently that current accommodation may not satisfy future housing needs.

Clearly this approach fails to provide a general theory of population movement since it is not all-inclusive, emphasizing housing needs at the expense of others. On the other hand, the life-cycle approach specifies particular stages when the propensity to move is high, and if employment motives can be superimposed the resultant framework might claim general application in explaining movement. At its simplest, the problem is that of reconciling migration decisions which are explicable as part of a common life-cycle pattern (movement on leaving school, on marriage, etc.) with those which are irregular and spontaneous (those activated, for instance, by desire for career advancement or the conscious decision to live in rural surroundings) and even with those which appear to be incapable of rational explanation. One method is to view the process of migration as the interaction between the family's values and aspirations, and its economic and social structure: in other words, as the attempt "to maximise the net balance of satisfaction derived from housing, employment, social intercourse and location" (1.38), within the constraints of life style and (financial) ability to move. This last point echoes claims that a 'migratory elite' has arisen (1.39), leaving stranded those on low levels of income who do not have the means with which to move out of declining rural areas, despite the financial incentive to do so.

All this is suggesting a complex interaction of physical and psychological stimuli which is as yet imperfectly understood, but it is nevertheless possible to discern (as indicated previously) the two major elements of population change in remoter areas: a regrouping of the rural population, and longer-distance migration related to employment opportunities. The first of these groups is normally motivated by housing need and is heavily weighted towards local movement; the average age of such migrants is relatively high. Included in this group is short-distance transfer from tied cottages to more modern accommodation, and movement to council housing in key villages. The second group comprises those moving for employment reasons, often over long distances, partly because of the absence of suitable work for young people in rural areas. Characteristically there is a heavy net loss of younger age groups.

Such a twofold classification is inevitably a gross oversimplification for a number of reasons, mostly alluded to above. Also of considerable importance is the marked difference in migration behaviour between school-leavers and other migrants, not only in terms of distance moved and employment-orientated migrants, but also in respect of family linkages, which play a far less important role, and knowledge of potential destinations, which is generalized and fragmentary. Nevertheless, lack of suitable employment is the factor which triggers the majority of movement on leaving school, allied to non-existent public transport in rural areas, which rules out short-distance commuting to nearby market towns.

The processes of population change, and their incidence, are thus relatively well explored. Yet the social and physical repercussions of sustained and selective out-migration, profoundly affecting not only the rural economy but also the quality of community and family life, are less well exposed, so that policies designed to alleviate rural problems are essentially disjointed and opportunist. The lack of far-reaching and integrated measures for improving rural facilities, stimulating non-agricultural employment and so on has resulted in an inevitable concentration of the older and poorer—those unable to move out—in declining rural areas, with little hope of reversing the trend towards extinction of smaller settlements. In some cases, of course, the trend has been actively encouraged, with the proposition that "the primary objective of any rural plan is to secure changes in the pattern of settlement that will increase the range of social, commercial and public services, and education and employment opportunities" (1.40); perhaps the most extreme example is that of County Durham, where reorganization included plans to completely run down certain villages.

In this case the villages concerned were declining in population with the diminishing local demand for labour from coal mining, but the principle is exactly the same as for traditional agricultural areas. Four categories of rural settlement were recognized in the County Development Plan, classified according to their anticipated population change, and the category D villages were expected to continue to lose population, partly an automatic process stemming from the small population of these scattered mining settlements, but partly because of the deliberate effort to channel new investment in housing towards a limited number of larger rural settlements (1.41). The plan was revised in 1964, and category D villages were re-classified into those where development would be discouraged but settlement would continue for a long period, and those where no new development would be permitted and wholesale clearance would take place. One-third of Durham's 370 rural settlements were included in these new categories, but "the elimination of small villages from the settlement pattern has been a gradual process, so that by 1970 only eight small settlements had been completely cleared and their sites assimilated into the surrounding country-side" (1.42).

The County Durham policy is unparalleled in modern Britain, but it is noteworthy that this type of implementation of key village policy—complemented by equally direct measures intended to attract employment into the key settlements—is considered necessary for success. Whatever the technique of implementation, however, the key village policy has achieved almost universal acceptance as the cornerstone of plans for population retention in rural areas. There is some evidence that the policy may simply strengthen a process which is inevitably operating in the British countryside at the present time, although population thresholds at which settlements become capable of retaining population and supporting basic services are a matter for conjecture. Thus Johnston found that population change in Nidderdale was related primarily to settlement pattern and suburbanization, rather than to changes in the nature and distribution of agricultural employment, with a positive correlation of 0.65 between population change and village size (1.43).

Edwards reached similar conclusions on the influence of settlement size (1.44), and produced a classification linking size to population trends:

(i)   below 120 persons (90 adults) population loss is rapid and social provision negligible; 120 was therefore considered as the threshold of minimum social provision;

(ii)   between 120 and 160, population losses are prevalent, and such settlements have over-representation of older people. Many such settlements are exclusively agricultural;

(iii) between 160 and 180, settlements have proved resilient and this should therefore be the minimum population for reorganised settlements;

(iv)   over 180, population change is erratic, although growth is normal for settlements of 450 and over.

The suggestion of a population as small as 160 as the minimum for regrouped settlements with 'more advanced social provision' would undoubtedly be disputed, as would the equally extreme claim that "a minimum population of about 5000 is needed to support a reasonable range of local facilities and this suggests a need for a policy aimed at the expansion of a few selected settlements and the acceleration of decline in the remainder" (1.45). In some British rural areas the largest settlements (even those which aspire to the description of market towns) would not qualify as service centres, and in any case problems of physical isolation in more sparsely populated upland areas would dictate some modification in the threshold.

The conclusion to be drawn, perhaps inevitably, is that considerable sensitivity is required in applying policies designed to redistribute rural population in a more efficient (and hopefully more enduring) pattern, and therefore that dependence on analysis of threshold sizes must be flexible, and qualified by frequent revision, since the critical threshold values will change with variations in the characteristics of the rural population. Finally, in this context, the dangers of blind adherence to key village strategies, yet to be proved

c

effective in resisting population losses in remoter areas, should be stressed; despite general agreement that a coordinated programme of development for rural areas has been required, none has emerged, and there is no guarantee that short-term and piecemeal policies for the reversal of population losses, developed in isolation from other policies, will be effective.

Urban population pressures in the countryside

Rural areas which are relatively accessible to urban concentrations of even modest size are increasingly under pressure in a number of ways, particularly where the landscape is of great scenic value or where other intrinsic advantages are present. Commuting to work becomes more common and more widespread, with a consequent distortion of local housing markets, to the disadvantage of the rural 'host' population. Recreational use of the countryside, even where it is concentrated both spatially and temporarily, causes traffic congestion, problems of litter and trespass and so on. Increasing second home ownership combines the effects of disruption of housing demand, and recreational use; in-migration to certain areas by retired people has a similar effect. Not all of these processes are detrimental to the area and population involved, of course, but the interplay of these urban-derived forces may precipitate migration of certain rural groups, yet virtually imprison other groups without the ability to move, and thereby substantially alter the character of rural communities in areas susceptible to such processes.

The processes under consideration operate specifically in rural areas fulfilling one or more of a number of criteria, including:

(i) location within the commuting hinterland of a town (although it should be emphasized that catchments vary with the size of urban area, and therefore that the London commuter belt embraces much of south-east and southern England, for example);

(ii) scenic attractiveness—which renders areas such as the North Downs and Chiltern Hills doubly vulnerable, of course;

(iii) traditional attraction for retirement migrants and/or recreational use (as with south coast resorts such as Lyme Regis).

The area subsumed under this set of criteria is so large, however, that it includes almost the entire lowland zone of England, except for particular areas which are excluded by virtue of their isolation, and specific but much smaller rural areas in Scotland and Wales. In such areas the appelation 'rural' may in itself be a misnomer, since the area is subjected to urban pressures of such an extent that it is, in all respects except those of physical form and location, as much a part of the city as a suburban housing estate.

The foregoing summary of the application and results of urban pressures on selected rural areas is a common interpretation placed upon census figures and other indicators, but there is in fact very little reliable evidence (particularly from small-scale detailed studies), even to the extent that "there is an obvious and desperate need for studies of rural areas in England and Wales which are experiencing acute pressures as a result of population growth and economic prosperity" (1.46). There is an evident place for research into, for instance, housing pressures in certain rural areas where in-migration resulting from increasing commuting from villages is significant. Nevertheless, there have been pioneer studies in this field, and the major conclusions from these are considered in succeeding paragraphs.

The classic case study, of course, is that carried out by Pahl in part of the metropolitan fringe in Hertfordshire (1.47). The study was set in the context of the planned decentralization of Greater London, a process involving massive redistribution of population from the congested core to the suburban fringe and in particular (during the period from 1951 to 1961) to what Pahl termed the Inner Country Ring, which recorded an intercensal increase of 585,000, or 46.5%. Of this increase, little more than half is accounted for by the eight new towns, which implies that existing towns and villages in the countryside immediately around the London suburbs grew in population by about 240,000 in the decade to 1961. Recognizing the social and structural implications of the virtual creation of a new 'fringe city' in the post-war period, Pahl sought to go beyond traditional geographical considerations of function and morphology to examine processes and inter-relationships in the fringe.

The policy of Hertfordshire County Council to stabilize the population at around one million was noted, together with the consequences of the policy—based on a restrictive green belt approach—particularly in respect of inflated land values in areas zoned for future housing development, of diversion of development pressure from the green belt area to its outer periphery, and of remarkable population increases in the rural areas of the county, *despite* rigid development control. A detailed study of two rural-urban fringe parishes with significant recent population increase, contrasted with a parish of 'traditional' character which had resisted development, established that there were fundamental occupational and social class differences between the established residents (largely skilled or unskilled manual workers) and newcomers (mainly professional or intermediate non-manual workers). The conclusion was drawn that an affluent, mobile, middle class element was effectively responsible for the in-migration into rural fringe areas—partly because the demand for private housing stimulated by this group had pushed house prices beyond the means of other social groups. Pahl was concerned to discover the extent of social segregation of the middle and working classes, and he demonstrated a geographical separation which was reflected throughout the structure of the communities studied.

Not only did the middle classes provide the majority of in-migrants, but they also accounted for the majority of commuters, and in particular commuters to London, many of whom had been born in and had previously lived in London. Certainly there was no evidence that the in-migrants were part of the drift to the south-east; rather, they were part of a selective middle class internal redistribution within the region. This selectivity was entirely based upon wealth: only the middle classes were in a position to accept higher costs of housing and the extra expenses involved in longer-distance commuting. Thus "rural-urban fringe parishes are attracting mobile, middle class commuters who live and work in distinct and separate social and economic worlds from the established populations" (1.48), normally to the detriment of hopes of establishing an integrated rural community structure.

This pessimistic view of the integration of newcomers into rural communities (and, indeed, of their aspirations in this direction) is, however, not supported by the study of the parish of Stratfield Mortimer in Berkshire (1.49). The specific objective was to explore trends in social integration in a growing village, the assumption having been made that certain qualities of village life were worthy of preservation, and that they might be threatened by current processes resulting from urban pressures. Most of the residents appeared to derive satisfaction from participation in various aspects of community life, and had acquired a sense of identity with the village; such measures of integration, however, indicate that the extent of assimilation varies with length of residence, and that the process is a slow one.

The usual paradox found in a village that has grown through the in-migration of commuters, that these recent newcomers become the most entrenched opponents of further expansion (with its connotations of dilution of the rurality to which they were attracted) appears to operate in Stratfield Mortimer, in that one of the main apprehensions of residents in the village was that too much growth would take place, with consequent loss of identity. Indeed, the point was made that a population of 2000 or so was large enough to ensure a reasonable choice of employment and services, public transport and communal facilities, but small enough for the traditional characteristics of the village to survive, albeit in a changed context. Even so, class segregation of the type found in Hertfordshire was seen to be encouraged by the physical separation of private and council housing estates within the parish, a separation which might have been avoided by more positive local planning. Nevertheless, "in a village which is not over-weighted with commuters, and in which most of them work within a 12-mile radius, there is no reason to expect the commuter to be less well integrated than the local worker"—given time.

A similar study of urban pressure on selected villages in Worcestershire stressed the sheer physical extent of the influence on housing demand of the West Midlands conurbation, both within its tightly restrictive Green Belt—where development on 'white land', perhaps originally intended to satisfy the natural increase of existing communities in the Green Belt, more commonly satisfies the needs of urban dwellers moving into the countryside—and for a considerable distance beyond, tempered only by considerations of service provision and accessibility (1.50). In a survey of two large villages in central Worcestershire, information was sought from samples of established residents and newcomers (those who had

Table 1.5   Reasons for moving to two villages in Worcestershire

	MARTLEY		KEMPSEY	
	Established	Newcomers	Established	Newcomers
Husband/wife born there	24	11	29	5
Husband/wife's family there	19	13	11	7
Marriage	7	5	2	—
Employment	22	34	18	21
Retirement	3	8	—	2
Convenient home	15	24	28	56
Death of relatives	1	—	1	—
Countryside	10	5	10	11

Note: figures are percentages of column totals
Source: RADFORD, E., *The New Villagers*, London, Cass, 1968

lived in the villages for four years or less) on economic and social status, occupational and geographical mobility, pattern of journeys to work, and attitudes towards and participation in community life.

The two villages, both situated a few miles from Worcester, and with easy access to the conurbation, nevertheless contrasted strongly in terms of the extent of urban intrusion. Reasons for moving into the villages were inevitably composite in many cases, although the determining reasons are given in Table 1.5. Availability of housing was clearly the major influence in Kempsey, where two large housing estates were completed in the early 1960s; change of employment was more important in Martley, a more traditional community with the remnants of village form and a substantial proportion of the labour force employed locally in agriculture. Kempsey, on the other hand, is in many functional and morphological respects more akin to a suburb, yet the motivation for movement into both villages was similar: housing reasons for those who had moved short distances, and change of employment for those who had come from outside the immediate locality. The villages were felt to represent settlements at different stages in the transition from truly rural to peri-urban, in that Martley acted as a dormitory for some 'urban' households but retained many of the features of rural life, whereas Kempsey in many ways functioned as a suburb of Worcester despite the survival of some rural attributes. In both cases the absorption of newcomers was relatively successful, although this apparently high level of integration might be due to the local origins of many in-migrants.

Between them the three case studies summarized above, and selected from a rather larger number now available, illustrate the concern for the continued existence of 'village life' or at least of the desirable characteristics associated with this commodity. Perhaps one of the most serious threats to the future of this sense of community, at least in certain rural areas, is the growth of the second homes phenomenon (1.51), a form of seasonal extension of suburbia which can destroy the basis of permanent settlement in rural areas. The establishment of second homes as weekend and holiday residences is a result of increasing leisure time and rising levels of disposable income, and as such is essentially a development of the post-1945 era. The suggestion that second home ownership will increase further to form a widely available extension of the urban-dweller's living space may encourage visions of a suburban country-side, in which the process of "the thinning out of the urban mass, together with its increase in area, (which) seems to have no natural or automatic limit" (1.52) has reached the stage where distinctions between urban and rural are purely academic.

However, the decentralization of the British city is largely to be measured in relation to permanent outward movement and its consequences for surrounding areas of countryside. Research has concentrated upon the social consequences of such pressures, as has been indicated in preceding paragraphs, with differing conclusions reached as to the extent to which in-migrants were accepted into rural communities. Hence Thorns contrasted the village-orientated working class, largely composed of agricultural workers and their families, with the middle class newcomers who perceived the village as a dormitory and nearby urban areas as the setting for most social contacts (1.53), and Lewis had added further grounds for differentiation between established and new residents in the Welsh context, in particular language and religious observance (1.54). Other studies, notably that of Stratfield Mortimer quoted previously, have tended to regard such differences as relatively minor and capable of erosion, and thus to accept urban diffusion into the countryside as a force which, wisely controlled, can complement and even reinforce rural communities.

Jennings goes so far as to suggest that "the essential, first characteristic of our countryside, now that so many of us are living in it, is not the urban-rural contrast but the traditional-modern one. Some villages are almost untouched, some have new commuter communities, some are almost swallowed up by neighbouring towns" (1.55). He observes that in every village there is a dwindling nucleus of long-established residents, but that with increased affluence and mobility the village as a closed, stable community rarely survives; in most villages there are the three distinct areas of old settlement, council estate and private residential estate, inhabited by people with different characteristics and lifestyles. In such areas as East Anglia, where isolation lasted longer, such development has been telescoped into the very recent past, with the intensified pressure to be expected in the last area in South-East England with some room for growth.

It is virtually impossible to quantify this urban overflow, since census statistics are tied to administrative areas which are of increasingly little use in separating urban and rural, and since in any case established and in-migrant groups live in juxtaposition in the same nominally rural areas. Certainly the generalization that one-fifth of the population lives in rural districts is increasingly irrelevant; perhaps a more meaningful statistic is that only 3 to 4% of the population are employed on the land. In one view, "it is by now clear that the greatest part of the inhabitants of British rural areas are either ex-urbanites, with households from which one or more travel every day to work in towns, or else they are retired folk who lived and worked in towns before coming to the rural areas where they are now rapidly buying up property vacated by people who formerly worked on the land" (1.56). This is an over-statement of the case, and certainly an under-estimate of the importance of intra-rural population movement, but the implications of this ex-urban domination are clear.

One implication contained in the above is that the rural housing market is being distorted by extra demand from outside the rural areas, and this is undoubtedly true. A crucial consequence of the amended operation of the housing market is that the inflation of prices makes it progressively more difficult for the children of established residents—perhaps working class and certainly with limited means—to obtain adequate accommodation. The twin results are enhanced out-migration of young people from the countryside and further encroachment of the commuting middle classes in the pursuit of peace and quiet, spaciousness and life in a small-scale community. Not only is there a displacement of population on an age-selective basis, but there is also a displacement of activities: local retail services suffer from falling demand with the increasing proportion of residents who are accustomed to shopping in town, and specialized services such as those dependent upon agricultural trade are withdrawn or relocated where the agricultural element is stronger. The new country-dwellers may therefore find that the effect of their decision to move to the country is to destroy part of the traditional rural economy which constituted a major attraction to them.

The suggestion was made in the previous section that the planning response to continued substantial population losses in the more isolated rural areas was piecemeal, stereotyped and therefore likely to be ineffective. Taking the argument a stage further, it is suggested that the lack of an overall strategy for the development of the countryside is likely to be positively harmful; that the absence of a policy review for more than thirty years has contributed to *laissez-faire* official attitudes which have operated against the interests of certain sectors of the rural population. One of the most crucial aspects of such a review would be the establishment of guidelines for controlling population pressures originating in towns and cities but directed towards the countryside. The absence of such guidelines has retarded the development of even embryonic planning measures in especially vulnerable rural regions, and has fostered a lack of urgency in the collation of data in this field; hence the CoEnCo sub-committee which debated 'urban pressures on the countryside' repeatedly complained that their debates were hindered by lack of adequate information, and their recommendations reflect this problem (1.57).

The sub-committee suggested a Royal Commission on the Countryside to consider the state of the countryside, current changes and their consequences, and resultant uncertainties, and to recommend appropriate planning methods to achieve its optimal capacity as 'an area for satisfactory living'. It might well be the case that more pragmatic measures are of higher priority in accommodating urban population pressures in the countryside. Some type of control of local housing markets may be necessary if the indigenous population is not to be denied access to housing opportunities in certain areas; with the domination of property markets by urban 'outsiders' has come the reluctance on the part of Local Authorities to provide council housing on a large scale when the potential demand for such accommodation may be diverted from the area by urban employment opportunities and sheer frustration at the difficulties of rural owner-occupation for the financially disadvantaged rural population. (This is discussed further in later Chapters.) An extreme response operated in Guernsey is that of 'open' and 'closed' housing markets, the latter of which is accessible only to islanders, with the declared intention of containing the influx of retired people, second home owners and other potential in-migrants. Such a policy might be socially and politically unacceptable if applied on a wider scale, but there is scope for experiment if urban population pressures are not to lead to unprecedented cultural changes in rural areas.

In reviewing such matters, however, it is important to underline the benefits accruing from the manifestations of urban population pressure. The diminuition of service provision in villages with declining or static populations was highlighted in the previous section, and it should be apparent that the same problem is present even in rural areas within the hinterlands of towns: services are increasingly concentrated in larger centres, as the economies of scale become more apparent and wider availability of private transport decreases dependence on local services. Yet the arrival of newcomers may ensure the continued existence of traditional facilities and services, and in a wider setting "an imaginative project to add to an existing village ... may very well produce a new and invigorated community in a relatively short space of time" (1.58).

To summarize, the process of urban decentralization, in the form of the creation of commuter communities within, or adjacent to, existing villages, of increasing second home ownership, and of all the ramifications of enhanced personal mobility, has brought with it problems of rapid population increase, difficulties of social integration of established residents and newcomers, and in certain circumstances the displacement of disadvantaged sections of the rural population affected by the free market system of house allocation. Planning and other statutory controls are rudimentary or non-existent in respect of population problems, and such policies as do exist (notably relating to development control in green belts and areas of attractive landscape) serve only to redistribute urban pressures in an intensified form in other rural areas.

Emerging patterns of population change

This final section of the chapter reviews the current position in British rural areas in respect of patterns of population losses and gains, and seeks to interpret indications of future variations in such patterns, within the framework of probable increase in policy responses as current problems become more pressing. It therefore recognizes the need for intervention to prevent the emergence of two locationally-differentiated rural regions, the one increasingly deprived of youth, skills and viability, the other subjected to severe urban population pressures on an unprecedented scale, surviving as countryside only through the application of progressively outdated and inadequate development control mechanisms.

Undoubtedly one of the most significant features of the recent past, and one which will grow in relative importance in the future, is the widening of rural-urban differentials (measured in terms of relative prosperity, life satisfaction and so on). This reduction in attractiveness of rural areas as a residential environment will inevitably be felt most in the more isolated districts, where provision of public utilities and other communal services will be restricted to key settlements, and existing facilities such as surviving rural public transport services, and mobile or static retail services, will be withdrawn. The effect of this economic retreat from the fringes of rural settlement will be to leave rural areas which, by reason of terrain, peripheral location relative to local and regional service centres, or inability to sustain labour-intensive farming types, are unable to retain their existing population, vulnerable to selective out-migration motivated by dissatisfaction with a relict life-style unaffected by modern influences. Allied to this may be growing disenchantment with the employment opportunities available in remoter rural areas, where not only isolation and lack of a substantial local labour market but also absence of essential ancillary services will deter new manufacturing and service industries from entering the area.

The net result of these pressures on inhabitants of declining rural areas is a perception of the area as one of disadvantage. Major causes of dissatisfaction include lack of variety of employment and falling demand in the agricultural sector; frequently, poor housing conditions, partly the result of the tied cottage system, and little prospect of improvement through either private or public initiative; rudimentary provision of services and facilities, and haphazard withdrawal of these as out-migration proceeds and demand falls; and knowledge, partly derived from previous out-migrants from the area, of greater opportunities in urban environments. Such disaffection is of varying importance, depending on age, sex, education, marital status, type of employment, income, and other more psychological characteristics, so that the likelihood of out-migration is highest with younger, educated, single, middle income residents who have no strong familial or other links with the area. The residual population, after a long period of selective depopulation, may therefore include higher than average proportions of the elderly and those with low incomes, amongst others, with a greater need for community services and a declining ability to contribute towards providing them.

This spectre of impoverishment consequent upon rural depopulation might well have become an almost universal reality in the British countryside, with villages reduced in some circumstances to a handful of prosperous farmers; there is still the prospect of such a future in some regions. In other areas the situation has been transformed by the startling increase in personal mobility in the second half of the twentieth century, coupled with the growth of a desire to live in rural surroundings, even (more recently) at considerable extra cost, related to higher costs involved in commuting and congestion in and around city centres. Previously the contact between urban man and the countryside was primarily recreational, of a transitory and superficial nature, but the growth of second home ownership, and, more permanently, the outflow of the urban middle classes into the newly accessible countryside as residents has created a new and more complex set of rural-urban relationships.

This attraction factor of rural living has created especially severe pressures around each of the major conurbations, with very rapid population increase seen by established residents as creating an entirely new type of rural community, less integrated and less self-sufficient than traditional rural settlements, and equally, population growth on a large scale and within a short time period seen by rural newcomers as eroding the facets of life in the countryside which they value most highly. The potential conflict between these two groups with very different preferences is clear. The problems of large-scale and concentrated in-migration to rural settlements have been relatively well researched, with emphasis laid upon the class differences between established and migrant populations, the physical isolation and social segregation which often exists between them, the different behavioural characteristics and use made of the village environment and facilities by the two groups, although with occasional glimpses of new integrated communities in the urbanized countryside.

There is some evidence, too, of the embryonic form of a chain reaction in which a certain proportion of in-migrants are, in a sense, reluctant rural dwellers. The problem lies, once again, in the uncontrolled operation of the housing market, with the result that accommodation in expanding towns meeting the needs of some of the overspill from conurbations is priced beyond the means of particular sections of the local population, whose housing opportunities are artificially constrained and directed towards cheaper accommodation in less accessible rural areas with lower standards of social provision and fewer services. The problem is only just emerging, but is potentially as damaging to the established population as the converse enforced migration of local inhabitants, namely the displacement of younger people from villages which are more accessible, and therefore subject to overwhelming competition for property from urban dwellers wishing to live in the countryside. The explosion in demand for second homes, coupled with inability to erect sufficient and suitable purpose-built weekend residences quickly, has merely added to the displacement effect and to the inevitable local discontent.

The forecast, therefore, is one of continuing polarization in population change in the rural areas of Britain, with further losses and resultant cuts in services, withdrawal of support, and so on, from the remoter areas, and further suburbanization of the accessible countryside, with the spread effects of urban decentralization held in check only by unsatisfactory controls in green belts and landscape protection areas, and by the imperfect process of development control. The theme of inadequate integration and cohesion in rural planning policies has been argued elsewhere, and echoed in the foregoing, but the wave of structure planning currently breaking over rural Britain has shown little sign of innovatory approaches to persistent problems. Faith is still placed in key villages to shore up stagnant and declining areas, despite the effect upon the remaining majority of settlements, and despite evidence that settlement reorganization is of strictly limited value as an agent of population retention. Planned reorganization of the settlement pattern, and imposition of a rigidly hierarchical settlement structure, is also viewed as helpful in centralizing services as an incentive for industrial relocation in rural regions—an unfulfilled strategy in the majority of cases.

At the other extreme, reliance is placed upon tightly restrictive land use zoning as a method of containing and directing urban pressures on particularly vulnerable countryside. Again, this policy has been shown, in Hertfordshire and elsewhere, to be ineffective in restraining population growth, distortion of the housing market, and the imposition of a new community structure upon such rural areas. It is difficult to envisage a suitably strengthened form of planning control achieving wide acceptance, however, so that the objective in accessible rural areas subject to urban population pressures must be to reconcile demands for the release of more and more land for development with conflicting claims for agricultural use and preservation as open countryside.

There is no easy solution to a set of problems which has resulted from free operation of public preference. Urban decentralization, essentially the outward movement of the middle classes, encouraged by rising real incomes and personal mobility, is the expression of disenchantment with city life and desire for an identifiable place within a small-scale and less complex structure. Rural depopulation in the remote countryside expresses frustration at rural-urban differentials in living standards, employment opportunities and so on. Clearly it is not economically feasible to produce a more even balance of satisfaction, and it may not be desirable to attempt to do so, but recognition of patterns of population change, as outlined in this Chapter, is merely a tool to be employed in planning to achieve expressed preferences, and this latter process has scarcely begun.

References

1.1   RAVENSTEIN, E.G., 'The laws of migration', *Journal of the Statistical Society*, 48, part II, 1885, p. 198.

1.2   *Ibid.*, p. 199.

1.3   NORTH REGIONAL PLANNING COMMITTEE, *Mobility and the North*, Newcastle, 1967.

1.4   SAVILLE, J., *Rural Depopulation in England and Wales 1851-1951*, Routledge & Kegan Paul, London, 1957.

1.5   *Ibid.*, p. 88.

1.6   VINCE, S.W.E., 'Reflections on the Structure and Distribution of Rural Population in England and Wales, 1921-31', *Transactions of the Institute of British Geographers*, 18, 1952, p. 76.

1.7   ROBERTSON, I.M.L., 'The Census and Research: Ideals and Realities', *Transactions of the Institute of British Geographers*, 48, 1969, pp. 173-187.

1.8   EDWARDS, J.A., 'Rural Migration in England and Wales', *The Planner*, 59, 1973, pp. 450-453.

1.9   HERBERT, D.T., 'Population Mobility and Social Changes in South Wales', *Town Planning Review*, 43, 1972, pp. 327-342.

1.10   GITTUS, E., 'Migration in Lancashire and Cheshire', *Town Planning Review*, 32, 1961-2, pp. 141-156.

1.11   JONES, H.R., 'Rural Migration in Central Wales', *Transactions of the Institute of British Geographers*, 37, 1965, p. 44.

1.12   EDWARDS, J.A., *op. cit.*, 1973, p. 450.

1.13   HOUSE, J.W. and KNIGHT, E.M., *Migrants of North-East England 1951-1961*, Department of Geography, University of Newcastle upon Tyne, 1965.

1.14   DICKINSON, G.C., 'The Nature of Rural Population Movement—an Analysis of Seven Yorkshire Parishes based on Electoral Returns from 1931-54', *Yorks. Bull. Econ. Soc. Res.*, 10, 1958, pp. 95-108.

1.15   DUNN, M.C. and SWINDELL, K., 'Electoral Registers and Rural Migration: a Case Study from Herefordshire', *Area*, 4, 1972, pp. 39-42.

1.16   DUNN, M.C., Patterns of Population Movement in Herefordshire: Implications for Rural Planning, Paper presented to IBG Annual Conference, Birmingham, 1973.

1.17   BRACEY, H.E., *People and the Countryside*, Routledge and Kegan Paul, London, 1970, p. 34.

1.18   HOUSE, J.W., *Rural North East England 1951-61*, Department of Geography, University of Newcastle upon Tyne, 1965.

1.19   MASTERMAN, C.F.G., *The Condition of England*, Methuen, London, 1909, p. 148.

1.20   GREEN, R.J., *Country Planning: The Future of the Rural Regions*, University of Manchester, 1971.

1.21   BEST, R.H. and ROGERS, A.W., *The Urban Countryside: The Land Use Structure of Small Towns and Villages in England and Wales*, Faber and Faber, London, 1970.

1.22   CAIRD, J.B., Population problems of the Islands of Scotland with Special Reference to the Uists, Paper presented to IBG Annual Conference, Aberdeen, 1972.

1.23   TURNOCK, D., Population Problems in Highland Scotland, Paper presented to IBG Annual Conference, Aberdeen, 1972.

1.24   JACKSON, V.J., *Population in the Countryside: Growth and Stagnation in the Cotswolds*, Cass, London, 1968.

1.25   DUNN, M.C., 1973, *op. cit.*, p. 8.

1.26   HEREFORDSHIRE COUNTY COUNCIL, *Review of the County Development Plan: Report on Population and Employment*, County Council, Hereford, 1968.

1.27   Dickinson, G.C., *op. cit.*, 1958.

1.28   Jones, H.R., *op. cit.*, 1965.

1.29   Johnston, R.J., 'A Reconnaisance Study of Population Change in Nidderdale, 1951-1961', *Transactions of the Institute of British Geographers*, **41**, 1967, pp. 113-123.

1.30   north regional planning committee, *op. cit.*, 1967.

1.31   House, J.W., *op. cit.*, 1965.

1.32   Saville, J., *op. cit.*, 1957.

1.33   Hookway, R.J.S., 'A Study of Rural Population Structure', *Journal of the Town Planning Institute*, 44, 1958, p. 212.

1.34   Lee, T., 'A Test of the Hypothesis that School Reorganisation is a Cause of Rural Depopulation', *Durham Research Review*, 3, 1960, pp. 64-73.

1.35   House, J.W. and Knight, E.M., *op. cit.*, 1965.

1.36   Mitchell, G.D., 'Depopulation and Rural Social Structure', *Sociological Review*, 42, 1950, pp. 69-85.

1.37   Cowie, W. and Giles, A., 'An Enquiry into the Reasons for the "Drift from the Land" ', *Selected Papers in Agricultural Economics*, 5, 1957, pp. 70-113.

1.38   Simmie, J.M., *The Sociology of internal migration*, Centre for Environmental Studies, London, University Working Paper No. 15, 1972, p. 23.

1.39   Musgrove, F., *The Migratory Elite*, Heinemann, London, 1963.

1.40   Green, R.J., *op. cit.*, 1971, p. 85.

1.41   Atkinson, J.R., 'Aspects of Planning', pp. 433-442 *in* Dewdney, J.C., (Ed.): *Durham County and City with Teesside*.

1.42   Clout, H.D., *Rural Geography: An Introductory Survey*, Pergamon Press, Oxford, 1972, p. 152.

1.43   Johnston, R.J., 'Components of Rural Population Change', *Town Planning Review*, 36, 1966, pp. 279-294.

1.44   Edwards, J.A., *The Settlement Factor in the Rural Problems of North-East England*, Unpublished Ph.D. thesis, University of Newcastle upon Tyne, 1964.

1.45   Green, R.J. and Ayton, J.B., 'Changes in the Pattern of Rural Settlement' quoted in Clout, H.D., *op. cit.*, 1972.

1.46   Edwards, J.A., *op. cit.*, 1973, p. 452.

1.47   Pahl, R.E., *Urbs in Rure: The Metropolitan Fringe in Hertfordshire*, London School of Economics, Geographical Papers No. 2, 1965.

1.48   *Ibid.*, p. 72.

1.49   Crichton, R., *Commuters' Village: A Study of Community and Commuters in the Berkshire Village of Stratfield Mortimer*, David and Charles, Newton Abbot, 1964.

1.50   Radford, E., *The New Villagers: Urban Pressure on Rural Areas in Worcestershire*, Cass, London, 1970.

1.51   Bielckus, C.D., Rogers, A.W. and Wibberley, G.P., *Second Homes in England and Wales*, School of Rural Economics and Related Studies, Wye, 1972.

1.52   Wibberley, G.P., *Rural planning in Britain: a study in contrast and conflict*, Inaugural lecture at University College, London, 1971.

1.53   Thorns, D.C., 'The Changing System of Social Stratification', *Sociologia Ruralis*, 8, 1968, pp. 161-178.

1.54   Lewis, G.J., 'Commuting and the Village in Mid-Wales', *Geography*, 52, 1967, pp. 294-304.

1.55   Jennings, P., *The Living Village*, Penguin, Harmondsworth, 1972.

1.56   Radford, E., *op. cit.*, 1970, p. 2.

1.57   committee for environmental conservation, *Urban Pressures on the Countryside*, CoEnCo, London, 1972.

1.58   Radford, E., *op. cit.*, 1970, p. 5.

Further Reading

CRICHTON, R., *Commuters' Village: A Study of Community and Commuters in the Berkshire Village of Stratfield Mortimer,* David & Charles, Newton Abbott, 1964.

HOUSE, J.W., *Rural North-East England 1951-1961,* Department of Geography, University of Newcastle upon Tyne, 1965.

JACKSON, V.J., *Population in the Countryside: Growth and Stagnation in the Cotswolds,* Cass, London, 1968.

JENNINGS, P., *The Living Village,* Penguin, Harmondsworth, 1972.

MUSGROVE, F., *The Migratory Elite,* Heinemann, London, 1963.

PAHL, R.E., *Urbs in Rure: The Metropolitan Fringe in Hertfordshire,* London School of Economics, Geographical Papers No. 2, 1965.

RADFORD, E., *The New Villagers: Urban Pressure on Rural Areas in Worcestershire,* Cass, London, 1970.

SAVILLE, J., *Rural Depopulation in England and Wales 1851-1951,* Routledge & Kegan Paul, London, 1957.

SIMMIE, J.M., *The Sociology of Internal Migration,* Centre for Environmental Studies, London, University Working Paper No. 15, 1972.

CHAPTER TWO

Rural Communities

Ian Martin

Types of community

Community, R.E. Pahl has noted (2.1), is a concept that has a high level of use but a low level of meaning. Certainly, as a weapon in the planning armoury, it ranks second only to 'amenity' in terms of imprecision and, with very little effort devoted to the choice of supporting words, 'community' can be guaranteed to draw nods of approval from directly opposed interests.

In a rural context, the term is diluted still further. Whilst it is comparatively easy to define the number of settlements in rural areas—Best and Rogers (2.2) have estimated that there are 17,000 settlements of 10,000 people or less in the countryside of England and Wales, or 18% of the national population—it is practically, and many would argue, theoretically, impossible to define the number of rural communities. Nevertheless, the planner often mistakes the two and equates the physically defined settlement, village or hamlet, with a rural community. In practice, this is rarely valid. On the one hand, it may be more accurate to describe many villages and small towns as comprising several communities inhabiting the same space whilst, on the other hand, the equation leaves the isolated farmer in limbo. He, too, has a social life in the widest sense, and will be a member of one (or more) communities. In short, physical, and social facts do not usually coincide.

If the physical fact of a village or other rural settlement is often self evident, the social fact is often obscure, especially to a casual observer, like the planner making a quinquennial visitation for the purpose of a local plan. But, elusive though social reality may be, it has to be understood before the planner can appreciate fully the problems inherent in rural community life and the ways in which he may help towards their solution. It will be necessary for him to know what rural community is, what are its major elements and how they interact, for these will also condition his contacts with the rural public before he, or they, can be moved to the problem formulation and solving stages.

If he is influenced by the media, pressure groups or even by literary sources, the planner may accept that rural communities are warm human places, having a considerable sense of security and a strong community spirit. Different in kind from the anonymous society of the towns, they shelter a way of life that is both precious and precarious. But, how far is this true? Is this a reliable guide for policy making or is it a myth, the countryside as we fondly imagine it to be, and not the countryside as it really is?

In his quest for help, the planner can turn to sociology for an analysis of contemporary social life and, as an area for investigation, community studies have proved to be fertile ground. In a famous paper, G.A. Hillery (2.3) identified and analyzed ninety-four different definitions of 'community' used by sociologists. For the cynical, this may be conclusive proof that sociology is simply semantics, but it is more reasonable to assume that sociologists have identified at least ninety-four different types of community or, equally likely, that there are at least ninety-four different ways of approaching the problem. Hillery's own conclusions were not helpful, "beyond the concept that people are involved in community there is no complete agreement as to the nature of community". He may have over-emphasized the disagreements, however, and in a reworking of Hillery's data, Bell and Newby (2.4) show that nearly three-quarters of the definitions agree that community incorporates three major elements: a group of people inter-acting; having some ties or bonds in common; and occupying a common geographic area.

The understanding of community life is not advanced greatly by such a minimal definition but, accepting that the variety of definitions mirror the diversity of social life, several attempts have been made to construct a continuum ranging from community life in a small, isolated, village to its antithesis in the big city. Apart from its sociological interest, the existence of a continuum, if proved, could be of considerable value to the planner; it could suggest an evolution of community types and help to anticipate the difficulties likely to be brought about by periods of change, of growth or decline. A German, Ferdinand Tonnies, writing in the 1880's, put forward the best known basis for a continuum by identifying two ideal types whose essence would be found in all kinds of social systems. These polar opposites are usually referred to as *Gemeinschaft* and *Gesellschaft,* their English translations, roughly 'community' and 'association', failing to convey the full subtleties of the original. Gemeinschaft is the more traditional type of society where relationships are personal, intimate and often enduring. The relationships are often ends in themselves and are functionally diffuse, in other words not formed for one limited purpose. The society in which they occur is homogeneous and immobile, there are relatively few cleavages or clashes of interest, every member knows and accepts his place, and the moral code of the society is clearly defined and generally upheld.

It is very tempting to associate Gemeinschaft with the small scale rural community and its polar opposite, Gesellschaft, with life in a metropolis. Gesellschaft typifies a society where relationships are chosen and employed for rationality and efficiency in achieving specific ends. Mobility, both social and spatial, is high. Life is dominated by impersonal and contractual ties and by an absence of traditional morality which "permits no consideration of means other than that of their perfect suitability for the obtaining of the end" (2.5). Central and Local Government bureaucracies and large commercial organizations are said to operate in a Gesellschaft manner.

Tonnies argued that these were ideal types only, standards by which reality may be recognized and described; nevertheless, a continuum linking one pole to the other was implied and has been central to much sociological thought. Unfortunately, for planners looking for a key to the understanding of community life and development, such continua are generally misleading. First, it is very rare for a continuum to describe more than a small part of the total relationships in society and those, like Tonnies', which are very broadly drawn may be dissected into several sub-elements, not all of which will vary to the same degree and in the same direction. Instead of one continuum, there may well be a hundred, each having some measure of 'independence'. Second, even if the broad gist of Tonnies' groupings is acceptable, they do not offer a satisfactory description of modern life. Relationships in the city are not always Gesellschaft-like in style or content. Wilmott and Young's study of family life in the East End of London (2.6) is not unique in

51

identifying a close knit pattern of relationships with a distinctly Gemeinschaft character apparently thriving in a city environment. Conversely, many small rural communities are more influenced by urban attitudes and organizations than by traditional rural ways of life. As Joe Bailey noted, "we see villages in our cities and cities in our villages" (2.7). It is to these cities in our villages that we now turn.

To help him understand the nature of rural communities in modern Britain, the planner is confronted with a plethora of detailed studies of individual communities. Some studies are almost microscopic in their approach and most tend to describe rural life as the background to a particular aspect which is under review, for example, commuters, or the strength of rural kinship patterns. Despite a variety of viewpoints, however, certain common themes begin to emerge from these studies and one of the most pervasive, as well as having most interest to planners, is urbanization.

Three studies illustrate the theme, each differing widely in place, beginning with R.E. Pahl's study of rural Hertfordshire. Pahl chose three villages for detailed study (2.8) but concentrated his attention on two villages within the Metropolitan Green Belt which had grown rapidly in population since 1945. The villages of Watton and Tewin with 278 and 340 households respectively, were analyzed by questionnaire techniques and Pahl was able to point to fundamental differences in background and life-style between the 'newcomers' (the post 1945 migrants), and the 'established' population. The newcomers differed markedly in terms of occupation, commuting, education and shopping places from the other residents. Newcomers, for example, were nearly eight times more likely to include representatives from professional or executive occupational groups. They contributed about 90% of the commuters from the two villages and their shopping habits, reflecting their mobility, were more likely to take them out of the local area into distant towns or into London. Although there were differences between the newcomers and the established, and between commuter and non-commuter, Pahl also demonstrated that many of these differences were sharpest when they were analyzed by social class and he concluded that selective migration into rural-urban fringe parishes was "attracting mobile, middle class commuters, who live and work in distinct and separate social and economic worlds from the established populations". The working class, Pahl has proceeded to argue (2.9, 2.10), is at an economic disadvantage by living in the countryside. The middle classes have more economic and social means at their disposal and enjoy a greater freedom to choose a 'place' to live. This has encouraged selective migration and has polarized communities socially. Class divides rural communities, and class or status characteristics are determined nationally, by the education and occupational systems. The mobility of the middle classes enables them to enter into 'communities of limited liabilities' where they can choose if they wish to opt in, and choose when they wish to opt out and move on, leaving their mistakes behind them. The social area that people inhabit depends upon their class, life style, residence, career and other factors. The same physical situation will be perceived differently by people with different social characteristics. Such an analysis leaves very little room for the traditional ideas about the cosiness or homogeneity of village life.

Pahl's conclusions were drawn from two Green Belt villages, a mere 25 miles north of London and heavily influenced by the metropolis. Does it follow that these conclusions are true of all rural settlements or does a different pattern emerge in villages more remote from large urban conurbations? Some answers are provided by a survey in 1966 of 75 parishes and 7 towns in Hampshire, mounted by Mass Observation on behalf of the County Planning Department (2.11). Winchester, which is roughly the geographic centre of the Hampshire, is 62 miles south-west of London and, although Southampton makes its presence felt in the southern part of the County, many of the villages are still far removed from the development pressures that have made a Green Belt designation essential to the Hertfordshire countryside.

The purpose of the Hampshire study was to provide a basis of facts against which current (1966) rural settlement policies could be assessed and, if necessary, modified. Data from seven towns were included for comparison. The results, it appears, surprised the authors of the report who had expected contrasts between town and village life but found instead that there were more similarities between them than points of difference; at least, in those aspects that the study investigated.

Similarities, some remarkably close, were found in many of the major characteristics and attitudes in town and country. In employment, villages had the same proportion of people at work, 55% of the population over 15 years, as the County as a whole. The proportion of people travelling out of their home village to work in the town was very close to the proportion of townspeople travelling from one town to another, and the distances travelled by villagers appeared to be no further, on average, than those in the town.

Similarities were evident in other aspects of life. Nearly one-fifth (19%) of villagers were born in the villages where they now lived while the comparable figure for the towns was 21%. People who were not born locally shared the same reasons for moving into their present town or village, 'work', at 37% and 34% respectively, being the prime motivator. Questioned on their attitudes towards possible improvements in their home areas, ranging from street lighting to swimming pools, few differences emerged and "the picture presented by these replies on the needs of the villagers suggests that they are not very different from those of the townspeople".

With these and other points in common, it should come as no surprise that the traditionalist view of the country, with its emphasis on the warm, close quality of community life, did not figure largely as an attraction for the modern villager. Most of the people who preferred the country to the town did so because it was more peaceful (55%) or because the countryside was more beautiful, more natural and healthier (53%). Only 27% referred to the supposed qualities of rural community life and these replies contained a disproportionate number from one particular socio-economic group (AB occupation group).

The report summarized its results with a distinct lack of enthusiasm. "Before the survey was carried out it was assumed that village life was somehow distinctive from, and had general characteristics which contrast with, life in towns. The survey was designed to illustrate contrasts if they existed. The results, however, show that there is no typical pattern of village life in respect of those aspects investigated, nor is there any marked difference between village life and town life in these respects, ..."

Although it discounts major differences between town and country, the report does allude to differences between the villages themselves and makes occasional distinctions between areas close to town and those which are 10 miles away or more. Should we turn, then, to the most remote villages to find a qualitative difference in rural life? Are urban influences and their apparent dominance over rural communities only diminished by great distance? Remote communities have exerted a fascination for social scientists; they exist at the common boundary of sociology and social anthropology and, as possible representatives of a way of life that is fast disappearing, they have been studied extensively. One such study is 'Westrigg', a parish in the Cheviot Hills, studied by James Littlejohn (2.12).

Westrigg is an upland parish with a population of 326 devoted mainly to forestry and to sheep farming. There is no village in the parish, no shop and no pub. It is 15 miles from the nearest town and is remote even by the standards of the Scottish Borders. 'Uncivilized' and 'wild' were epithets used by townspeople to describe the parish. Yet, in these unpromising circumstances, Littlejohn felt compelled to emphasize the similarities between Westrigg and urban centres. The way of life in the parish had altered profoundly in recent times. Changes were seen in agriculture, with 'agribusinesses' replacing the family farm and employer—employee relationships superseding master and man. There were changes too in the administration to local needs, with the decline of parish based services and the growth of the impersonal but more equitable supervision of the distant bureaucrat. Mass consumption, reducing the need for the exchange of goods among parishioners, more public transport and more leisure time, have all combined to make relationships between the people in the Westrigg "much more like those among the population of any industrial area than they were fifty years ago".

These broad conclusions, about the spreading influence of the outer, urban world, have been endorsed by other studies in isolated western and highland areas of Britain. Littlejohn's analysis was based on survey work between 1949 and 1951 and, if the trends that he observed were strong then, they have many times the force now. Indeed, the myth of rural life was being debunked much further back than the late 1940's. Disraeli (2.14) scarcely bothered to differentiate between country and town:

> ' "There is no community in England; there is aggregation, but aggregation under circumstances which make it rather a dissociating than a unifying principle . . ."
> "It is a community of purpose that constitutes society", continued the younger stranger; "without that, men may be drawn into contiguity but they still continue virtually isolated".
> "And is that their condition in the cities?"
> "It is their condition every where, but in cities that condition is aggravated." '

When Christopher Hall of the Council for the Protection of Rural England asserts that "the English Village . . . is dying, is being done to death" (2.14) he is probably right, albeit one hundred years after the event.

The lesson of these studies is not that rural life is identical with the town but rather that their coincidences over-ride their contrasts to a much greater extent than popular or professional sentiment is prepared to allow. Differences will still remain, a function of the small scale of rural life rather than of rurality *per se,* and, although they are subordinate to the main theme, they can have an influence in the approach to, and in the resolution of, community problems.

Superficially, these differences may vary from village to village, as in the status granted to the squire and clergy. Many of these idiosyncracies, however, are legacies of the past, their rationale derived from the social and economic conditions of days gone-by, but the traditional manners and ways of behaviour persist, ghostlike, long after the substance has dissolved. Much more important to the planner is the network of social relationships around the village and the effects wrought upon that network by the small scale of the village and its physical isolation. Bearing in mind the risks attendant upon any broad generalization, rural life tends to be characterized by multiple role relationships, that is each person will be linked to many other people in the community in a variety of different but overlapping ways. Thus, one man may have several links with another, as a neighbour, as a colleague at work and as a fellow member of the parish council, sporting or voluntary clubs. In the town, these relationships tend to be discrete; the large scale and patterns of segregation in urban life will usually ensure that the neighbour, the work colleague and the club member will be three different people, not combined into one. It follows that social networks in the rural areas are more closely knit. Two people will have more friends, or activities, in common than in the town where it is a rare coincidence for two strangers to find that they share a mutual acquaintance. As a direct consequence, rural community life will be dominated by caution. If a man has to share a range of social contacts with a relatively limited number of people he will hesitate before taking attitudes or actions which will offend and which may be carried over into other spheres of social life that he shares with them. The implications of this analysis illuminate many village problems and will be discussed later.

Transport

As links with the outer world grow in volume and intensity; the village or rural community becomes less self-suffici-ent in meeting its own needs and relies increasingly upon contacts with specialist services from urban centres. Some of these con-tacts, television and the media generally, exert a great influence upon rural life but are beyond the purview of the Local Planning Officer. Others, and in particular, personal mobility and public transport can be controlled by locally based decision makers. In an urban orientated society, the ease of getting out of the village is one of the reasons that makes village life tolerable and those to whom mobility is denied form the deprived groups of rural areas. Transport is a means of meeting the deficiencies of village life and it has become a key area in the solution of community problems.

It is worthwhile looking hard at the facts concerning car ownership in rural areas for they can be used to conceal rather than to reveal the true situation. About 50% of all households nationally have the use of a car and in rural areas the figure is higher. Recent Department of Environment surveys showed 74% of households in Devon (2.15) and 73% in Suffolk (2.16) with at least one car, while the comparable figure in an Oxfordshire parish study by P.E.P. (2.17) was 67% and a report on Merioneth for the Welsh Council showed 64% (2.18). The conclusion, that a relatively small minority of rural households, between one-quarter and one-third of the total, are without the use of a car would be strictly true but grossly misleading. Apart from diverting attention away from disadvantaged and needy groups in society, it ignores the high degree of use of cars for journeys to work (70% of all car owning households in Merioneth, 76% in the Oxfordshire parish) in effect, making the remaining members of the household non-car users for most of the week. It is not households but people without the use of cars that show the true extent of rural deprivation. On this revised base half of all adults in Merioneth and Oxfordshire are carless, and women in Merioneth (68%), more so than men (27%). By age, the elderly and the late teens have least access to private cars, three-quarters (76%) of all pensioners in Oxfordshire, and in Merioneth a detailed analysis by age groups showed 90% of women and 52% of men over 65 years had no regular use of a car. In the words of Age Concern (2.19), "Elderly people are virtually prisoners to their immediate neighbourhood". The only other age group to approach these levels are the teenagers, 14-24 years, where nearly half (47%) the men and nearly three-quarters (71%) of the women are without private transport.

The Welsh Council also measures the likelihood of car ownership against family income and their figures suggest a statistical correlation of 0.93. Most families with an income of £1000 p.a. or less do not own a car (November 1972 figures) and include low paid workers and most pensioners. The extent to which families in rural areas pay

57

more for their transport, a basic necessity for life, is found in the Household Expenditure Survey where a greater percentage (15.3%) of the rural disposable income pays for transport than in the town (13.1%). And, it must be remembered that in some rural areas incomes are about 25% below national levels.

Evidence of this sort postdates the Department of Environment surveys in Devon and Suffolk but it is disappointing to see how the Department failed to realize the importance of accessibility by specific groups in the population and referred instead to the 'residual' needs of a "small minority of the population" ignoring, it seems, the results of its own survey which showed that "the availability of a car is strongly related to sex (men more than twice as likely as women), to social grade (AB about three times as likely as DE) and to age (25-44 nearly three times as likely as those 65 or over)". The survey work was based on two rural areas, where the number of passengers travelling by stage bus services had been declining for many years. Overall, only 6% of the people interviewed used public transport regularly, about the same proportion for work journeys and personal business trips, rather more for shopping (13%), but very few for leisure purposes. This type of analysis begs the question of the availability and convenience of bus services in the area as well as the importance of the bus services to its users. For example, in Merioneth, 41% of all bus journeys were for health purposes and 35% for shopping, many times greater than the use of the household car which, by contrast, had more journeys for social purposes.

The two reports had identical remits but they differ strongly in tone. An awareness of certain basic social needs is obvious from the conclusions to the Suffolk report: "Is it too much to hope in this compassionate society of ours that a small part of its almost unlimited potential can be diverted, now and then, to solve the hardship of the old, the young and the needy?". The Devon report, however, is unmoved by such considerations and betrays an astonishing complacency. After documenting the incidence of lift begging, especially in areas poorly served by public transport, and noting that over one-third of all respondents had felt unable to make journeys because of a lack of public transport, it concludes, "clearly people have adapted to the absence of a bus; those who could not presumably left some time ago". Or, presumably, do without. The social implications are not pursued.

In looking to the future, passenger transport services will continue to decline as private car ownership slowly expands among the lower paid occupational groups. There will always, however, be a group without the use of a car, either because they are too poor or because age or physical infirmity prevent them driving. "The belief that the rural transport problem will disappear with the rise in car ownership" says the Welsh Council report, "is an Utopian illusion", though the eventual size of this group has not been determined. Too many railway tracks have been dismantled and too many track beds have been sold for the train service to resume a significant role in rural passenger transport, and the public bus, supplemented by car-based and other services, is the most feasible pattern. The crucial question revolves around the level of subsidy *vis-à-vis* the level of need. The disadvantaged are not likely to be the most articulate or knowledgeable advocates of their cause and, as Connell (2.20) noted in four Surrey parishes, the two car, professional families who understand the workings of Local Government bureaucracy are not bothered by the problems of the immobile council housewife; their preoccupations are on different matters, conservation not transportation is their concern. Partly as a result, local authority subsidies for bus services are low, usually no more than 10% of the total highway budget, excluding trunk roads, in rural Counties and it is not difficult to spot some apparent inconsistencies in different counties with more money spent subsidizing car parking than bus services (2.21).

In passing, it must be acknowledged that subsidies are an emotive and complicated issue and the presentation of bald statistics relating to bus services alone gives a one-sided picture. Thus, the level of subsidies does not equal total savings in the event of the closure of a subsidized route. Passengers often interchange routes as part of their journey and because of the network effect, the closure of one route would have an adverse effect upon passenger levels on the other routes that link with it. Some costs would be thrown onto other services altogether. The Ambulance Officer in the former County of Denbigh estimated a 15% increase in patients and mileage for non-emergency purposes should the loss-making rural bus services be withdrawn (2.22). Other studies in the same County showed how the catchment area for mother and child clinics was limited to the town and that very few mothers travelled in from the country. "In effect this means that the population in the surrounding country areas are making relatively little use of clinic facilities and find themselves giving an informal and involuntary subsidy to the town possibly through the inadequacy of rural transport."

Despite some differences in approach, the studies in Devon, Suffolk and Merioneth come to broadly similar conclusions. All agree that the solution lies in the co-ordination of transport policies and services with the County Council exercising a dominant role through its allocation of grant aid under Section 34 of the Transport Act 1968. Stage bus services should be retained for all journeys judged important within the County context: in other words inter-urban services and between towns and major villages, with the County ensuring that buses required for school contracts would also be available for stage services for the rest of the day. (The Merioneth report goes so far to suggest that the number of buses needed for school journeys should dictate the numbers available for stage services. By using part time drivers and a one shift system—labour accounts for 72% of total running costs—and by relying upon postal buses and cars to serve the smaller settlements it should be possible to retain a basic service and halve the amount of subsidy. The only people to suffer in this proposal would be those travelling to work, who are probably the least vulnerable group.)

In the more isolated areas, school buses can be used to take fare paying passengers and a similar flexibility is available under Section 30 of the Transport Act 1968 for taxi services and mini buses to charge separate fares and pick up passengers en route. Norfolk County Council are currently grant-aiding a mini bus project using volunteer drivers centred on six villages near Sheringham. With some slight legislative amendments private cars could also accept payment for lifts given on a fares basis, and here there is a role for Parish Councils to put forward schemes for organizing lifts in their own areas. Parish Councils and their umbrella bodies, the County Associations of Local Councils, can offer much sound advice in a transport coordination programme as Hertfordshire has recently demonstrated (2.23).Following parish and public involvement, spare bus capacity in off-peak hours has been used to reorganize and extend shopping and evening services at little or no extra cost.

Postal buses were considered but have limitations. Their flows do not match the needs of many potential passengers as they start from the town early in the day to go out to the villages at a time when passengers will require journeys in the opposite direction. Their routes are often circuitous and very slow (1 hour to cover 5 miles) and with only one delivery and collection a day in some parts of the country, there may be no return journey from town. Notwithstanding these drawbacks, postal buses operate in Devon, Mid-Wales, and Scotland, at a profit, and provide a service for shopping and other purposes where exact timing is not of over-riding importance. They operate best on linear routes, along valleys (reminiscent of their

Swiss ancestry) and may reach their full potential only in the highland areas of Britain.

The social car service, is very different in character. It has similarities to the hospital car service but is not confined to the movement of patients and is intended to meet emergencies and 'important but irregular needs' experienced by the poor and handicapped who do not normally have access to private cars and for whom public transport is not available. The service, which began in Lincolnshire (Lindsey) and has since spread to other parts of the country, is founded upon local volunteers as drivers and as village organizers who receive requests for assistance and arrange the appropriate lifts. Since the County Council's role, as fund giver, is limited to the cost of administration and petrol and does not pay for the time of the volunteers, the burden on the public purse tends to be low. An experiment in the Maelor area of Clwyd, with population of 5000, cost a mere £239 over a twelve month period, or 85p a trip.

Transport always has been a problem in rural areas, even in the days of the horse drawn carrier asking if anything was needed from the town. As a 'liberator', which has freed the villager from forced dependence upon his neighbours for goods and services, it has still some way to develop before it overcomes the basic paradox, outlined by Political and Economic Planning, that those areas with the least facilities to offer are generally those with poorest public transport. The people living in these areas have nothing to go to locally, nor do they have adequate means to get out to facilities elsewhere. Although the solutions proposed for public transport embrace some controversial and possibly undesirable aspects, notably the implications in the Devon report that the State should shed some of its obligations on to voluntary service agencies, the flexible use of resources in trying to meet a problem is a characteristic of other community services in rural areas. They, too have encountered difficulties in servicing a small and scattered population and they, too, have been forced to re-examine their initial approach, to question whether solutions derived from a large scale urban society are necessarily appropriate to small scale dispersed communities.

Education

In education, the main theme in rural areas has been reorganization and consolidation into fewer, larger schools. Primary schools have suffered greatly in this process. In the former East Riding, the number of primary schools dropped from 235 in 1946 to 151 in 1970, a decrease of 36% in 24 years. The impetus underlying this movement has been part educational and part economic, with the sceptics laying stress upon the latter. Labour represents a proportionately larger cost in small schools and the minimum 'economic' size is probably a one form entry school with roughly 210 pupils. Of late, the pace has slackened as the extra costs of transporting children has outstripped the savings made by school closures. There has also been a major report, Gittins on Primary Education in Wales (1967) and, although influenced by conditions within the Principality, it suggested certain standards by which all local education authorities could judge their own problems. Gittins proposed a minimum size for primary schools of 60 pupils (say, three teachers) but even this has provoked opposition from defenders of smaller schools. Many schools are still well below the Gittins lower limits and, in practice, it seems that only those with less than 40 pupils are in danger of 'reorganization'.

The educational arguments against small rural schools take their cue directly from the modern world (2.23). At the upper end of the primary school, the curriculum has expanded so rapidly, to cover subjects such as French, Science, and Music, that there are now too many and diverse interests for one or two teachers to cover adequately and children in small schools could be disadvantaged by the limited range offered to them. Very similar arguments apply to equipment and materials. Economics apart, it may be physically impossible to house all the equipment considered essential for modern education in a small, out-dated building. Activity spaces, music rooms, television, film projectors and cookery bays, are all extensive in their use of space—which is at a premium in small schools.

The arguments have a psychological and social slant as well. Psychology stresses the dangers inherent in a small school where the dominance of one teacher may be unrelieved; the school could thrive under the influence of a good teacher but equally it may suffer under a mediocre one. Sociology refers to the influx of people from the town into country areas and their demands for urban standards of education which, it is said, are superior and cannot be met within the limitations of a small school. Use is also made of the resources argument familiar to planners. Schools must adapt to the changing patterns of population and work place and if certain villages are selected for growth, education must be responsive and go where growth is directed.

The proponents of the small school are not without arguments of their own to stress. There are advantages derived from small, vertically grouped classes where children of different ages help each other, the older children gaining particularly in terms of responsibility and self-expression. The value of this traditional teaching method has been demonstrated by its adoption in larger, urban schools. Young children also benefit from the confidence and security obtained from smaller groups and from the individual attention allowed by a low pupil-staff ratio and low staff turnover. Discipline is rarely a problem and the vitally important links between home and school can be strong, a point which readily merges with a more general one, namely the social advantages that can be gained by the use of the school as a focal point for community life. Turning to the expanding horizons of the modern world, a demand for a variety of interests could be met by peripatetic teachers serving a group of village schools (and cheaply too, the costs of transporting one person are less than an entire school), whilst the educational administrator may prefer smaller units for the flexibility they give in meeting unforeseen population changes and the grouping of children into secondary school catchment areas.

Both sets of arguments have their merits and the compromises now being discussed, or implemented by some Authorities like Northumberland, incorporate the best features of large and small schools. The Northumberland Scheme proposed three levels of schooling, a primary school from 4+ to 9 years, a middle school 9 to 13 years and a high school 13 to 18 years. Of the three levels, the primary school is the most locally based and may well include some two teacher schools with less than 60 pupils. At the age of 9, the child transfers to a middle school accommodating roughly 200 pupils and serving a group of villages. Finally, there is the high school, of which there will be six across the County.

Besides trying to achieve a gradation in size, the Northumberland Scheme also tries to maintain ties with the local community and this it does in two ways. First, by ensuring that where village schools are closed, the buildings are used for alternative educational uses and this has led to a comprehensive programme for outdoor education by converting eleven former village schools into Field Study Centres with residential accommodation. At least a quarter of the courses taught are concerned with the acquisition of skills necessary for living in remote areas. Second, by encouraging the development of youth and adult associations, based on high, middle and secondary schools, educational and recreational programmes can be provided in association with the school in areas where commercial facilities or entertainments would not be viable.

In its involvement of youths and adults with local schools, Northumberland probably owes a debt to the Cambridgeshire Village Colleges founded and developed in the 1930s by Henry Morris, the former Director of Education for the County of Cambridge. Morris's idea was to "shift the centre of gravity of education from childhood to youth and maturity" and he proposed to do this by making places of education the centre of village life. Believing that education is a process that continues throughout life, he created within one complex of buildings, cultural, educational and recreational facilities for all sections of the rural community and refused to countenance any rigid divisions in the use of the centres; adults for example should use the centre in the daytime as well as in the evening. Each village college serves a group of villages. Sites were chosen with an eye to the natural beauty of the environment and are associated with county secondary schools. There are currently fifteen village colleges in Cambridgeshire and the idea has spread to other Counties.

Northumberland and Cambridgeshire demonstrate a flexibility in the use of scarce resources which is essential for meeting the needs of rural communities. The dual use of facilities in a community school maximizes the use made of buildings and equipment and has, as a most valuable side effect, the integration of education into village life. Flexibility is required in the use of rooms and equipment so that they can be adapted to the changing circumstances and demands throughout the day or, indeed, throughout the year. A new housing estate built near the village may throw a heavy burden upon the school in its first few years before declining to more normal levels; temporary accommodation is probably the best response and not, as it is so often presented, an admission of failure to anticipate demand. Flexibility is needed in the use of funds, for, invariably when integrated schemes are proposed, finance will come from many different sources and problems of coordination arise. Above all else, flexibility is required of the personnel, the policy maker and the teacher, who should recognize the drawbacks of a compartmentalized, urban approach to the problems of a small scale rural society and should devise a system that is adaptable to local circumstances and not be imposed as a rigid pattern. This is a point which can be generalized to cover other rural services.

Health and community services

The tendency towards the wholesale grouping of facilities in education has also been evident in the provision of health services, but here again there has been a reassessment as the costs of centralization became too great to ignore. These costs extend to the inconvenience felt by the patient, pupil or whoever is on the receiving end of the service, and more emphasis is now placed upon small units. As an example, the hospital service, whilst still pushing forward with a programme of large specialist hospitals with wide catchment areas, has now begun to buttress this programme by a series of smaller community hospitals, often using former cottage hospitals in small market towns. The role given to the community hospital is to provide locally based services for patients not in need of acute treatment, where general practitioners may treat their own patients, thus providing a firm link with the family doctor, the man who still comes to your home.

Similar considerations have affected clinic based services. Basic medical facilities dictate the minimum size of a clinic and very often these facilities would be under-used in rural areas. The usual response was to provide clinics only where they could be justified by theoretical population catchments, until it was realized that this penalized many patients who found they could not reach the clinic. Three alternatives presented themselves. First, to reverse normal procedures and, instead of taking the patient to the specialist, bring the specialist or technician out to the patient's home area. It has been argued that the time of people dispensing specialist services was too valuable to be spent travelling but transport costs have escalated so much that the equation has been overturned. Second, to provide clinics in areas knowing that they will not be fully used but planning to share the surplus capacity with similar users in education or the social services. Third, to develop the use of mobile clinics and services. Conventional mobile clinics are usually unsatisfactory because they contain no w.c.'s or waiting room space, but a new concept, a specialist clinic which can be moved from village to village and plugged into a core of fixed basic facilities shared with other users, may overcome these limitations.

Services dispensed from mobile units are often disparaged as second best, yet their flexibility in meeting the needs of a changing population or of a scattered one are unequalled, as the Clwyd

Library Service has shown. The County is schizophrenic, with the eastern, English speaking, urban half experiencing tremendous population growth in the past ten years while the Welsh speaking and rural west is still slowly declining in numbers. Faced with these very different demands, the County inaugurated a joint mobile-trailer library system where the trailer is routed to a large housing estate or village for one or more days while the attendant mobile library detaches itself and journeys to the smaller settlements in the hinterland. Two or three days later the mobile rejoins the trailer and moves to another location. Far from being expensive, this service is as cost-efficient in the allocation of books as fixed libraries, mobiles in Clwyd accounting for 18% of all books on loan to adults but only 15% of all costs. Admittedly there are some hidden overheads to be added but the general picture is not challenged.

So far, general principles have been drawn from the public services and they are not necessarily applicable to commercial concerns which obviously have to pay regard to maintaining their competitive position. The option of the dual use of facilities and of premises is not presented in the same form and alternative strategies have to be devised whereby the commercial operator can overcome the disadvantages of scale yet refrain from imposing limitations upon his independence. One such strategy is the cooperative, for buying or for selling, which has been adopted by farmers and by shop keepers.

The village shop is one of the traditional focal points for community life but has found itself to be at a severe disadvantage in competition with supermarkets. Because of the small scale of his operations, the shopkeeper is not able to negotiate comparable discounts and finds that his higher prices lose him customers. And it is his best customers that he loses first, the most affluent being the most mobile who can afford to shop around and buy in sufficient bulk to make a trip to a distant supermarket worthwhile. The village shop is left to cater for a diminished and increasingly impoverished clientele and a downward cycle sets in that may end with the closure of the shop and exacerbate the hardships felt by the immobile, disadvantaged groups in rural society. There are other ways in which supermarkets can have detrimental effects upon people in rural areas. A supermarket situated on the edge of a small town will draw customers away from town centre grocery stores. Some of these town centre stores operate rural delivery services and when the contraction of trade threatens their profit margins, these relatively expensive delivery services are the first to be cut. Thus, once more, the immobile and impecunious suffer because of an economic system which is geared to the needs of the affluent.

With these adversities, the banding together of shopkeepers into a cooperative could give them the price advantages of a large buying organization and several companies (such as Mace, Spar, and V.G.) now operate in Britain and, although not cooperatives in the true sense, perform the same functions. To join the Mace organization a fee is required of the shopkeeper and an undertaking to purchase a minimum amount (say £200) of goods each week. In return, Mace supplies goods at relatively cheap rates and delivers them to the village shop. It supplements this basic task with a variety of advertising, promotional and other retailer services. At the end of the year most shopkeepers can obtain a discount based upon their turnover. The shopkeepers are grouped into regional units and have representatives on the Mace Retailer Committee, whom they elect directly. They have, therefore, a considerable influence upon the policy of the company.

Planning declining communities

The difficulties in serving rural communities that are attributable to the small scale, isolation and dispersed population patterns, are essentially components in a static analysis. Few communities, however, are stable in numbers. Most are in a process of growth or decline and the problems they face cannot be understood without regard to the additional complications that ensue when the size of the community itself is changing.

Depopulation is a minority phenomenon, even among the minority who live in rural areas, and is largely confined to the western and northern peripheries of Britain with occasional pockets elsewhere. It is also an unfamiliar problem in the sense that it goes against national experience. The whole tenor of national life since the war (at least until the oil crisis) has been founded on growth and planners have been trained to meet the demands of an expanding economy, not of a declining one. But although unfamiliar for the majority, depopulation has had a long and consistent history, and parts of highland Britain for example have been losing people steadily for over 100 years.

Community problems associated with depopulation stem, in part, from the overall number of people lost and, in part, from the special characteristics of those who migrate. Looking, first, at overall numbers, a gradual decline could lead, paradoxically, to depopulated areas enjoying some of the highest standards of provision of social and other services of any part of the U.K. The original population levels may contract but their services, in terms of buildings and fixed equipment, are not so flexible. To take an extreme example, settlements with two or more meeting halls dating from late Victorian times may now find that they can only make economic use of one. Even staff numbers are not capable of fine and instantaneous adjustments. There is considerable inertia built into organizations whose services hinge upon personal relationships; they may see their clientele reduced over a period of say ten years to give a staffing ratio that would be the envy of any urban area but raises serious doubts about the fullest use of valuable skills. Similarly, redundancy is also created in the provision of public utilities. A water main may now serve only one farm instead of two; if the costs of provision are unaltered and the revenue has been halved, the subsidy required to maintain the service is increased.

The under-utilization of resources caused by a reduction in overall population levels may be a lesser problem than the effects brought about by the differential rates of migration between sections of the population. It is the young who migrate, predominantly in the 15 to 34 age group. To quote the Welsh situation again, figures for the former counties of Merioneth, Montgomery and Radnor show that they had 18% of their population in this age group compared with 22% in England and Wales in 1971. These proportions have changed little since the report, *Depopulation in Mid-Wales* (2.25) was published in 1964. A point made in the report and confirmed by the 1971 census is the high rate of migration among young women (28% more than men, in the 15-34 year group) leading to a low marriage rate, a low rate of natural increase, and to yet another cycle of deprivation.

Selectivity applies even among the young. As the Mid-Wales report noted, the stream of migrants comprises "those of the younger generation possessing ambition and initiative, and more particularly those who have attained a high level of education". Some may be attracted by the bright lights of the city. Many more will leave in search of job opportunities that are not available locally. This applies especially to those with an advanced education for, it has been argued (2.26), that the urban nature of our educational and examination system makes its recipients unsuited to living and working in the countryside. Not only does the system instruct them in the ways of the urban world but it forces them to join that world to seek their economic salvation. Rather like the tribute extracted by feudal lords, the depopulation of the young is a tribute levied by an urban society upon remote rural areas. When the high level of subsidies to upland areas is discussed, and, usually deplored, it must be remembered that upland areas 'pay' heavily for their subsidies, through the forced migration of their young.

The effects of this movement upon community resources and services are stark. There will be a squeeze on the economically productive age groups who will have to support a proportionately larger unproductive population of pensioner age. This results, in turn, in a lower per capita income and less financial resources, public and private, for improvements to housing and community services that may be deficient in standards. In fact, one of the few 'growth' points likely to be found in a depopulating area is the growth in the numbers of old people. An absolute growth obviously strains depleting local authority resources but the effects of a proportionate growth may be equally severe. The migration of the young leaves fewer people to discharge traditional family responsibilities and more old people who, bereft of family support in times of need, have to turn to the Local Authority for assistance.

Finally, there is the delicate matter of community leadership. Without doubt, the migration of a substantial proportion of the young diminishes the pool of potential leaders. If the Mid-Wales report is correct and it is the more able who migrate, leadership will be monopolized by the older, conservative age groups and by the remaining and, possibly, complacent young who will have little incentive to alter a system from which they, at least, derive some sustenance (2.27). The leadership thrown up by depopulated areas, therefore, is likely to exhibit one of two contradictory traits. It will either be a conservative force unwilling to consider change and unable to adapt satisfactorily to measures required to halt depopulation, or it will be so desperate to reclaim its lost youth that it will demand development, any development, regardless of its suitability to the area or possible adverse consequences. Very often, of course, the two traits coexist and give rise to the man, who is quite prepared to consider change as long as it does not affect him. Thus, the planner finds that his technical problems are compounded by the attitudes of the population, and the latter may be the more difficult to resolve. This sort of problem is encountered in Scotland where the impact of oil development on remote communities has thrown up situations of great sensitivity, requiring tact and understanding to resolve.

Growth in rural areas, and the difficulties brought in its train, has been more in line with the national experience than has depopulation, and has attracted more attention. When the Mid-Wales report complained that areas of economic growth were receiving too much emphasis, it was echoing the sentiments of William Cobbett nearly 150 years earlier (2.28): "These new enclosures and houses arise out of the beggaring of the parts of the country distant from the vortex of funds. The farm houses have long been growing fewer and fewer; . . . The labourers' houses disappear also. And all the *useful* people become less numerous". Cobbett knew where to put the blame, the new houses were built on a spot "not far distant from the Stock-Jobbing crew. The roads to it are level. They are smooth. The wretches can go to it from the "Change without any danger to their worthless necks". A picture, many would argue that differs only in details from the present time.

The Development Commissioners (themselves London based) illustrate some of this preoccupation by their investigation of three studies of rapidly expanding rural communities on the fringe of urban areas. They chose to study villages in Monmouth, Hampshire and, surprisingly, West Cumbria, and although only the latter two have so far reported (2.29) it is interesting to observe how different teams in widely differing areas come to similar conclusions.

Planning for expanding communities

While it would be misleading to suggest that growth is a mirror image of depopulation, nevertheless, it may be helpful to adopt a similar approach and to recognize, first, the problems that result from an increase in the size of a community and, second, the problems that result from the distinct character of the migrants themselves, when seen against the established population.

Both the Hampshire and the Cumbria reports identify the provision of facilities as a major deficiency in planning for growth. There was a considerable time lag between the arrival of new residents and the expansion of social facilities to cater to their needs. Public utilities are usually functioning prior to arrival but it seems that social facilities are still an after-thought, despite the warnings sounded in *The Needs of New Communities* in 1968.

Policy documents which concentrate almost exclusively on the physical aspects of planning (the situation reported by the West

Cumbrian Study) and ignore the social needs of the inhabitants, may therefore assign a lower priority to social facilities and services than public opinion requires. Very often, of course, villages selected for expansion are those with some slack in the basic physical infrastructure and while planners can congratulate themselves for getting expansion 'on the cheap', the villagers may get no improvement in their social services and the experience merely serves to exacerbate the problems of living in a rural area. Thus, in Hampshire, it was difficult to find any new social facilities that had followed expansion in the four villages except schools, and the situation with regard to playing fields, youth facilities and community halls was generally much worse. Commenting on the opportunities to alleviate these problems by the dual use of school premises and equipment, the Hampshire report remarked that "despite encouragement from central government, the evidence for much movement in this direction is somewhat slender". Where existing facilities are taken into account in planning for expansion, it seems that the attention they receive is frequently meagre. It is not sufficient merely to note the presence of a certain facility or building without going on to consider whether it has the capacity or flexibility to accommodate growth, or changing patterns of needs.

What the villagers expect from an expansion of their settlement, and what they actually get, is a neglected aspect of the growth process. Many villagers begin with the attitude that bigger can only be better; their subsequent disappointments breed apathy and cynicism which can make solutions even more difficult to attain and place yet another obstacle between the planner and the public he serves. The two studies agree that the planner must shoulder much of the blame. He under-rates the provision of social facilities because he has not bothered to sound public opinion, and, conversely, he frequently fails to supply the same public with information about his intentions and about the changes that the plan may bring. Rumour thrives in a situation of uncertainty, expectations are allowed to mount and the disillusionments will sour later dealings.

There are reasons which go some way towards explaining this unsatisfactory state of affairs. Statistical projections upon which the justification for services may hinge, are very unreliable in small area studies and extraneous factors can have a major disturbing influence. The programme of the entire development, too, may be out of the planners' hands. It will be the developer who usually controls the pace and the Local Authority is placed in the unenviable position of reacting to the developers' plans unless, of course, it chooses to gamble with public money and provide facilities in advance of a predicted need—which may never come about. Even if the planner is aware of social needs in the village, he may be unable to provide for them adequately. The village centre may have no space for additional public buildings and they will have to be relegated to a subsidiary centre or to sporadic, 'back street' sites, assuming of course, that the sponsoring Authority does not wish to bear the additional expense of buying property or land already used for some other (non-agricultural) purpose. Regardless of choice, costs will inevitably impose a heavy burden. The very mechanisms of growth encourage a general rise in land values and the purchase price for land for community services will increase proportionately, or more so, if key village centre sites are sought.

Whether such problems can be overcome will depend partly upon the physical structure of the village, a precondition over which the planner has little control. But the same cannot be said of the new residential areas and the physical forms that they take. In Hampshire and in Cumbria, there were strong criticisms of the layouts of residential areas. Village extensions were described as a series of linked housing estates, with the layouts encouraging a separate identity on each estate and going no way towards promoting a sense of 'community' between the newcomers and the established residents. If the thesis is accepted, that physical form can influence social contacts, then one answer may be to plan an inverted Radburn-type layout. The intention would be to deliberately design housing estates that are outward looking and to maximize the casual and accidental contacts between the estate and the village, rather than to continue with 'village green' type designs which are usually spurious in tradition and may fragment life by giving rise to groups of social isolates.

The scale of development, too, can give rise to concern. Some residential estates have grown too fast, and by too much, for the host village to absorb and, once again, a separate neighbourhood identity has been encouraged. To avoid social divisions and to allow newcomers and established residents time to adjust to a new situation, the allowable rate and scale of growth should be related to the size of the village and to its social characteristics. Few studies have been directed to this problem.

On the available evidence, however, it must be admitted that the form and scale of new development is of less significance to the social life of the village than the characteristics of the migrants who come to live in the new houses. The migrants in the four Hampshire villages (mainly owner occupiers, with professional or skilled occupations and upwardly mobile) appear to differ very little from those studied by Pahl on the fringes of the metropolitan Green Belt or by Elizabeth Radford (2.30) in her survey of newcomers to Worcestershire villages within commuting distance of Birmingham. The pattern is a very familiar one and even extends to North Wales, with the additional complication that Merseyside commuters intermingle with a migrant retirement population; nevertheless both groups appear to share a common social and economic background—apart from age (2.31).

Although there may be similarities across the country between migrant populations, the contrasts with their respective host populations are marked. The established 'villagers' often comprise more unskilled workers, have less personal mobility and lower educational standards. With the introduction of a migrant element, especially on a large scale, social and class divisions could be accentuated and village 'solidarity' reduced. The type of migrant attracted, will depend upon the type of house offered, and if the builders are allowed a free rein, they will naturally supply the most profitable market, usually executive houses. Thus, in Hampshire, the social balance of some villages has been allowed to change, unwittingly, by the differential migration of the middle classes. It would be unrealistic to expect the developer to accept the notion of a balanced community, which may cut into his profit margins, but it is disappointing to note the extent to which planners have either failed to impose this concept upon new residential development, or have never bothered to try.

The village of Broughton in West Cumbria was reported as an example of an unhappy marriage, between a new housing estate and a host village. The village itself is largely working class in composition and any extension should have paid regard to its existing character (as in architecture, so in social planning); instead, a middle class estate was added to the village. As well as being physically separate, the newcomers found that the largely working class culture gave them few opportunities to enter village life; it is difficult to imagine a rising young executive joining the pigeon fanciers club. As a result there were two 'villages' in Broughton and the benefits of an increased population to the social life and 'community spirit' of the village were minimal. It may seem an obvious point, but the social life of the village should be examined to see whether it has enough points of contact to absorb newcomers, before a decision for growth is taken. However the number of planning studies that treat the variety of village activities and the composition of its population as a major element in a successful plan are regrettably few in number.

Participation

The problems of growth do not stop at the mixing of disparate elements. In a democratic society, all factions are entitled to a voice and will assail the planner with contradictory opinions, magnified by the tensions that accompany growth. If he is to profit by this advice and if he is to fulfil the spirit as well as the letter of his public participation obligations, the planner must be aware of the local power structure and appreciate that the nature of leadership in rural areas will reflect aspects of the society that nurtures it. This refers to a point made earlier about the qualities of social relationships in a small community, of informality, of face-to-face dealings, and of overlapping roles. Rural societies are often conservative and place a high value on individualism and self-reliance. They are also personal and more likely to exhibit decisions which are seemingly irrational, but quite understandable, when viewed against the people and the temperaments involved. Being small in scale they can be suspicious of large, impersonal and calculating organizations and treat the Planning Officer, especially the County Planner, as a representative of an alien body.

Faced with what amounts to a cultural gap, the planner must discard elaborate decision making models applicable to urban areas and, following Travis (2.32), heed instead a range of individuals who are the critical decision makers and opinion moulders in the countryside. To an urban orientated mind, these individuals are to be found in the most unlikely places, in the Women's Institute and in the Church Men's Society as well as the more formal Parish Council or local branch of a farmers' union. The special role of the land owner in rural leadership must be acknowledged, together with the consequences that flow from a simpler pattern of land ownership. Compared to urban areas, there are fewer and larger blocks of land, but controlled by smaller managerial units where family and personal motivations may be strong enough to over-ride the emotionless promptings of the commercial world. Bearing in mind that it is the landowner who retains the initiative in the development process, and may continue to do so, notwithstanding the Community Land Act, an analysis of the local power structure in these terms may help to explain the unpredictability that dogs planning matters in rural areas.

Returning to the growth situation, the immigrant population may be equally guilty of misreading local patterns of power and how they are applied. Institutions like the W.I. are susceptible to take-overs and, by abruptly applying new manners and attitudes, the migrants may alienate the local people. However, they will rarely alienate the planner to whom their specialist and professional approach is instantly recognizable and, often, welcomed. Thus, the danger exists that the planner will be beguiled into known and accustomed ways, giving more attention to the views of the migrants than to the locals whose own knowledge of bureaucratic manipulation may be relatively slight. Public meetings, despite being well attended, may be no more effective in sounding rural opinions than they are in the towns and a search must be made for an appropriate local vehicle which will fit in with the casual, informal approach often found in rural areas.

Whatever means are selected, public expressions of opinion will be heavily influenced by overlapping roles. In other words, the same faces will recur, wearing different hats and trying to reconcile their multiple roles by voicing curiously contorted and not entirely consistent opinions. The outsider may be confused but attempts at elucidation will not be welcomed, for confusion caused by ambiguity is one of the social mechanisms whereby the sharp cutting edges that may disturb life in a small community are blunted and overcome. A closely related mechanism is caution, or the apparent inability to suggest any solutions to what may be generally recognized as a serious problem. To propose a solution—or even an exact definition of a problem—may be to disadvantage a fellow inhabitant or a group in the village and, rather than upset a delicate social balance, only the most cautious statements are uttered. In an extreme form this may find expression in total silence which, far from being a sign of indifference, is often an indication of the difficulties preventing a solution. Another device, more unsettling still than silence, is the use of the planner as a communal scapegoat. The rural community may externalize its schisms and make the planner responsible for all the conflicts that the community is incapable of resolving itself, at least, without aggravating considerable social divisions. This device is used more frequently than in the towns (despite the planner having less powers of control thanks to the considerable exemptions enjoyed by farmers), again, for the simple reason that the various interests in a rural community are much more closely inter-twined and internal conflicts much more costly.

The planner in his erstwhile role as a 'professional', asking rational questions and expecting rational replies, may well be disconcerted by this approach but the planner, as Community Development Officer, ought to be delighted. It gives him the opportunity to partially define a problem and throw it back to his audience in a reiterative process that gradually forces the community to come face to face with its own problems and to devise socially acceptable solutions. All the time the planner acts his role as the whipping boy, effectively disguising and easing the internal adjustments that have to be made within the village before a solution is found.

With so many demands on scarce resources, village self-help is often the only way to counter many deficiencies and the planners' new role must include helping the community to recognize and to consider how it can best meet its own needs. Participation is the core of this decision making process. People will join in more readily if they are convinced that important decisions will be responsive to their activities or opinions, and not be arbitrarily imposed from above. A key element in this process is the Parish Councils, called Community Councils in Wales, which now enjoy enlarged powers through the Local Government Act, 1972. The new Councils are no longer hampered by the old limitations on expenditure and have a range of spending functions from swimming pools to industrial promotion. (There will be Community Councils in Scotland, too, but they will be largely advisory and can vary widely in their constitution.) Some have begun to employ planning consultants but it must be admitted that the majority have not discarded their pre-reformation attitudes and are seemingly unaware of the possibilities open to them. So far as self help is concerned, this can be a two-way process. The Parish Council can work in tandem with the planner, augmenting his resources by collecting and supplying him with information and learning a great deal about its own area while doing so. In turn, the Council can use the planner as an advisor as it prepares its own, self-help, village plan. The Planning Officer begins by outlining the broad policy framework but thereafter there is no reason why the Parish Council should not involve itself and the whole community in a study of parish problems, priorities and the form that solutions should take. Such a plan will have no statutory force and its authority will come from the community itself. By applying expert local knowledge, it could relieve the planner of some of his burden and, at the same time, encourage the village to think and to act for itself.

An early example of this approach was shown in 1970-2 in the Northumberland village of Stocksfield (population 2500). Local Government reorganization provided the impetus and the Parish Council decided to set up a Community Working Party "to identify the needs and aspirations of people in Stocksfield and go on to produce an environmental and social plan for the village" (2.33). It looked at the complete range of services in the village, from highways to medical facilities, the needs of individuals in the community and the physical appearance of the village. Recommendations were costed and their report is a highly professional document that stands comparison with the best that Local Authorities have prepared. The strength of the report lies in its grass-roots participation. It claims that 2000 people, or 80% of the population, contributed to all stages of the project and offered a variety of specialist skills (for example, a statistician to analyze the results of a questionnaire survey) that are normally unavailable to all but the largest Local Planning Authorities (2.34).

Since the Stocksfield experiment, similar projects have been undertaken by Parish Councils in other parts of the country and are known under the generic terms of 'village appraisals'. The exact form of the appraisal varies with village resources and needs but they are usually based on a thorough survey of the village and focus upon the social and economic needs of the community as well as assessing the physical fabric of the village. Two common strands underlie all these appraisals. First, they represent village interests and claims in a coherent and reasoned form to outside bodies responsible for providing rural services, and second, they help the village to identify areas where it can help itself—whether it is simply tidying up a derelict site or promoting a more ambitious scheme to give shopping help to elderly people disadvantaged by a lack of transport.

Many of these village appraisals have been fostered by a corps of Countryside Officers operating through a three year experiment in sixteen Counties and financed by the Development Commission. The Countryside Officers enjoy the blessing of Local Authorities but are independent of them and work through the Rural Community Councils. Their terms of reference are broad. They are charged with strengthening cooperation between voluntary groups and Local Authorities; examining environment problems, solutions and projects; and, of great significance for the Local Planning

Authority, they must "assist local communities in formulating views on their needs with reference to local plans and major strategies affecting their future, particularly at the formation stages of the planning process".

Some of the flavour of their work is given by this extract of a summary report of the Community Initiative in the Countryside Conference, held in Leicestershire in July, 1974: "bringing Parish Councils together (Northumberland) to consider what they would like to see in plans for rural settlements and to formulate suggestions to the Authority; the possibility of using parish meetings as forums (Cornwall): encouraging village appraisals and local surveys, a concern for the village among the people living there, in advance of statutory plans, in order to have a basis for judgement and comment on County and District plans (Wiltshire)".

To a considerable extent, the Countryside Officers are already undertaking the community development role mentioned earlier. For the planner this presents an opportunity or a danger. The danger is that the planner, for a variety of reasons, may retreat before this new wave of participation into splendid bureaucratic isolation, leaving the Countryside Officer to cultivate the rural voice and thus widening the division between planner and public. The opportunity is for the planner to work with the Countryside Officer (for structural reasons, he could never supplant him) to learn how to present relevant advice so that rural communities can work out their own responses to their own problems, based on local circumstances.

Strategic planning

Whether solutions which are a direct response to local circumstances will be accepted by the Local Planning Authority is a moot point. Instead of beginning at grass roots level and working up to a sub-regional framework by a process of assimilating and reconciling diverse local demands, regional and area policies are usually imposed from above and work their way down. By the time they reach ground level, they may have lost much of their relevance to the problems of an individual settlement. Thus, decisions are taken and villages categorized before a village plan is prepared, and its scope in meeting the needs of a village will be pre-empted by a regional strategy. All this follows from the main thrust of rural strategies today which is how to apportion scarce resources in an economically efficient manner, and not how to meet the problems of individual settlements, except in the most general way.

This approach to community problems has flowered most frequently as the 'key village' or growth centre policy, whereby one village is selected for expansion and as a focal point for the concentration of public and private resources, while other villages are assigned the passive role of satellites, looking increasingly towards the key village for their main community services. One of the first Counties to adopt this policy was Cambridgeshire where it was linked to the otherwise admirable Village College movement. Since then, it has spread across the country from Devon to Durham. Central Government, too, has looked favourably upon the idea; it is currently part of the Development Commission policy and is incorporated in its memorandum on 'The Submission of Action Plans for the Rural Areas', July 1975.

The theory underlying the policy is simple and almost exclusively economic. The provision of services to a scattered population is most cost efficient when they can be located at one main point and not dispersed at several. Only by concentration can economies of scale (of buildings and equipment, of specialist services and of administration) be earned, and if all services are grouped into common centres valuable cross-service linkages or 'trade-offs' might also be achieved. Finally, transportation is greatly simplified by the resulting radial settlement pattern. Such a policy carries with it certain implications for the settlements not selected for growth and these are usually explained as static or, at most, change limited only to infilling. Stripped of its trappings, the implication is that the rural settlement pattern is out-moded and needs to be radically altered by the possible demise of certain settlements but, for political reasons, these ultimate goals are rarely acknowledged.

To those concerned solely with the allocation of scarce resources, a growth centre policy is probably a valid tool in an attempt to reconcile the conflict between the rationalization of services and the need to maintain levels of personal accessibility, but it does so by the simple expedient of shifting the burden from the public sector to the private citizen. It may well be administratively convenient to group services at one central point but the costs of this reorganization have to be borne by the private citizen who finds that his local school, clinic or whatever, is no longer available to him and an equivalent service can only be reached by an increased journey, costly of time and of money, to a distant key village. Unfortunately, these 'costs' of centralization are not the sort that appear on the public account sheet and the policy is given a validity in cost terms which it does not deserve. Nor is this the only 'cost' that the public accounts omit. They do not consider the social capital already invested in the satellite villages and the costs of under-use by the restrictions imposed on growth. Second, they do not consider the extra costs imposed on the key village itself by the accelerated rate of growth that it is forced to accommodate, and, third, the pattern of key villages fails to recognize that services will have different thresholds and that a pattern which is 'economic' for one service may be 'uneconomic' for another (2.35). Most serious of all, however, is the charge that a growth centre policy is based upon a complete misreading of rural settlements and their interactions. In short, its advocates are not, as they imagine, fostering trends which are inherent in the rural settlement structure, but, quite the contrary, by the crude application of principles derived from an urban society, they are promoting a revision almost as radical (though hardly as dramatic) as the fortified village policy in South Vietnam.

The accepted picture in most planning studies is that rural settlement patterns can be analyzed into a hierarchy of centres corresponding roughly to the size of the settlement, its catchment area and the number of shops and other services that it contains. This picture is derived from a straightforward aggregation and counting of different functions in each settlement and it usually pays no attention to the way in which they interact with other functions in other settlements. Rather than looking at the rural pattern conventionally, in terms a sun surrounded by totally dependent satellites, it may be more accurate to describe it as a co-operative of unequal partners. Thus each village regardless of size may contribute an attribute or service which is unique or relatively uncommon in the area. For these 'unique' functions, a village will have a much wider catchment area than its own residents, and people in adjoining villages, instead of going to progressively higher order and, probably, more distant centres for specialist services may turn to neighbouring villages; to one for electrical goods, to another for furniture, to a third for shoe repairs and so on. This is a pattern that has been observed in the U.S.A. and, nearer home, in Peak District villages along the Derwent Valley (2.36). To impose a crude key village policy on this pattern, could disrupt a delicate system of inter-relationships. Ultimately, it may detract from the identity of each village by undermining the functions that make it distinctive and will result in a reduction and reorientation in the flow of outside contacts.

Whatever the aspect of community problems under discussion, from the grouping of villages into clusters to the detailed provision of one service in an individual settlement, the main theme must be that of flexibility in seeking solutions—flexibility, first, in meeting unforeseen situations. Technological and social change dominate the scene in rural and in urban areas, and the planner has to work with the knowledge that unless he can incorporate flexibility into the structures that he is now designing, they may well become obsolete within his own lifetime. Flexibility is necessary also because different communities will throw up different problems, with the result that transplanting stereotyped solutions from other parts of the country may not be the best way of meeting the needs of local people. By allowing rural communities to suggest their own solutions, free from dogma or theoretical niceties, the planner places his skills at the service of local people and helps them to meet and to adapt to social change with a minimum of disruption. There is a strong feeling that there is too much change in rural areas and the planner should take care not to compound the situation by proposing policies which ignore existing patterns of rural life.

That change has been, and will continue to be, important in overcoming the under-privileged past of rural areas is not denied. "As for the wistful paternalism . . . and talk of old-style village self-help and charity, mention of such things causes her to smile and shake her head the merest fraction. 'Certainly people were more neighbourly then. They went in and out of each other's houses to help with what was needed, and thought themselves well paid with a cup of tea, yet (a small smile at the paradox) it wasn't better than now. It was worse, much, much worse' ". (District Nurse, Akenfield (2.37)). But change, especially that which affects social and economic relations, generates conflict and it must also be the planner's duty to identify, minimize and defuse potentially hazardous situations before they can run their course and threaten to disrupt community life. In this and in the other roles that he is now seeking to adopt, the planner has more in common with the social worker than he has with the geographer, the architect or the engineer.

References

2.1   PAHL, R.E., *Whose City*, Longman, London, 1970; quoted by BAILEY, J., *Social Theory for Planning*, Routledge & Kegan Paul, London, 1975.

2.2   BEST, R.M. and ROGERS, A.W., *The Urban Countryside*, Faber & Faber, London 1973.

2.3   HILLERY, G.A., 'Definitions of Community: Areas of Agreement', *Rural Sociology*, **20**, 1955.

2.4   BELL, C. and NEWBY, H., *Community Studies*, George Allen & Unwin, London, 1971.

2.5   TONNIES, F., *Community & Society—Gemeinschaft & Gesellschaft*, translated and supplemented by LOOMIS, C.P., Michigan State University Press, 1957; quoted in *A Dictionary of the Social Sciences*, GOULD, J. and KOLB, W.L., (Eds.), Tavistock Publications, London, 1964.

2.6   YOUNG, M. and WILLMOTT, P., *Family and Kinship in East London*, Routledge & Kegan Paul, London, 1957.

2.7   BAILEY, J., *Social Theory for Planning*, Routledge & Kegan Paul, London, 1975.

2.8   PAHL, R.E., *Urbs in Rure. The Metropolitan Fringe in Hertfordshire*, London School of Economics, Geographical Papers, No. 2, London, 1964.

2.9   PAHL, R.E., 'The Rural-Urban Continuum', *Sociologia Ruralis*, **6**, 1965.

2.10   PAHL, R.E., *Patterns of Urban Life*, Longman, London, 1970.

2.11   HAMPSHIRE COUNTY COUNCIL and MASS OBSERVATION LTD., *Village Life in Hampshire*, Winchester, 1966.

2.12   LITTLEJOHN, J., *Westrigg, The Sociology of a Cheviot Parish*, Routledge & Kegan Paul, London, 1963.

2.13   DISRAELI, B., *Sybil or the Two Nations;* quoted in *The Long March of Everyman*, BARKER, T. (Ed.), Andre Deutsch, London, 1975.

2.14   HALL, C. in a paper to the Rural Life Conference, 1974, published by the National Council of Social Service.

2.15   *Study of Rural Transport in Devon*, Report by Steering Group, The Department of the Environment, London, 1971.

2.16   *Study of Rural Transport in West Suffolk*, Report by Steering Group, The Department of the Environment, London, 1971.

2.17   HILLMAN, M., HENDERSON, I. and WHALLEY, Anne, *Personal Mobility and Transport Policy*, P.E.P., London, 1973.

2.18   *A Study of Passenger Transport Needs of Rural Wales*, Welsh Council, Cardiff, 1975.

2.19   *Age Concern on Transport*, Age Concern England, London, 1973.

2.20   CONNELL, J., 'Green Belt County', *New Society*, 25 February, 1971.

2.21   Noted in *Changing Directions*, Report of the Independent Commission on Transport, Coronet Books, London, 1974.

2.22   *Rural Bus Services in Denbighshire*, Report of Working Party, Denbighshire County Council, Ruthin, 1971.

2.23   HISLOP, M., 'The Rural Bus Problem in Hertfordshire', *The Village*, **30**, 2, Summer 1975.

2.24   See, 'Aspects of Education', *Journal of the Institute of Education*, The University of Hull, 17, 1973, for articles devoted to rural education and a useful bibliography.

2.25   *Depopulation in Mid-Wales*, HMSO, London, 1964.

2.26   THOMAS, J.G., 'Population Changes and the Provision of Services' in *The Remoter Rural Areas of Britain*, ASHTON, J. and LONG, W.H., (Eds.), Oliver & Boyd, Edinburgh, 1972.

2.27   FUGUITT, G.V., 'Some Demographic Aspects of the Small Town in the United States', *Sociologia Ruralis*, **12**, 1972.

2.28   COBBETT, W., *Rural Rides*, 1830, reprinted in Penguin English Library, London, 1967.

2.29   *Rapidly Expanding Rural Communities*, Reports to H.M. Development

Commissioners by The Hampshire Council of Community Service, 1975, and by the Cumbria Council for Voluntary Action, 1974.

2.30   RADFORD, Elizabeth, *The New Villagers,* Frank Cass & Co. London, 1970.

2.31   *Rural Housing in Denbighshire,* Denbighshire County Council, Ruthin, 1974.

2.32   TRAVIS, A.S., 'Policy Formulation and the Planner' in the *Remoter Rural Areas of Britain,* ASHTON, J. & LONG, W.H., (Eds.), Oliver & Boyd, Edinburgh, 1972.

2.33   *An Experiment in Democracy,* Stocksfield Neighbourhood Working Party, Stocksfield, Northumberland, 1972.

2.34   The Chief Planning Officer for Tynedale, whose area includes Stocksfield, notes that the report made people more aware of their surroundings and possibilities regarding future changes. In this case the majority of the proposals were capable of action at a parochial level. Whether it is worth repeating elsewhere will depend upon the priorities of each community but it requires the presence of at least one very interested and dedicated individual able to devote a great deal of time to it. He concludes by pointing out that Local Plans produced by the District Planning Authority will also require a great deal of local involvement. H.J.A. Phillipson, Chief Planning Officer, Tynedale in a letter dated 14th November, 1975.

2.35   TRAVIS, A.S., *op. cit.*

2.36   HAHN, A.J., 'Planning in Rural Areas', *Journal of the American Institute of Planners,* 34, 1, January, 1970. The Peak District reference is based on survey work undertaken by the author in 1966.

2.37   BLYTHE, R., *Akenfield,* Allen Lane, Penguin Press, London, 1969.

Further Reading

JONES, G., *Rural Life,* Longman, London 1973.

FRANKENBERG, R., *Communities in Britain, Social Life in Town and Country,* Penguin Books, London, 1966.

BLYTHE, R., *Akenfield,* Allen Lane, The Penguin Press, London, 1969.

WILLIAMS, W.M., *The Sociology of An English Village: Gosforth,* Routledge & Kegan Paul, London, 1956.

BROADY, M., *Planning for People,* The Bedford Square Press, N.C.S.S., London, 1968.

CHAPTER THREE

Rural Housing

Alan W. Rogers

Introduction

This chapter concentrates on problems of rural housing. The emphasis is naturally on the post-war situation, but present problems have to be seen in their historical context and so there is first a review of legislative developments during the present century. Such a review emphasizes a basic theme in rural housing which should be made clear at the outset. In the nineteenth century rural housing problems were equated essentially with problems of living conditions and were legislated for with this view in mind. During the present century, however, rural housing has increasingly been placed in the wider context of town and country planning. As will be seen, rural housing conditions now generate relatively little concern, and problems are considered more from the viewpoint of land use planning rather than public health, a change which in many ways parallels the development of planning in its broader sense.

By the turn of the nineteenth century, the concern for rural public health as the main problem area of rural housing was very much the province of social reformers. Ebenezer Howard underlined this view in his consideration of the 'country magnet' in his book *Garden Cities of Tomorrow* (3.1) and he was under no illusions as to true living conditions in the countryside: "Even the natural healthfulness of the countryside is largely lost for lack of proper drainage and other sanitary conditions, while, in parts almost deserted by the people, the few who remain are yet frequently huddled together as if in rivalry with the slums of our cities". The absence of sanitation, the pollution of rudimentary water supplies, and chronic over-crowding, combined to make the spread of cholera, typhus and related diseases almost inevitable in many rural communities. There was, however, a distinct element of moral concern in the call for improved housing conditions. Hugh Aronson's tract of 1913 (3.2) illustrates this view well, and a chapter was characteristically headed 'The effects of bad housing on morals and character'.

This view of the rural housing problem, concerned essentially with public morals and with public health, provided the main focus around which rural housing problems were considered until only a generation ago. The Scott Report, 1942 (3.3) considered it axiomatic that "the improvement of rural housing is an essential prerequisite of a contented countryside"—a phrase which highlights concern for a law-abiding countryside as much as for a healthy rural popula-tion. The Report took an attitude which had appeared many times before—that good housing was essential, not just for the contented lives of the rural population, but for the maintenance and progress of an efficient agricultural industry.

The assumption that an improvement in rural housing condi-tions could be justified on economic as well as on grounds of social justice, though often implicit in some nineteenth century writing, was essentially a twentieth century innovation. This contention not surprisingly coincided with the deterioration in the livelihood of the private rural landowner with the onset of the agricultural depres-sion of the late nineteenth century. The private provision of agricul-tural cottages became more and more difficult. Cottages fell into disrepair when owners could not afford to maintain them, and demands for the public provision of rural housing increased. The Land Enquiry Committee reported in 1913 that at least 120,000 new houses were needed in rural areas and, although the Land Agents Society estimated the need at only half this figure, the need was nonetheless substantial in the context of the time.

It was increasingly argued that this demand could only be satisfied with the help of central government funding, although this was only made possible after World War I. Thus a survey of the views of Local Authorities organized by the National Land and Home League in 1912 (3.4) concentrated on the question of national as opposed to local responsibilities for rural housing improvements. Only eight of the 332 Authorities which replied considered that they could build cottages to meet the needs of agricultural labourers without causing a burden on the rates, and only thirty nine Authorities were opposed to the idea of a central housing authority.

Until Government help for house construction and improvement was forthcoming, it remained certain that declining demand due to population migration to the towns and the generally meagre financial base of most rural counties would ensure that relatively little new building would take place. Weber (3.5) has shown clearly that rural housebuilding was sluggish through most of the nineteenth century. New construction in rural areas in England and Wales averaged only just over 9000 houses per year from 1841 to 1891. Rapid urbanization naturally resulted in many more houses being built in urban areas, but more importantly the rural house building record also showed none of the marked fluctuations of the building cycle which characterized the urban market. Construction did increase after about 1890, however, and totalled 241,000 houses built in rural England and Wales in the period 1901-11, though it should be noted that a substantial proportion of this total was located on the periphery of towns and cities, and as such were not truly rural.

Official views of the rural housing problem were translated into legislation, usually as part of general provisions made for all housing. Rural areas benefitted to differing extents from the various Housing and Planning Acts which followed the *Report of the Royal Commission on the Housing of the Working Classes* in 1885 and the subsequent Acts of Parliament in 1886 and 1890. The Select Committee formed by the Campbell-Bannerman Liberal administration in 1907 to study the amendment of these Acts made special note of the fact that bad housing conditions were not just confined to urban areas. Indeed the Committee followed Ebenezer Howard in considering that poor rural housing was instrumental in driving people townwards, and thus were causing overcrowding in urban areas (3.6). They recommended that agricultural housing should be improved, tied cottages should be done away with and that the agricultural wage should be increased so that the farm worker could afford reasonable housing. More significantly they suggested that County Councils should take responsibility for health and housing and that the Treasury should make cheap interest loans available to Local Authorities for new housing construction.

Despite the fact that some of these provisions were built into the subsequent Act of 1909, very few schemes for new housing in rural areas were forthcoming. Yet hopes that something would result at this time were obviously high in the agricultural community. A writer in 1914 (3.7) considered that "the legislature, as part of a scheme to improve rural conditions, may shortly introduce measures that will result in the erection of many thousands of cottages throughout the country". But the provisions made for rural housing in the 1909 Act proved as ineffective as the rest of the Act and little had been accomplished by the outbreak of war.

An interesting sideline to the concern for improved rural housing in the first decades of the twentieth century was the plans and descriptions of 'model' farm cottages produced to meet what were regarded as the "practical requirements of the rural labourer". The magazine *Country Life* even ran a competition in 1914 for a pair of three-bedroomed cottages which would together cost no more than £250.

These model designs were, however, much more characteristic of the social reformer's view of rural housing rather than that of the town planner. Plans to help the private landlord to improve the lot of his workers became less common after World War I, and their place was taken by official 'standards' for the construction of new housing in rural areas. The *Report of the Departmental Committee on Buildings for Small Holdings* suggested "adequate minimum standards of accommodation" and the Ministry of Health produced recommendations after the First World War on the size of cottage accommodation. Designs for new and reconstructed cottages were still produced, though these were generally addressed to Local Authorities rather than private landlords. C.S. Orwin (3.8) provided designs for reconstructing cottages in north Oxfordshire, while M.F. Tilley (3.9) produced a series of designs to meet Ministry of Health recommendations on size as late as 1947.

Rural housing between the wars

Legislation between the two World Wars again centred largely on the general housing and planning Acts. This mainly concerned the 1919 Housing, Town Planning Etc. Act (the so-called 'Addison' Act) and the Housing (Financial Provisions) Act of 1924 (the 'Wheatley' Act). Subsequent legislation in 1930, 1935, 1936 and 1938 encouraged Local Authorities and, in some cases, private individuals to build new houses. The Housing Act 1936 had provisions for new building to tackle overcrowding and was applied to some villages, while the Housing Act 1938 provided a subsidy for the construction of agricultural workers' cottages. The poor state of the agricultural economy and the advent of war made this last piece of legislation largely ineffective.

In terms of generating new houses in rural areas, inter-war legislation was by no means insignificant. C.S. Orwin (3.10), writing two decades later in 1944, was in general terms quite complimentary of the effect of the 1919 Act. He reckoned that most villages had benefited by the addition of a few new houses in those authorities which took notice of their new statutory duty to consider the needs of the working classes. Though these 'Addison' houses took little account of local building styles, he considered them "not unsightly", and could comment: "from the point of view of occupation they mark a distinct advance".

Official estimates made in 1943 (3.11) suggested that no less than 870,610 houses had been built by public and private enterprise in Rural Districts since the 1919 Act. More recent estimates of the inter-war building programme (3.12) suggest that the Addison Act resulted in nearly 34,000 new Local Authority houses in rural areas while an additional 64,000 Council houses were gained by rural areas between the passing of the Wheatley Act and 1934. Moreover, it is significant that the 1924 Act made a distinction between houses for agricultural use and those for general residential purposes, and larger Treasury subsidies were available for the former. All the evidence suggests, however, that these measures did comparatively little to benefit agricultural workers and new houses continued to be used for other uses and even for some weekend accommodation for city dwellers. Far too many Rural Districts were discouraged from building houses for agricultural workers by the arbitrary definition of the areas to which the extra subsidy applied, the relatively high cost of building in rural areas and the conditional contribution from the rates which these subsidies required. But the basic reason why agricultural workers did not benefit as was hoped centred on the low level of farm wages which often made it impossible for a farm worker to take on the rent payments of a Council house.

Inter-war increases in the rural housing stock were, however, generally low in relation to what was being done in some urban areas, and in the rural Counties of Wales, and parts of East Anglia, the South-West and certain other rural areas of England, there was a majority of Local Authorities which carried out no building under the new provision (3.13). Despite the fact that conditions were still bad and the Treasury subsidy for new housing under the 1924 Act was higher for 'agricultural parishes' (£12.50 over 40 years compared with £9.00 in urban areas), many rural Authorities did little to improve their housing.

The Housing Acts of 1931 and 1934 followed the previous legislation by providing financial encouragement to Local Authorities to build houses but again with only limited success. Lord Addison (3.14) was of the opinion that less than 34,000 houses had been built in rural areas as a direct result of these Acts, and he doubted whether more than 20,000 were occupied by agricultural workers. In Scotland the position was worse. The Scottish Housing Advisory Committee, reporting in 1937 (3.15) considered that, "with the exception of the subsidy provided by the Housing (Rural Authorities) Act, 1931, the subsidies for the erection of houses for general needs which were available from 1919 to 1933 were inadequately used by County Councils of rural counties and, in the absence of any direct subsidy for the purpose, County Councils of rural counties are unable at present to erect houses for the general needs of rural workers".

Inter-war activity tried to do more than simply encourage new building. An amendment to the 1919 Bill tried to limit gross housing densities in rural areas to eight houses per acre (20 per hectare), but this was defeated before the Bill became law. But Rural Districts with populations in excess of 20,000 were required to produce simplified plans for development which would inevitably take account of housing matters. In practice, however, this provision was generally ignored by those few rural Authorities (3.16) which were of this size.

Density control was, however, considered important in some rural areas, largely as a means of preserving the countryside rather than as a way of improving rural living conditions. Local Authorities wishing to safeguard a particular piece of countryside could generally only hope to do so by making a private agreement with the landowner (3.17). Land could thus be zoned either for agricultural use alone, where no residential development would be permitted, or for controlled development at densities varying from one house to two acres to one house to 100 acres. Though conflicting in theory at least with the attempts to build more houses, it is doubtful whether these zoning arrangements had any substantial influence upon housing problems and they were generally applied only to areas of outstanding landscape quality such as the South Downs.

The other main contribution which interwar legislation tried to make to the rural housing question was in the improvement of existing properties and the relief of overcrowding. Loans were made available for cottage improvement under the 1919 legislation, but the Housing (Rural Workers) Act of 1926 made a more positive move in this direction by providing grants of up to two-thirds of the cost of reconditioning, subject to a maximum of £100. Unfortunately the encouragement given to landlords to improve their properties was largely counteracted by provisions in the same Act which required that any house which was reconditioned with the help of a grant should not be let at higher than agricultural rent. Thus landlords were effectively deprived of the means of seeing an increased return on their investment, and were not attracted to the scheme. Though later Acts made modifications to these grant rates and conditions, the initiative had probably been lost.

The *Report on Rural Housing in Scotland* (3.18) produced by the Scottish Housing Advisory Committee in 1937 provides a useful comment on the effectiveness of the 1926 Act, at least in Scotland. The overall conclusions are probably fairly applicable to England and Wales. The *Report* declared that "in the administration of the Housing (Rural Workers) Acts there has been a grave waste of public money" (p.70). As noted previously, the Committee found that County Councils had, with few exceptions, not carried out their duties under the various Housing Acts which applied to Scotland (notably 1925 and 1935) which required them to make inspections of working-class housing in their districts, and that staff involved in housing duties was inadequate.

The problem of overcrowding was specifically tackled in the Housing Act of 1935. The Survey which followed the Act (3.19) revealed that over 40,000 rural houses were overcrowded by the terms of the standard adopted. It found that there was a higher proportion of overcrowded families in rural areas living in Local Authority housing than in privately-owned houses (3.7% as compared with 2.8%), despite the fact that most of the Local Authority houses were less than seventeen years old. The 1935 Act provided a special agricultural subsidy to Rural Districts to build agricultural cottages to relieve overcrowding. Between the passing of the Act and the outbreak of World War II Rural Districts built 8098 houses to relieve overcrowding, claiming a subsidy of £8 paid annually for forty years from central Government. The fact that the contribution from the rates required to match this subsidy was only £1 from the Rural District and £1 from the County Council made this provision much more successful than the subsidy arrangements made under the 1924 Act.

The inter-war period saw a further major change in the rural housing situation. At the end of World War I most houses in rural areas were in owner-occupation, except for those cottages which were tied to estates and a very few houses built by Councils under the Housing Act of 1890. Subsequent Housing and Planning Acts, which, as has been seen, added substantially to the total number of houses, also made an important change in the tenurial picture. Over 160,000 new houses were built by the Rural Districts in England and Wales under the various housing Acts between 1919 and the Second World War and, although this was probably less than one-tenth of the total rural housing stock, it introduced an element of public housing into the countryside which had hardly been present before. The Council house became a commonplace sight, since most villages, particularly in lowland England, had their quota.

The progress made between the wars in the problems of rural housing were undoubtedly substantial. The fact that many people were still disturbed by the problems of overcrowding, housing shortage and poor sanitation in rural areas at the end of the Second World War and that they were often critical of the operation of the various pieces of legislation which had been enacted, should not obscure the fact that major changes had been made. As many houses were built in rural England and Wales in the twenty years before 1939 as in the seventy years up to 1914. Though some writers (3.20) might argue that perhaps 20% of the rural housing stock in 1945 should be condemned as unfit for human habitation, the fact was that nearly 30,000 houses had been demolished between 1919 and 1943 and a further 22,000 had been reconditioned under the 1926 Act.

Some idea of this progress can be gained from the *Third Report of the Rural Housing Sub-Committee* of the Central Housing Advisory Committee, under the chairmanship of Sir Arthur Hobhouse, in 1944. Though critical of past progress, particularly as far as housing for agricultural workers was concerned, and concerned at the deterioration which had occurred during wartime, the Sub-committee was not unmindful of the progress which had been made. Their investigations in different districts showed that some Authorities had been very active in the housing field and they had no criticism of these "active and progressive Authorities and their achievements" (3.21). They found other Authorities, particularly those with small populations and low rateable values, where progress had been negligible and where little opportunity had been taken of the various grants and subsidies which had been made

Table 3.1   Houses Provided in Rural Districts in England and Wales, 1919-1943

	Rural District Councils	Private Enterprise	Total
1. *Housing Acts*			
Housing, Town Planning, etc. Act, 1919; (for general needs)	34,284	1631	35,915
Housing (Additional) Powers Act, 1919, (for general needs)	—	15,979	15,979
Housing, etc. Act, 1923, (for general needs)	8,410	109,851	118,261
Housing (Financial Provisions) Act, 1924, (for general needs)	62,370	4577	66,947
Housing Acts of 1940, 1936 and 1938, (for slum clearance)	31,746	1246	32,992
Housing Acts of 1935, 1936 and 1938, (for abatement of overcrowding)	7205	123	7328
Housing Acts of 1925 and 1936, (for general needs), without subsidy	11,548	495	12,043
Housing (Financial Provisions) Act, 1938 (Section 2), (for agricultural population)	3584	29	3613
Housing (Financial Provisions) Act, 1938 (Section 3), (for agricultural population)	—	1148	1148
Total under the Housing Acts	159,147	135,079	294,226
2. *Houses built other than under the Housing Acts* (including those built by County Councils without subsidy)	4936	571,448	576,384
Grand Totals	164,083	706,527	870,610

Source: Third Report of the Rural Housing Sub-Committee of the Central Housing Advisory Committee, 1944

available. The record of Welsh Local Authorities was particularly bad in this respect.

Nationally the inter-war picture in England and Wales can be seen from Table 3.1 which records the performance of both private enterprise and rural housing Authorities between 1919 and 1943 and details of specific contribution made by each of the Housing Acts. Houses in the Rural Districts had increased by 870,000, an increase of 50% on the 1919 total. The contribution of private enterprise provided, of course, the major element in this total, but it is arguable that the importance of the Local Authority contribution was out of all proportion to its numerical size. Though only one in five of all new houses were provided by the Rural Districts, the responsibility of the Local Authority for housing in rural areas was made clear for the first time. Though primarily aimed at improving housing conditions in general, it is significant that some legislation towards the end of the period specifically highlighted the housing problems of the farm worker—problems which in some respects are still present forty years later. Finally, Local Authority activity in housing introduced a new element into the landscape of the village which is now taken for granted.

A further assessment of the rural housing situation by the start of World War II can be gained from the Scott Report. The members of the Committee were very concerned at the low housing standards which still prevailed in many villages and also of the effect of these standards on the drift from the land: "Thousands of cottages have no piped water supply, no gas or electric light, no third bedroom and often only one living room with no seperate cooking and scullery accommodation. For the great majority of rural workers a bathroom is a rare luxury".

Though the Committee was conscious that some progress had been made in improving rural living conditions, the evidence which they considered showed very clearly how much there was still to do. In 1939 about one-third of all rural dwellings were not yet served by electricity, and no more than one-tenth of farm houses were served in this respect. At the same time at least a million rural dwellers did not have the benefit of piped water, despite the improvements after the Rural Water Supply Act of 1934, and over 5000 parishes were lacking sewerage systems.

Rural housing in the post-war period

The spirit of reconstruction after the Second World War made no exception of rural housing in its concern for the future. The importance given to rural housing problems in the Scott Report coupled with the reports of the Central Housing Advisory Committee served to remind the Government of its responsibilities in this direction and a modest start was made before the end of the War. But good intentions did not necessarily lead to good results, and indeed some suggestions for rural housing improvement were probably unworkable from the outset. The Scott Report had even suggested that new rural houses might be built ready equipped for electricity, gas and water, even though there was no immediate prospect of these services being provided. Not surprisingly, and with justification, the relevant Government departments criticized this recommendation as a waste of resources (3.22).

The *Third Report of the Rural Housing Sub-Committee, 1944,* of the Central Housing Advisory Committee had recommended that each County in England and Wales should set up a Joint Advisory Committee on rural housing problems which would bring together Local Authorities and other interested parties. A first task of these committees was to be a comprehensive survey of rural housing conditions throughout the country.

The Ministry of Health accepted this recommendation in 1944 and committees were set up in every county except London and Middlesex. Surveys commenced in many counties but, to all intents and purposes, the matter rested there. The post-war survey of rural housing, which was to provide the basis for the rural component of the housing campaign, petered out, and with it went the other activities of the Joint Committees. By 1952, when the *Second Interim Report* on the Housing Survey in Rural Areas (3.23) was published, thirty four Counties had started the survey, but only three had completely finished even though eight years had passed. In two Counties work had either not started or was in abeyance, while six further Counties had yet to reach the half-way mark. Moreover, no less than twenty five Joint Committees had completely ceased to function. Roughly one-third (29.3%) of the houses in the survey were thought to be in need of major repair or reconditioning and a further 12% were totally unfit for habitation and not capable of repair. Minor repairs were needed in another 27% of houses.

It was felt that the survey and the work of the Joint Committees had lost their impetus largely as a result of the general problems of post-war reconstruction. The government had made the provision of new housing a major priority (3.24) and local committees found that schemes for reconditioning old properties were regarded with less interest and urgency than they had originally hoped. Though some Local Authorities obviously carried out their duties conscientiously (3.25), and had some hopes of reviving the pre-war concern for reconditioning rural houses, this enthusiasm was not matched by central Government. Rural housing problems had received passing reference in general statements on the rebuilding of Britain after the war, and the problem of tied cottages in agriculture had been mentioned in Labour's 1945 manifesto, although no real action followed. The country faced problems which were understandably regarded as more pressing than those of rural housing, despite the exhortations of private individuals and interested organizations (3.26, 3.27).

Subsequent concern for problems of rural housing has been subsumed within the general problem of the nation's housing. With justification perhaps, the problems of inner city areas, of urban slum clearance and of the housing conditions of 90% of the population, have tended to take attention away from the problem of housing in rural areas. Poor housing conditions still exist in the countryside, but the focus of political concern is urban rather than rural. Some of the old problems remain, most notably that of the tied cottage in agriculture, but new rural housing problems are frequently caused by increased wealth rather than deprivation. Rural houses as desirable goods, rather than damning indictments of the rural economy, have tended to provide the focus of housing problems in the post-war situation.

Desirability as a function of relative scarcity provides a further reason why rural housing has been regarded in a different light in the last thirty years. The planning machine which was set up from 1947 put a tight control on new housing in rural areas which has meant that, far from encouraging rural Authorities and private enterprise to build houses as in the 1930s, there has been active discouragement, particularly with regard to building in the open countryside, except in cases where it can be proved that new housing is necessary for essential agricultural workers. The twin objectives of urban containment and countryside preservation which have been explicit in land use planning since the Second World War have inevitably had repercussions for rural housing. The basic argument should again be emphasized that, if rural housing in the nineteenth century was decidedly wedded to public health legislation, then its mid-twentieth century equivalent is as firmly based in the field of land use planning.

Inevitably these post-war themes of major urban problems and strict development control in rural areas, together with minority issues such as second homes and tied cottages, provide something of a *leitmotif* for rural housing policy since 1945. Rural housing has, of course, been treated as part and parcel of the total housing problem, and Government action on this front has generally been equally applicable to the rural sector (3.28). In some cases legislation has contained special provisions to encourage the construction of agricultural workers' cottages, though this has had no effect upon the problem of tied cottages. Grants for improving property were introduced in the Housing Act, 1949 and so the financial aid which had previously only been available for farm cottages was now extended to all housing. It is certain that many such grants have been made by rural Local Authorities for the improvement of rural housing, but it is debatable whether this aid has benefited those who need it most, even though legislation has tried to prevent the use of these grants by urban speculators and, latterly, by second home owners. From the viewpoint of housing conditions and quality, much progress has been made in the post-war period as part of the general improvement in living standards. Rural housing problems undoubtedly remain, however, but they are more often those involving social equity and privilege than questions of poor sanitation and overcrowding.

The rural housing stock

The 1971 Census of Population recorded some 4,377,600 dwellings within the areas of the old Rural Districts in England and Wales and in the landward areas and the small burghs of Scotland. This rather arbitrary definition provides something of a starting point for a discussion of the rural housing stock and so highlights the problem of defining what is meant by the term 'rural' housing. This gross figure presents an increase on the 1961 total of around 24%, although it should be realized that a large part of this increase is accounted for by suburban extensions of urban areas into the administrative areas of Rural Districts. Urban growth provides the main explanation for the substantial increases in the number of houses in rural areas over the last forty years or so. The total dwelling count in Rural Districts in England and Wales in 1951 was 2,410,707, an increase of over 30% on the 1931 total, while the gross increase from 1951 to 1961 was of the order of 23% (55,652 dwellings). These substantial changes have, of course, been matched by changes in the rural population. Rural Districts recorded an increase in the 1971 Census of nearly 1,700,000 people since 1961—a rate of 16 or three times the national figure, and an illustration of the dispersal of population that is taking place from urban areas throughout the country. But large areas of Wales, northern England and Scotland recorded decreased populations as people moved from isolated and deprived rural areas to towns or to the more attractive rural regions of lowland England. This pattern of movement is described by Dunn in Chapter 1.

Yet the relationships between housing and population totals and increases are by no means straightforward (3.29), and changes in household formation and family size are as significant as they are in urban areas. The size of households in rural areas has continued to decline over recent decades. In 1961 the average size of rural households in England and Wales was calculated as 3.13 (3.30). Ten years before the figure had been nearly 3.30, while in 1971 it had declined to only 3.04 (3.31). The national trend for young people to form households at an earlier age than previously may be constrained slightly in some rural pressure areas where young married couples are forced to live with parents because they cannot afford inflated house prices, but this seems to have had little effect overall.

Population increases coupled with a higher rate of household formation would, by themselves, create some problems of housing pressure. But the picture is complicated further by the recent decline in house-building in rural areas, mainly in the public sector, and the additional competition for private housing generated by commuters and second home owners. The change of Local Government boundaries in England and Wales in 1974 (and Scotland in 1975) and the consequent disappearance of the old Rural Districts has now made it virtually impossible to apply even an arbitrary administrative definition of 'rural' to the available statistics. However, figures published by the Department of the Environment up to 1973 illustrate the decline in rural house building since the end of the 1960s, particularly in the public sector. Though this decline in house building has been shared, and even exceeded, in urban areas, it nevertheless provides cause for much concern in rural areas.

Table 3.2 traces the rural house-building record in the constituent parts of Great Britain from 1969 to 1973. The substantial decline of nearly 40% over this period in the number of houses built by rural Local Authorities is particularly noticeable. Indeed two years previously, in 1967, the total number of completions in the public sector had been around 35,000, nearly twice the number six years later. This trend seems likely to continue in many rural areas in the face of severe cuts in Local Government expenditure and gives much

Table 3.2   Rural House-building by Local Authorities and Private Enterprise, Great Britain 1969-73

	1969	1970	1971	1972	1973
Public Sector					
England	13,436	12,802	12,800	10,101	10,156
Wales	2270	2099	1465	1014	864
Scotland*	14,566	15,526	13,088	10,193	7398
Subtotal	30,272	30,427	27,353	21,308	18,418
Private Sector					
England	59,370	52,466	59,901	59,868	57,237
Wales	4016	3799	4205	4571	5247
Scotland*	5976	6073	8530	8856	8775
Subtotal	69,362	62,338	72,636	73,295	71,259
Total					
England	72,806	65,268	72,701	69,969	67,393
Wales	6286	5898	5670	5585	6111
Scotland*	20,542	21,599	21,618	19,049	16,173
Grand total	99,634	92,765	99,989	94,603	89,677

*Aggregate of landward areas and small burghs of under 10,000 population
Source: Housing and Construction Statistics No. 9, 1974, HMSO

cause for concern. The fact that private house building in rural areas has not suffered in quite the same way does not necessarily alleviate the problem. In the first place private housing rarely helps the problems of those relatively deprived members of the rural population, particularly the old and those on low incomes, who simply cannot afford the inflated cost of private house. Secondly, private housing takes little account of policies to help declining rural areas and tends to be built where a demand, often from a nearby urban area by commuters, exists. If two other factors, which will be examined in detail later, namely the growing demand for second homes over this period and the probable future decline in the number of privately-rented houses following successive Rent Acts, are also considered, the outline of what is a major problem in rural housing becomes clearer. A decreasing pool of rented housing in rural areas is available to a part of the rural population which is least able to take advantage of the private market.

The tenurial structure of rural housing corresponds broadly with that in urban areas, with roughly half the housing stock in private owner-occupation (Table 3.3). Only in Scotland does the proportion of owner-occupied houses drop to one third, and here the greater importance of council-rented property again mirrors the

Table 3.3   Rural Housing in Great Britain, 1971—Tenure

	Owner-occupied	Rented from Local Authorities etc.	Rented privately (unfurnished)*	Rented private (furnished)	Not stated
	%	%	%	%	%
England	56.6	22.0	18.2	3.1	0.1
Wales	55.0	27.4	15.3	2.1	0.2
Scotland†	32.3	51.5	13.9	2.3	—
Great Britain	51.9	27.9	17.2	2.9	0.1

*includes housing associations

†aggregate of landward areas and small burghs under 10,000 population

Source: Calculated from *Census of Population*, 1971, Housing Tables

urban situation. Yet there are important regional differences within Britain which these generalized data tend to hide. Truly rural areas of England, for example East Anglia, Lincolnshire and Shropshire, show a generally lower than average proportion of owner-occupied households, while 'urban' areas, particularly those near towns and cities in south-eastern England, show an above-average proportion, reflecting among other factors, the predominance of private house-building for sale in these areas within the last forty years. Conversely the proportion of privately-rented houses and, to a lesser extent, of Local Authority housing, is often higher in these rural areas (3.32). In Scotland, as has been noticed, the position is rather different (3.33). Owner-occupation, while relatively low nationally, is particularly important in the northern crofting counties of Sutherland, Ross and Cromarty and the Western Isles, while private renting is characteristic of eastern and central rural areas and the Border country. The combination of a long tradition of estate houses and tied cottages in these areas largely explains this distribution. Local Authority housing provision in Scottish rural areas is often relatively low, except, of course, in lowland counties where the bulk of the population live.

Roughly one in five rural houses in 1971 was rented from a private landlord, mostly as unfurnished property, which represents a rather higher figure than that found in urban areas. Traditionally this form of tenure was very much more common when village housing was owned as part of a local estate, and the occupants were employed as retainers of the landlord working on the estate. The break up of these aristocratic holdings has decreased this element, but examples can still be found where housing availability and conditions are in the hands of the local lord of the manor (3.34), even if he is now in practice represented by a city company. Private rentings, both furnished and unfurnished, have declined in common with the national situation, and the general opinion is that this trend has been accelerated by the Rent Act, 1974. The increased security given to tenants of both furnished and unfurnished lettings will, in the opinion of some authorities, encourage landlords to sell property and thus progressively remove an element of the housing market which was available to those who could not contemplate owner-occupation. Despite the publicity given to bad housing conditions in some agricultural tied cottages, it is probable that privately-rented houses now show few of the really bad conditions which were common before the Second World War. In a situation where Local Authorities are effectively decreasing the provision of Council

101

houses, the loss of the privately-rented sector is especially worrying.

A few rural houses are provided from sources other than the Local Authority or the private landlord. Three important examples may be quoted. The Ministry of Defence has built a surprisingly large number of houses for its employees, particularly following the withdrawal of troops from overseas territories from the mid-1960s. Between 1965 and the early 1970s about 25,000 houses were built by the Ministry, generally in conjunction with military air bases (3.35). Secondly the Forestry Commission has for long had a policy of building housing for forestry workers, often in special villages but sometimes as additions to existing settlements. Finally some special agencies have provided housing or grant aid for housing, notably the Scottish Special Housing Association and, through the operation of the Crofter Housing Scheme, the Department of Agriculture for Scotland.

Housing quality, though now relegated well below housing availability in rural areas as a problem, remains an important concern for a small proportion of rural dwellers. The housing stock, particularly in the more remote rural areas, suffers from the fact that the average age of property is substantially higher than in urban areas and this means that housing standards are often lower and improvement costs are higher. Surveys in Norfolk, for example, showed that in the 1960s half the rural housing stock was built before 1900 (3.36) and the regional estimates made in 1964 by the National Institute for Economic and Social Research (N.I.E.S.R.) (3.37) recorded similar figures for predominantly rural regions. The average age of housing stock in North and Central Wales was 79 years and 48% of properties in the sample were built before 1881. The corresponding figures for the South East Region were 50 years and 21% respectively.

The same survey also considered housing conditions at a regional level, and recorded figures for 'very poor dwellings' in the mainly rural regions of North and Central Wales and East Anglia which were over three times as high on the national average of 1.9%. Yet these figures refer to relatively small numbers of houses, and important changes have taken place since this survey. The House Condition Survey of 1971 (3.38) showed that major improvements in the rural housing stock had taken place since the previous survey in 1967. Within Rural Districts in England and Wales about 255,000 houses were estimated as being unfit, a decline of 41% on the 1967 figure of 430,000. This figure represents about 6.9% of the rural housing stock, compared with 8.1% of houses in conurbations which were regarded as unfit. The regional disparities which the N.I.E.S.R. surveys noted, in Wales, are confirmed by the Welsh House Condition Survey, 1968 (3.39). Based on a sample of 4800 dwellings, the parts of Wales excluding the Valleys and industrial South Wales, recorded 15.1% of the housing stock as being unfit.

The relatively good record for the improvement of rural housing conditions in recent years is to be explained largely by the problems which are faced by inner city areas in the matter of housing improvement. Housing in urban areas deteriorates at a faster rate than in rural areas and thus offsets progress made in improvement by redevelopment and reconditioning. The fact that many rural houses prove attractive to people who have the financial resources to improve their own property provides a secondary reason for this disparity between urban and rural areas.

Recent housing improvement in many rural areas also shows itself in the availability of household amenities. Changes of definition and tabulation between the different Censuses makes comparisons over time very difficult, but some comments are possible. Thus in 1951 37% of rural households in England and Wales either shared or were entirely without a water closet, and under half had exclusive use of the five basic amenities recorded by the Census. By 1971 85% of rural households in England and Wales recorded the exclusive use of the three amenities of hot water, a fixed bath and an inside toilet. The House Condition Survey, 1971 suggested that rural areas were on balance better equipped from the viewpoint of household amenities than the conurbations and other urban areas—only 13.1% of the sample had none of the five amenities recorded, while the corresponding figure for conurbations was 18.3%.

Major improvements in rural living since the Second World War provide the major explanation for these changes. Local Authorities have, despite the relatively high cost of provision, continued to connect rural settlements to main sewerage systems, and all but the most remote areas are now served by piped water and electricity. Compared with many inner-city areas, the quality of rural living in terms of household amenities is very high, particularly in areas which have seen influxes of people from the towns able to improve any deficiencies at their own expense. Conversely, of course, there remain some glaring regional disparities, notably in rural Wales and the Highland Counties of Scotland. In areas of the old Counties of Radnor and Montgomery (now Powys), one-third of rural households lacked one or other of the three basic amenities recognized in the 1971 Census. In contrast, parts of the Home Counties and the south-east of England have barely 5% of households in the same position.

In one final respect, rural housing is at a distinct advantage compared with urban areas. Shared occupation of dwellings is comparatively rare and there is little evidence of the overcrowding which was common in the nineteenth century. Barely 1.5% of households in Rural Districts in England and Wales recorded densities in excess of 1.5 persons per room in 1971, and only in some of the western areas of the Scottish Highlands and Islands, which have a long tradition of rural overcrowding, does the proportion rise above 5%. Residential land densities in small settlements are correspondingly low (3.40), even though infilling has been common in many village settlements.

Problems of rural housing need

It was suggested at the beginning of this Chapter that whereas rural housing problems in the nineteenth century were primarily concerned with housing conditions, those of the second half of the twentieth century are concerned with the conflict between housing *demand* and housing *need*. The two concepts should be clearly differentiated. One deals with the ability or inability to pay, while the other considers the essential requirements of people, irrespective of their financial capacity to afford them. To many people housing in rural areas has become very desirable and an increasing number find themselves able to indulge this desire.

Of course this view of the rural retreat as a desirable goal for the successful is no new phenomenon (3.41), but the number of people, both absolutely and relatively, who can now afford this goal has increased substantially. Rising living standards and increased personal mobility probably explain this increase, and there is little sign that such increases will not continue in the foreseeable future, though they may be modified by changes in the costs of transport and the economic climate generally.

These pressures from an urban source are, of course, not universally applicable to all British rural areas. Areas of population dispersal, particularly in the hills and uplands, have their own problems of housing need where housing demand is frequently low or non-existent. Yet numerically speaking, these areas are less important than those rural pressure areas where housing needs and housing demands conflict on a variety of fronts. The situation is complicated by the fact that old-established rural residents, for all their lack of bargaining power in financial terms, are increasingly aspiring to urban living standards. The end result is conflict between different housing needs on the one hand and demands on the resources of rural areas which are frequently ill-equipped to supply them on the other. Ray Pahl has considered that "one of the most crucial problems in Britain during the last quarter of the twentieth century will involve the unprecedented demand for an urban range of choice in a rural setting" (3.42).

Certain groups of people in the countryside have an undeniable and often very specific need for housing in rural areas. The most obvious groups, of course, are those directly involved in the agricultural industry at the farm level. Though the numbers of both farmers and farm workers are declining (3.43), there are still some 600,000 people making up these two groups in Great Britain, and, if their families are included, some idea of the primary need for rural housing can be gained. By the time those rural households which are connected with forestry, the extractive industries and some transport and service trades are added to this basic figure, there are perhaps some four to five million people in Great Britain whose livelihood virtually requires them to live in rural areas.

At least as many people again make up that group of rural dwellers which Dudley Stamp termed the 'adventitious' population. A rather more detailed analysis of social groups in the countryside has been provided by Ray Pahl (3.44) and is referred to in Chapters 1 and 2. Though not complete and referring particularly to lowland England, his list recognizes eight groups which provide something of a starting point for a discussion of competing housing needs. Pahl's eight groups are: large property owners; salaried immigrants with some capital; 'spiralists' (highly mobile young executives); those with limited income and little capital; the retired; council house tenants; tied cottagers and other tenants; local tradesmen and owners of small businesses.

This classification can be criticized for its incompleteness and for the fact that some groups, notably small tenant farmers, fit unhappily into the system. Equally Pahl seems to equate tied cottagers with the rural poor, a correlation which begs questions rather than provides useful answers. However, this simple scheme provides a first idea of competing housing needs, not least because Pahl considers these groups particularly from the viewpoint of their housing requirements and demands.

Inevitably, perhaps, there appears a dichotomy between those groups whose position in the countryside is a direct function of employment, of birth or of force of circumstance, and those who have entered the rural housing market in both a conscious and a well-equipped way. All too frequently problems arise when members of each side find themselves in competition over the same rural property. In a way which is far less common in towns and cities, except perhaps in areas of gentrification, competing social groups are in pursuit of the same good. Though the wealthy commuter or aspiring second home owner may assess a cottage from a different viewpoint from that of a farm worker or a retired rural schoolmistress, they are each bidding, albeit unequally, for the same property.

The recognition of this unequal competition which inevitably operates against the less wealthy local resident has been slow to be translated into local housing policy. Even now there seems to be the view that the problem only exists in certain areas of the Home Counties where Pahl's marauding urbanites have come into erstwhile rural areas. Yet more and more is it certain that rural housing pressure is far more widespread than this, and is to be found in most parts of lowland England which are reasonably accessible to an urban centre.

A study of housing pressures in the Peak District by Penfold (3.45) highlights this problem in a situation where it has been exacerbated by planning controls in an area of high landscape quality. Though referring to part of a National Park, the study is by no means an unusual one because of the particular circumstances. Special areas, delineated because of their landscape quality, cover a high proportion of the countryside and, even where this constraint does not apply, the application of standard development control procedures means that housing pressure is virtually assured. Penfold's work touches on many of the issues which are now seen as characteristic of areas of rural housing pressure. The increasing numbers of commuters from Sheffield, coupled with the demand for second homes in the Park, has forced up the price of property so that it is out of the reach of many local people, particularly young married couples. At the same time, the supply of privately-rented accommodation has decreased substantially and so cut off another element of housing choice. Both circumstances show themselves in an increased demand for Council housing such that the waiting list kept by Bakewell Rural District had increased from 336 in 1961 to over 500 by May 1973.

Conflicts between local residents and incoming urban dwellers are most clearly seen in the much-publicized demand for second home properties. Although second homes are far less important in the British countryside than in many European countries, the total has grown at a surprisingly high rate. From a figure of under 25,000 built second home properties in England and Wales at the end of the Second World War, the estimates were put at around 200,000 in 1970 (3.46). To this should be added estimates for Scotland of between 30,000 and 40,000 at the same time (3.47). An ailing economy, following the growth period of the 1960s and the early 1970s, certainly had some effect upon the upward trend, which seemed to reach its peak in about 1972 with a total of about 370,000 built second homes in Britain. There has been suggestions that the number of second homes in Britain has declined very substantially since this time—one estimate making the 1975 total for Britain below 200,000. It is probable that many second homes have become retirement properties, that many people have not been able to buy holiday homes, as they may have intended and that the total would thus have decreased. It may be significant, however, that property experts do not necessarily consider that the demand for second homes in the future will continue to drop and that there will, moreover, be an increasing market for purpose-built second home developments (3.48).

Whatever the future demand for second homes, problems of housing conflict undoubtedly exist now, although they may have been exaggerated by the press. Particularly in Wales local opposition to outside interests buying up rural houses for holiday retreats has been especially vocal. Auctions have been disrupted by members of the Welsh Language Society, and Plaid Cymru has campaigned for controls on second home development (3.49). At a broader level, Shelter has taken the same line in equally outspoken terms (3.50). The concern is with the erosion of community spirit, with speculation and the inflation of house prices out of the reach of local people, and, above all, with the situation of some people having two houses while others have none: ". . . to the homeless and the ill-housed . . . (second homes) can constitute a social affront" (3.51).

The supporters of second home development, particularly those professionals who are increasingly interested in the commercial possibilities of large scale purpose-built development, naturally reject these arguments. They argue that second homes bring capital and employment to declining rural areas, that the homeless exist largely in the cities and that erstwhile derelict rural houses are irrelevant to the general problem of homelessness. Further they contend that second home owners make a positive rather than a negative contribution to the social capital of the area and act as a conscious and enthusiastic support to the small rural community.

The evidence for both sides is fragmentary and both arguments are over-played. Even if the opposition case is well-founded in some areas, control on second home development is difficult, although there have been suggestions of higher rates, increased stamp duty on purchase, mortgage limitations and even local taxation. Government has responded in a small way to the opposition and Local Councils are now generally unable to give improvement grants for second properties. Yet for many people the problem remains and, for all the cold logic of the newly-emerging professional second home developer, they find themselves basically unhappy with an attitude which seems to consider rural homes as rich pickings for urban speculators (3.52).

Another area of conflict in rural housing need is that dealing with tied accommodation in the countryside. In practice this means the case of the agricultural worker and the tied cottage, but it should not be forgotten that there are other groups which may be similarly affected. Situations where whole villages are owned by one landlord are relatively rare, but some mining villages are effectively in the hands of the National Coal Board. Equally there are several thousand clergy who live in tied accommodation provided by the Church Commissioners (3.53). Armed service personnel are frequently housed in tied accommodation usually located on military bases in rural areas, but the problems which this situation brings are somewhat different and are dealt with separately.

It is fair to say that the public *debate* about tied cottages in agriculture should not necessarily be equated with the *problem* of tied cottages in agriculture. Serious problems only really arise when there is conflict between worker and employer, usually when the loss of a job requires the loss of the house. Between 1000 and 1500 cases each year reach the courts and an order for eviction is approved; perhaps 300 families are subsequently evicted from their homes. The National Union of Agricultural and Allied Workers has been assiduous in ensuring the maximum publicity for these occasions. With some justification they argue that these extreme situations hide the bulk of the tied cottage problem and that many workers are intimidated by the control which their employer has upon their home as well as their livelihood.

The best estimates of the number of agricultural tied cottages suggest that there are between 70,000 and 80,000 in England and

Wales, with perhaps a further 20,000 in Scotland (3.54, 3.55). Though the absolute numbers are decreasing as the farm labour force shrinks, the relative provision has in fact increased since the last war. Whereas there were 35.3 tied cottages for each 100 full-time hired men in England and Wales in 1947, the corresponding provision in 1972 had risen to 54.2 (3.56). Thus the evidence suggests that, though numbers are decreasing, tied cottages are becoming more important to the agricultural industry, with a corresponding hardening in the attitudes of the farmers towards criticisms of the system.

The abolition of the tied cottage system has been mooted by the Labour Party at least since the end of the Second World War, though little has been done. The N.U.A.A.W. has campaigned in effect since 1909 for farmworkers to be given 'the freedom of the rent book', and proposals to this end contained in a consultative document were put forward by the Labour Government in July 1975 (3.57). Legislation would probably extend the protection under the Rent Acts to farm workers, where previously they had been specifically omitted.

Opponents of abolition, notably the National Farmers Union, naturally contend that this will simply create more problems. Farmers, not surprisingly, argue that the tied cottage is essential to an industry which often needs workers on the spot at a moment's notice, and in a situation where workers have come to expect housing as part of the job. In their view productivity will suffer and labour will become more difficult to recruit. Workers will remain in housing after they have left the job, thus preventing the farmer from securing replacement labour. Moreover, if tied cottages are abolished and become part of the decreasing quantity of privately-rented accommodation, there will be even greater pressure upon rural housing authorities to provide Council housing for agricultural workers. The poor record which most rural Authorities have for housing provision makes this consequence of abolition seem even more problematical, even though some use could presumably be made of the relatively high number of farm cottages, perhaps around 12,000, that are empty at any one time. Equally there seems to be little consistency in the treatment which Local Authorities give to evicted farm workers (3.58), and this situation gives even less confidence in the ability of Local Authorities to cope with the changes implicit in abolition.

The forcible eviction of a family, particularly one which is dependent for its existence on work in one of the poorest paid of all industries, is an undeniable housing problem, and many people would argue further that the total commitment which many work-ers have towards their employers for housing is both degrading and unnecessary. Yet there is the paradox that relatively few agricultural workers support the N.U.A.A.W. in its demands for the total abolition of the system. One survey in 1975 found only 5% in favour of complete abolition, although more than half the sample felt that insecurity of tenure was a major disadvantage of the system (3.59). There are views which suggest a middle-ground approach to the problem. Some would favour the approach of the 'Warnford Charter' (3.60), which, while not changing the tied cottage system, makes the system and its responsibilities explicit to all parties, and thus tries to prevent misunderstanding and ill-feeling. Many more would reject this approach as maintaining the very paternalism which is criticized in the whole system, and would say that 'freedom to depend' is no freedom at all. A second approach has been put forward by Shelter (3.61) which has proposed a system whereby some tied houses remained but only for key farm workers such as stock-men whose presence near to the holding is clearly necessary. All other tied cottages would have to be licensed with the Local Authority and annual renewal of the licence would allow a check to be made on housing standards. If such a key worker were to leave his job, rehousing would be guaranteed by the Local Authority and thus the property would be available to the farmer for letting to his new employee. The majority of houses, which are at present 'tied' to the farm, would then be subject to the Rent Acts, with the security of tenure which this would mean.'

Any proposals along these lines inevitably raise those issues which are at the base of so many rural planning problems. The shortage of rural housing, particularly for renting at relatively low rates, and the poor house construction record of rural Local Author-ities have undoubtedly helped to bolster up the system, aided by the poor bargaining power and the low wages of the agricultural worker. Simple abolition could well cause severe hardship to both sides if Local Authorities are not persuaded to provide alternative accommodation. It may well be, as Shelter has argued, that, since political power in rural areas is frequently in the hands of landown-ing interests, the means of persuasion lies well within the power of the farmers to see that this hardship to both is minimized.

Away from areas where commuters and second home seekers are generally to be found, in the upland areas of Britain, there are still problems of rural housing need. In essence they are really very little different from those of the rural pressure areas. A small and usually dispersed population which is also generally one that can generate little demand in the private housing market, is also handicapped by its poverty as far as Local Authority housing is concerned. Only in certain rather special areas where, for example, Rural Development Boards have operated for a short time, has there been much hope of breaking out of the high cost/low income situation which typifies most of the hill lands of Britain. Occasionally organizations such as the Highlands and Islands Development Board or the Council for Small Industries in Rural Areas may generate sufficient investment in particular areas for housing demand to be encouraged, but the overall effect has been slight. Paradoxically, of course, once invest- ment at a significant level does come into a previously neglected rural area, then problems of housing pressure become common. Such is the case with the Moray Firth area which has seen all the problems of house price inflation and shortage in recent years with the expansion of oil production from North Sea fields.

Problems of housing need also exist for other, often relatively small, groups in the countryside. In particular there are problems regarding the increasing proportion of the rural population which has reached retirement age. In some cases, of course, members of this group are well able to fulfill their own housing needs and the pressure for retirement bungalows, particularly in seaside areas of the south of England, provides ample evidence for this. In some areas, indeed, such as the south-west of England, it may well be that the demand for retirement houses in rural areas acts to the disadvan- tage of the local population in much the same way as the demand for second homes. More significant, though, from the viewpoint of social welfare, are those ageing populations which are unable to control their own housing environment in this way. The problem is often compounded by the fact that old people are frequently left in older, substandard properties for which they have no resources in terms of repair and improvement. They may be old retainers staying on in privately-rented or tied accommodation where the landlord may be equally unable or perhaps unwilling to improve the pro- perty. Such groups are frequently in a poor bargaining situation since they see themselves as dependants within the rural social framework and the protection of housing legislation is often irrele- vant in their case. To the Local Authority they provide another problem since their housing need may require special facilities and expensive wardening services and these can be costly to provide in rural areas.

Finally there should be noted the irregular demands upon the rural housing market which can be made by the armed services. As has been seen already, service personnel are usually housed in purpose-built bases which present particular problems to Local Planning Authorities (3.62). They can, however, enter the market for private housing and the concentration of such a demand both in space and time can cause price inflation and housing pressure. The fact that military bases are for strategic reasons usually sited in areas of dispersed population simply reinforces the imbalance between the newcomers and the local people in the housing market. Where military bases are themselves concentrated, as for example in parts of eastern England, this situation is made even worse.

Problems of rural housing provision

Problems related to the provision of rural housing are usually those of an absolute shortage of housing in a rural area or of a relative shortage of the right type of property. As in urban areas Local Authorities attempt to match housing need in terms of type and location with the housing stock which they have at their disposal. Yet, as has been seen, new Council housing has tended to decline in recent years and the prospects for the immediate future are no better, while the privately-rented sector has also decreased substantially. Although the Government has tried to encourage the activities of housing associations as a 'third arm' in the housing market (3.63), these bodies have relatively little importance in rural areas, except perhaps in some small towns. Even where they can satisfy a particular need, housing associations still have to cope with higher building costs than in urban areas and also often have to contend with opposition from powerful pressure groups in existing small settlements which see such developments as an unwanted intrusion.

In theory Local Authorities have a wide brief in the management of housing within their area. As a prime objective they have a responsibility under the Housing Act, 1957 to see that adequate and suitable housing is generally available to meet the needs of the area. Three subsidiary aims follow from this main task and each can be related to the different tenure groups in housing. First, Authorities have to manage their own housing stock efficiently from the viewpoints of allocation, new construction and repair and mainte-nance. Secondly, they should seek to improve the quality of private housing, for example through improvement grants, and to provide mortgage backing to private purchasers where this is appropriate. Thirdly, they have a duty to protect private tenants under the terms of the Rent Acts and other legislation. A number of further responsibilities are also involved, such as housing for special groups, aid to housing associations and the control of private caravan parks.

which centre mainly on policies for the construction and management of Council housing. As has been seen, virtually all rural Local Authorities have from time to time built housing for their own use, and accordingly they operate policies for the allocation of Council accommodation. The most obvious point where housing need meets housing policy is the housing waiting list, both in terms of eligibility for the list and in the ability of those on the list to be transferred to housing. It could well be argued that problems of rural housing provision centre almost exclusively on a situation of increasing waiting lists, and too few houses to allocate, with complementary problems of eligibility for Council aid and the high cost of housing provision which serve to make matters worse. Significant discrepancies in the way in which different Authorities operate their policies complicates the picture further.

The provision of housing by Local Authorities in Oxfordshire provides a good illustration of some of these points (3.64). While the house completion record improved after the slump of the early 1970s, the growth of waiting lists for Council accommodation exceeded the number of families housed by the District Councils. Excluding Oxford City, new registrations in the year 1974/75 exceeded the number of families housed by virtually two to one (3.65). Although Local Authority housing programmes for the future may suggest an increase in house completions, these forecasts may be optimistic and it is more certain that waiting lists will continue to grow out of proportion. Moreover, comparisons of gross numbers of house completions and of those on waiting lists tend to hide discrepancies in the type of accommodation available. Many rural Authorities have problems of too few small houses which are suitable for newly-married couples and for the growing number of old people who are now without families and, conversely, perhaps too many larger houses for which there is less demand and which are costly to maintain. As will be seen, the small, one- or two-bedroom house is rarely built by private developers except as retirement bungalows, and so these types must be provided by Local Authorities.

Two key issues in this problem are the lack of building land and the cost of providing new housing—both problems which are also found in urban housing situations. In the Oxford survey, three of the four District Councils outside the City considered that shortage of building land provided a major constraint to new house construction despite Government encouragement to adopt a more flexible approach to 'white' land development for housing (3.66). There is evidence however, that such land shortages exist only insofar as Local Authorities are unable to develop land for which planning permission exists, rather than there being an absolute shortage. The situation is certainly worse, however, in those areas where Green Belt or similar restrictions have been placed on rural land and where the normally restrictive processes of development control are reinforced.

The cost yardstick, within which Authorities have to provide new housing, represents another problem, particularly when the increased costs of building and servicing in rural areas are considered. Some indication of this last point can again be given from the Oxfordshire study. Whereas the average weekly cost in Oxford City of a new three-bedroom house in 1974/75 was estimated at £6 (with Government subsidy), the corresponding figures for the four, largely rural, Districts ranged from £19 to £27 (3.67). The need for smaller, two-bedroom houses may help with the problem of the cost yardstick, but only to a small extent.

Rural housing is an expensive commodity to provide, whether by Local Authority or by private developer. The figures quoted for Oxfordshire may be criticized because they provide a notional, rather than a real, estimate of some of the true costs of rural housing, but the contrasts between rural and urban are probably of the right order of magnitude. Over and above the higher cost of building, the provision of services such as power and sewage can often be three or more times more expensive than for comparable properties in urban areas. Housing provision was one of the items which Gupta and Hutton considered in their comparisons of economies of scale in Local Government services (3.68), and specific diseconomies were evident at the Rural District level which were not found in higher-order settlements.

These diseconomies are, of course, related to the problem of the optimum size of rural settlements. The tendency in the past for many rural Authorities to locate a few Council houses in most large villages may have been justified on social grounds, but has almost certainly led to increased costs. Diseconomies are seen in their most extreme form in the upland areas of Britain where housing is

114

frequently isolated and scattered over great distances. Tender prices in 1971 for Local Authority housing in some of the Scottish islands were up to 80% higher than comparable figures for the central lowlands. Studies carried out for the Highland and Islands Development Board by Gaskin (3.69) showed that transportation costs were a major factor in these contrasts, but other items (a shortage of local contractors, poor labour productivity, difficult site conditions) were also important and are probably applicable to many other rural areas.

Two further problems of Local Authority housing provision remain to be considered: eligibility for waiting lists and the control of housing standards. The wide range of criteria which can be applied by Local Authorities in deciding eligibility has been reviewed by Niner (3.70) and, although only one of her sample areas was a Rural District (Ludlow R.D.), evidence from other sources confirms her broad conclusions. Variation between Authorities in the importance given to such factors as the lack of household amenities, family size and eviction from a service tenancy, are complicated by the fact that people may be eligible for inclusion on the lists of two or more Districts. The discrepancies between qualifications and the possibility of duplication provided two important reasons for the formation of the joint working party on housing problems in Oxfordshire in 1974 and it would seem likely that this initiative will be followed elsewhere.

The control of housing standards is one area where a Local Authority intervenes directly in the private housing market. Nationally the record of rural housing quality has improved enormously but there are still problem areas. Rural Authorities are hampered by a poor financial base and rural houses are frequently scattered throughout the countryside, making inspection both expensive and time-consuming. The national improvement in standards has thus not been found in some rural Authorities and it has been argued that there will be little future improvement unless more funds are provided by central Government (3.71).

Both in terms of existing houses and of new construction, of course, the private developer is more important than the Local Authority, though he plays virtually no role in housing provision for the various underprivileged groups in the countryside. His activities are essentially a response to housing demand rather than housing need, and it should come as no surprise that this situation has frequently been criticized from a variety of standpoints. Local Authorities, through their housing and planning departments, attempt to regulate the activities of the private developer, but they must nonetheless be dependent on him for meeting a high proportion of rural housing demands. Indeed it has been argued that this regulation is less concerned with fulfilling social objectives related to housing need than planning objectives related to landscape quality (3.72). Planning control on private housing has traditionally been concerned with the visual quality of settlements and countryside and the loss of agricultural land, rather than with problems of underprivilege and poor housing. This attitude is clearly apparent in the guidelines for developments in rural areas (3.73) where it is stated at the outset:

"One of the most important aims of planning is to see that the need for building land is met without spoiling the countryside or wasting good agricultural land. Building in the open country, away from existing settlements or from areas allocated for development in development plans, is therefore strictly controlled."

This policy has operated since 1947 and is well entrenched despite the pressure on housing lists and the continued demand from private purchasers. The objectives of planning control, as traditionally defined, should be reconsidered in the light of obvious housing pressure in rural areas.

The policy of concentration of housing development in existing settlements has also meant that most private house building, other than infilling, has been in the form of estates. Development has increasingly been carried out by national firms rather than small builders and this has resulted in a trend towards uniformity in rural housing. Such uniformity can be criticized on grounds of design, since it frequently involves the construction of semi-detached houses, bungalows or terraced (so-called 'town') houses, which can be out of keeping with the rural idiom. But a more serious criticism concerns the market for which these houses are built (3.74). Put briefly, much private development is of a type, and consequently at a price, which effectively excludes many of those rural people who have the greatest need for housing. Houses are often too large and too costly for both newly-married couples and for older local residents. Thus it seems that the planning permissions which are given by one department of the Local Authority are not used to help solve the housing problems which are the responsibility of another.

A case study of a Rural District in Denbighshire (now Clwyd) provides some evidence for these views (3.75). Applications for planning permission over the period 1963-1972 increased in average size over the period, at least for applications to build within village envelopes. Of the 559 dwellings for which permission was given, only 272 had been built by 1973 and yet there was the seeming paradox of 180 people on the Council waiting list. Problems with the supply of building materials might have accounted for some of the shortfall, but the main explanation comes back essentially to the conflict between housing need and housing demand. The evidence of a social survey of new residents suggested that new houses within the Rural District were in general built to meet a non-local demand for small retirement properties or larger houses for commuters, and, moreover, there is a clear suggestion that this building was largely speculative. Builders were 'storing' land with planning permission and using it as the private demand and their own resources made construction possible. Both applications and planning consents tended to be concentrated in the more favoured western areas of the Rural District away from those areas of the east where residual local population had problems of poor housing amenities. Thus land which had in effect been earmarked for housing development was lying idle while housing need remained in the area. Clearly market forces were doing little to help the situation but, by the same token, the Local Authority was unable to help, even though the planners could argue that no absolute shortage of land existed.

Conclusion

Viewed in an historical perspective, rural housing in Britain today contrasts very favourably with its nineteenth and earlier twentieth century counterparts. The rural population is, by and large, well-housed and when compared with many urban situations, rural areas are clearly much favoured. No longer is there any truth in the parody of nineteenth century romantic verse which appeared in *Punch* as:

"The cottage homes of England,
Alas! How strong they smell;
There's fever in the cesspool
And sewage in the well" (3.76).

Yet rural housing problems remain. Often there are problems of the relative deprivation of particular groups within society which are often powerless to help themselves. The homeless, the old and the poor are the most obvious groups thus affected. From time to

117

time the plight of some of these groups may hit the headlines and action may be taken. The situation with regard to the tied cottage in agriculture is a case in point. For the most part, however, the system is left to provide specific solutions from general policies and, perhaps inevitably, the system is seen to fail.

This prompts the question of future policies and the form which they should take. Many would argue that solutions are possible within the system. An answer lies in encouraging Local Authorities to build more houses to meet the pressure of waiting lists, helped by new powers for land acquisition, or that schemes of voluntary housing or of co-ownership can help where minority groups are disadvantaged by the process of the private housing market.

Other critics see the problems as more deep-seated and solutions as realistic only in terms of radical changes in the system. Peter Ambrose has argued strongly that the system of public and private housing which has developed in Britain is offensive on several counts (3.77). It is socially and spatially divisive insofar as it separates the Council estate from the private development, the commuter from the farm worker. Secondly, that it distributes wealth upwards and so favours those who have rather than those who have not. And finally, and perhaps most important, that it fails to satisfy housing need. Four-fifths of new housing in rural areas comes from the private sector and is a direct response to economics rather than social welfare. The remaining fifth is supplied from the public sector, ostensibly to underwrite the deficiencies of the private market, but in a form which is complicated and contentious to administer and with resources that are far from adequate. Changes in the system may indeed be what are needed, but they can be effective only with changes in attitude to housing as a social service rather than an economic good.

The early part of this Chapter considered the change in attitudes towards rural housing problems at the beginning of the twentieth century. The concern of social reformers was gradually taken over by the concern of the planners, and this change was mirrored in legislation. It may be that this process has now gone far enough and that housing problems have become so firmly embedded in land use planning, that the problems of society which they reflect have been all but forgotten. The planning of villages, with the delimiting of conservation areas and of village 'envelopes', the concern with landscape and layout and the production of guides by Local Authorities to help in the choice of 'good' design in the countryside simply emphasize this seperation of the material from the human. It may well be, therefore, that future policies for rural housing should be based more on the ideas of nineteenth century social reformers than on twentieth century land use planners.

References

3.1   HOWARD, E., *Garden Cities of Tomorrow*, Faber & Faber, 1902/1946.
3.2   ARONSON, H., *Our Village Homes: Present Conditions and Suggested Remedies*, Munby, 1913.
3.3   MINISTRY OF WORKS and PLANNING, *Report of the Committee on Land Utilisation in Rural Areas*. Cmd. 6378 HMSO, 1942. p. 91.
3.4   ARONSON, H., *op. cit.* pp. 135-140.
3.5   WEBER, B., 'A New Index of Residential Construction and Long Cycles in House-building in Great Britain, 1838-1950', *Scottish Journal of Political Economy*, **II**, 1954-5, p. 120.
3.6   MINETT, J., 'The Housing, Town Planning Etc. Act, 1909', *The Planner*, **60**, 5, 1974, p. 677.
3.7   ALLEN, C.W., 'The Housing of the Agricultural Labourer', *Journal of the Royal Agricultural Society of England*, **75**, 1914, p. 21.
3.8   ORWIN, C.S., *Country Planning: A Study of Rural Problems*, Oxford University Press, 1944.
3.9   TILLEY, M.F., *Housing the Country Worker*, Faber & Faber, 1947.
3.10   ORWIN, C.S., *op. cit.*, p. 116.
3.11   RURAL HOUSING SUB-COMMITTEE OF THE CENTRAL HOUSING ADVISORY COMMITTEE, *Rural Housing, 3rd Report*, HMSO, 1944.
3.12   JENNINGS, J.H., 'Geographical Implications of the Municipal Housing Programme in England and Wales, 1919-39', *Urban Studies*, **8**, 2, 1971, pp. 121-38.
3.13   MARSHALL, J.L., 'The Pattern of Housebuilding in the Inter-war Period in England and Wales', *Scottish Journal of Political Economy*, **XV**, 1968, p. 187.
3.14   Quoted in TILLEY, M.F., *op. cit.*, p. 42.
3.15   SCOTTISH HOUSING ADVISORY COMMITTEE, *Report on Rural Housing in Scotland*, HMSO, 1937.
3.16   CHERRY, G.E., 'The Housing, Town Planning Etc. Act, 1919', *The Planner*, **60**, 5, 1974, p. 684.
3.17   CHERRY, G.E., *The Evolution of British Town Planning*, Leonard Hill, 1974, p. 103.
3.18   SCOTTISH HOUSING ADVISORY COMMITTEE, *op. cit.*
3.19   MINISTRY OF HEALTH, *Report on the Overcrowding Survey in England and Wales*, HMSO, 1936.
3.20   TILLEY, M.F., *op. cit.*, p. 42.
3.21   RURAL HOUSING SUB-COMMITTEE OF THE CENTRAL HOUSING ADVISORY COMMITTEE, *op. cit.*, p. 24.
3.22   CULLINGWORTH, J.B., *Environmental Planning, 1939-1969: Volume 1, Reconstruction and Land Use Planning, 1939-1947*. HMSO, 1975, p. 41.
3.23   ASSOCIATION OF COUNTY SANITARY OFFICERS, *Housing—Second Interim Report on the Housing Survey in Rural Areas (England and Wales)*, ACSO, 1952.
3.24   The Government's plans were put forward in the White Paper, *Housing*, Cmd. 6609, HMSO, 1945.

3.25 For example, SCOTT, W.B., 'Housing Conditions in a Rural District', *The Medical Officer*, 23rd August, 1947. pp. 81-2.

3.26 ORWIN, C.S., *Problems of the Countryside*, Cambridge University Press, 1945, pp. 45-7.

3.27 COOPER, J.B., *Memorandum upon Rural Housing, with Particular Reference to Standards, Costs and Subsidies*. National Housing and Town Planning Council, 1946.

3.28 For a good review see WATSON, C.J., 'The Housing Question', chapter 3 of *Urban Planning Problems*, CHERRY, G.E., (Ed.), Leonard Hill, 1974, pp. 57-83.

3.29 HOLE, W.V., and POUNTNEY, M.T., *Trends in Population, Housing and Occupancy Rates, 1861-1961*, HMSO, 1971.

3.30 *Census of Population, 1961, England and Wales*, Housing Tables, Part III, Table 26.

3.31 Calculated fron the *Census of Population, 1971, England and Wales*, Housing Tables.

3.32 For a brief review of the regional differences shown by the *1961 Census of Population* see STORRIE, M.C., 'Household Tenure in the British Isles', in *Population Maps of the British Isles, 1961*, HUNT, A.J., (Ed.), *Transactions of the Institute of British Geographers*, 43, 1968.

3.33 See the maps produced as part of the *Census of Population, Scotland, 1971: Housing Report*, HMSO.

3.34 For example the villages of Ardington and Lockinge studied in HAVINDEN, M.A., *Estate Villages*, Lund Humphries, 1966.

3.35 MILLER, T., 'Military Airfields and Rural Planning', *Town Planning Review*, 414, 1973, p. 36.

3.36 GREEN R.J., and AYTON, J.B., 'Changes in the Pattern of Rural Settlement', paper given to the Town Planning Institute Conference on *Planning for the Changing Countryside*, 1967.

3.37 STONE, P.A., *Urban Development in Britain: Standards, Costs and Resources 1964-2004*, Cambridge University Press, 1970, p. 90.

3.38 DEPARTMENT OF THE ENVIRONMENT, *House Condition Survey, 1971; England and Wales*, Housing Survey Reports no. 9, HMSO, 1973.

3.39 WELSH OFFICE, *Welsh House Condition Survey, 1968*. HMSO, 1969.

3.40 BEST, R.H., and ROGERS, A.W., *The Urban Countryside: The Land-Use Structure of Small Towns and Villages in England and Wales*, Faber & Faber, 1973.

3.41 WILLIAMS, R., *The Country and the City*, Chatto and Windus, 1973.

3.42 PAHL, R.E., 'Commuting and Social Change in Rural Areas', chapter 1 of *Whose City? and other Essays on Sociology and Planning*, Longman, 1970.

3.43 For a good review, see GASSON, R., 'Resources in Agriculture: Labour', chapter 6 of *Agricultural Resources: An Introduction to the Farming Industry of the United Kingdom*, EDWARDS, A. and ROGERS, A. (Eds.), Faber & Faber, 1974.

3.44 PAHL, R.E., 'The Social Objectives of Village Planning', chapter 4 of *Whose City? and Other Essays on Sociology and Planning*, op. cit.

3.45 PENFOLD, S.F., *Housing Problems of Local People in Rural Areas: The Peak District Experience and Discussion of Policy Options*, Study No. 7, Department of Town and Regional Planning, University of Sheffield, 1974.

3.46 BIELCKUS, C.L., ROGERS, A.W., and WIBBERLEY, G.P., *Second Homes in England and Wales*, Studies in Rural Land Use No. 11, Wye College, 1972.

3.47 Data from *Audits of Great Britain Ltd.*, quoted in AITKEN, R., DOWNING, P. and DOWER, M., *Second Homes in Scotland*, report of Dartington Amenity Research Trust to the Scottish Countryside Commission and other sponsors, 1975. All subsequent estimates of second home numbers are based on this source.

3.48 Anon, 'Is There a Future for Second-home Development?', *Property Letter*, 232, 1974, pp. 7-16.

3.49   ALLISON, S., *et al.*, *Holiday Homes/Tai Haf*, Report No. 3, Welsh Language Society, 1972.
3.50   MAHON, D., *No Place in the Country*, Shelter, 1973.
3.51   *Ibid.*, p. 1.
3.52   *Property Letter*, *op. cit.*
3.53   CONSTABLE, M., *Shelter Report on Tied Accommodation*, Shelter, 1974.
3.54   IRVING, B.L., and HILGENDORF, E.L., *Tied Cottages in British Agriculture*, Tavistock Institute for Human Relations, 1975.
3.55   GASSON, R., *Provision of Tied Cottages*, Occasional Paper No. 4, Department of Land Economy, University of Cambridge, 1975.
3.56   *Ibid.*, p. 45.
3.57   Department of the Environment and Ministry of Agriculture, Fisheries and Food, *Abolitoon of the Tied Cottage System in Agriculture: Consultative Document*, HMSO, 1975.
3.58   JONES, A., *Rural Housing: the Agricultural Tied Cottage*, Occasional Papers on Social Administration, No. 56, Bell, 1975.
3.59   CONSTABLE, M., *An Alternative to the Abolition of the Tied Cottage in Agriculture: An Informative Document on Licensing*, The Arthur Rank Centre, National Agricultural Centre, Kenilworth, Warwickshire, 1975.
3.60   REED, B., and QUINE, C., *Freedom to Depend: A Study of Service Accommodation on an Agricultural Estate*, The Grubb Institute, 1974.
3.61   CONSTABLE, M., *op. cit.* 1974.
3.62   MILLER, T., *op. cit.*
3.63   *Widening the Choice: The Next Steps in Housing*, Cmnd. 5280, HMSO, 1973.
3.64   JOINT WORKING PARTY ON HOUSING STUDIES, *Housing in Oxfordshire*, Joint Oxfordshire County and Districts General Committee, 1975.
3.65   JOINT WORKING PARTY ON HOUSING STUDIES, *Oxfordshire Housing Statistics, 1975*, Joint Oxfordshire County and Districts General Committee, 1975.
3.66   DEPARTMENT OF THE ENVIRONMENT, *Land Availability for Housing*, Circular 241/73, HMSO, 1973.
3.67   *Oxfordshire Housing Statistics, 1975*, *op. cit.* Table 4.
3.68   GUPTA, S.P., and HUTTON, J.P., *Economies of Scale in Local Government Services*, Royal Commission on Local Government in England, Research Study 3, Institute of Social and Economic Research, University of York, 1968.
3.69   GASKIN, M., *Freight Rates and Prices in the Islands*, Highlands and Islands Development Board, 1971.
3.70   NINER, P., *Local Authority Housing Policy and Practice—A Case Study Approach*, Occasional Paper No. 31, Centre for Urban and Regional Studies, University of Birmingham, 1975.
3.71   FLETCHER, P., 'The Control of Housing Standards in a Rural District: A Case Study', *Social and Economic Administration*, 3, 2, 1969, pp. 106-120.
3.72   LIVINGSTONE, J., *Rural Housing in the Context of Current Planning Practice*, unpublished M. Phil. thesis, University College, London, 1975.
3.73   MINISTRY OF HOUSING AND LOCAL GOVERNMENT/WELSH OFFICE, *Development Control Policy Note 4: Development in Rural Areas*, HMSO, 1969, p. 1.
3.74   This criticism is raised in AMBROSE, P., *The Quiet Revolution: Social Change in a Sussex Village, 1871-1971*. Chatto and Windus, 1974. pp. 190-191.
3.75   JACOBS, C.A., *Rural Housing in Denbighshire*, Denbighshire County Council, 1974.
3.76   Quoted in WOODFORDE, J., *The Truth About Cottages*, Routledge, 1969.
3.77   AMBROSE, P., *op. cit.* Chapter 14.

Further Reading

BRACEY, H.E., *People in the Countryside,* Routledge and Kegan Paul, 1970.

GREEN, R.J., *Country Planning: the Future of the Rural Regions,* Manchester University Press, 1971.

JACKSON, V.J., *Population in the Countryside: Growth and Stagnation in the Cotswolds,* Frank Cass, 1968.

THORBURN, A., *Planning Villages,* Estates Gazette, 1971.

WHITBY, M.C., ROBINS, D.L.J., TANSEY, A.W., and WILLIS, K.G., *Rural Resource Development,* Methuen, 1974.

CHAPTER FOUR

Rural Employment
Andrew W. Gilg

While Britain, in landscape terms at least, is still a rural country, the numbers involved in working in rural employment have dwindled over the years until they now comprise only about 5% of the total labour force. However, wherever the presence of employment in nearby urban areas makes commuting a practical proposition, the numbers living in rural areas have increased since the Second World War. Though working in towns many of these commuters may be indirectly employed in extracting production from rural areas. Such is the case of those involved in the manufacture of agricultural equipment or fertilizers, the financing of agriculture, or in the distribution and marketing of produce from one agricultural area or another. In other words a great deal of rural employment is now centred within urban areas. Other examples could, obviously, be given, but without elaborating, it is clear that the employment situation in Britain today is so complex and interrelated that it is virtually impossible to distinguish between rural based and urban based employment, at least throughout those parts of the country that lie within the commuting orbits of the main centres of population.

Accordingly this Chapter concentrates on the problems of rural employment in the remote rural areas, away from the main commuting areas (4.1). These remote rural areas are usually defined as consisting of the following parts of the country: the Highlands and Islands of Scotland, the Scottish Border Country, the Lake District and Northern Pennines, Central and Northern Wales, East Anglia and the South-West (4.2). These areas have a number of factors in common, the most important being: their low population density; the distances between their main centres of population; their isolation from main centres of economic activity; and their poor population and employment structure.

Employment problems

Little study has been made of the employment structure of rural areas, partly because of the difficulty of distinguishing between rural and urban employment as outlined above, and partly because most of the administrative units used for data collection are unsuitable since they usually contain large towns. What work has been done (4.3) has been largely of a historical nature. By tracing the evolution of employment structure, these studies have, however, thrown a useful light on to the problems encountered today.

Since 1801, three periods of change have been distinguished by these studies. During these periods the labour force has taken characteristically different forms (4.4). In the first period between 1801 and 1831 the general pattern of movement from agriculture to industry was established. During the second period between 1831 and 1911 agricultural employment continued to decline, but employment expansion occurred in the mining and transport sectors rather than in the manufacturing sector. The real change occurred, however, in the third period from 1911 onwards. In this period, employment in both the manufacturing and service sectors expanded at the expense of all other sectors, though in recent years manufacturing employment has declined as service employment has become dominant. Since 1911 modern service and manufacturing industries have relied for their expansion on rising prosperity and a consequential demand for their products caused by either a growing population or rising productivity in manufacturing industry. However in most rural areas neither of these factors has generally occurred, more often than not the reverse has been the case. In most remote rural areas the population has declined, and industrial production has also often declined as old plant has become redundant and outdated. The employment pattern of many such areas is thus characterized by an antecedent structure. This is the result of traditional industries not being replaced, as they become outmoded, with dynamic new industries. Most rural areas have thus not participated in the growth of the third period.

Tables 4.1 and 4.2 show examples of these employment structures and demonstrate the considerable differences that still exist between the national, regional and local levels. For example, the percentage employed in the primary sector varies from a low of 4% nationally to a high of around 40% in some local areas. Within this diversity a number of common themes can be found. The gas, electricity, water, transport and communication sector, for example, shows virtually no national, regional or local variation. Similarly other employ-

Table 4.1   Distribution of all Employment by Type and County 1961 and 1971

Type of Employment		County (County Boroughs excluded) 10% Sample					
Percentages in each		Devon	Kent	Norfolk	Westmor-land	Radnor	England +Wales (Including County Boroughs)
Groups I+II Agriculture	1961	17	6	27	17	40	6
fishing, mining and	1971	15	5	16	13	28	4
quarrying							
Groups III-XVII†	1961	22	38	21	26	10	43
Manufacturing and	1971	25	35	32	30	22	40
construction							
Groups XVIII+ XIX*	1961	8	9	5	8	8	9
Gas, electricity,	1971	5	8	4	6	5	8
water, transport and							
communication							
Groups XX+XXIII°	1961	32	26	26	30	22	24
Distributive trades	1971	33	26	27	30	24	22
and miscellaneous							
services							
Groups XXI+XXII•	1961	13	13	9	13	11	12
Insurance, banking,	1971	16	19	15	17	12	16
finance, professional							
and scientific services							
Group XXIV#	1961	8	8	11	5	8	6
Public administration	1971	6	7	6	4	9	10
and defence							

Sources: 1961 Table 4 of the appropriate County volumes of Occupation, Industry Socio-Economic Groups of the 1961 Census.
1971 Table 3 of the appropriate County volumes of Economic Activity County Leaflets of the 1971 Census
†In 1971 Census Groups III+XX °In 1971 Census Groups XXIII+XXVI *In 1971 Census Groups XXI+XXII •In 1971 Census Groups XXIV+XXV #In 1971 Census Groups XXVII

Table 4.2 Distribution of all Employment by Type and Region 1971

Type of employment

Percentages in each group	England and Wales	North (R)	Yorks and Humberside (R)	North West (R)	East Midlands	West Midlands (R)	East Anglia	South-East (R)	South-West	Wales	Scotland (R)
							Region (Conurbations excluded)				
Groups I–II Agriculture, forestry, fishing, mining, and quarrying	4	10	10	4	12	7	9	4	6	9	8
Groups III+XVII Manufacturing, construction	42	41	42	49	24	48	37	34	35	40	37
Groups XVII+XIX Gas, electricity, water, transport, and communication	8	7	8	7	9	6	7	8	7	8	7
Groups XX+XXIII Distributive trades, miscellaneous services	23	22	22	22	29	20	25	26	25	21	23
Groups XXI+XXII Insurance, banking, finance, professional and scientific services	16	14	14	14	18	13	15	18	16	15	16
Group XXIV Public administration and defence	7	7	5	5	7	6	7	10	10	7	8

Source: Table 20 of the Economic Activity Tables (Part III) of the 1971 Census (R) Denotes a region where the conurbation has been excluded.

ment groups within the tertiary service sector show little variation, compared with the variations exhibited by the primary and secondary sectors. It is thus clear that one of the employment problems of rural areas is that of an unbalanced employment structure, with too much employment in the primary sector, but with too little in the employment generating secondary sector. This problem is largely due to the historical evolution of rural areas, which have been left behind in the economic changes taking place in the more urban parts of the country.

An unbalanced employment structure is, however, but one of the employment problems of rural areas. The principle employment problem of the remote rural areas is lack of opportunity for work. This problem occurs in two forms. First there are few jobs available and second what jobs there are, are of a limited scope and tend to be in a declining sector of the economy (4.5). The population of these areas, especially the younger people, when faced with the prospect of no job at all or a job not really to their liking, have for the last hundred years or so taken the decision to leave and migrate to areas of greater employment opportunity. The consequent depopulation of these areas, especially of the younger age groups, has frequently set off a vicious circle of both population and economic decline. This can eventually lead to the complete death of a community, a situation which has in fact occurred in several islands off the west coast of Scotland.

A second employment problem of these areas is the low activity rate of the population. This index does not refer to the laziness or otherwise of the population, but instead to the ratio of people employed or registered as unemployed to the number of people of working age. Accordingly, low activity rates reveal the extent of *under*employment in an area, or put in a more positive way, they reveal substantial labour reserves capable of productive work. In the remote rural areas low activity rates are caused by three main factors. First, the apparent hopelessness of finding a job deters many women from registering as unemployed and thus eligible for work. Second, there are few job opportunities for women. Third, many men in their late fifties or early sixties retire to these areas. Table 4.3 demonstrates that the two major problems are low female employment and high unemployment among young people.

In addition to these problems, most of the remote rural areas also suffer from an abundance of infrastructure deficiencies, for example poor roads, outdated hospitals, schools and other social services. Furthermore most of these areas have few basic resources worth

Table 4.3   Economic Activity Rates and Economically Active out of Employment by Region 1971

Region	15-24				25-44				45-64 Sex and Age Groups			
	MA	FA	ME	FE*	MA	FA	ME	FE	MA	FA	ME	FE
North	78	59	10	7	98	49	6	4	92	51	9	3
Yorks and Humberside	78	57	8	6	98	50	5	4	94	56	6	3
East Midlands	78	59	6	5	98	50	3	4	95	57	5	2
East Anglia	75	56	6	5	98	46	3	4	95	53	5	4
South East	74	59	6	5	97	52	3	4	96	61	4	3
South East	74	55	6	6	98	47	3	4	93	52	5	3
West Midlands	79	59	7	6	99	52	4	4	96	60	5	3
North East	78	59	9	7	98	54	6	5	94	61	6	3
Wales	75	52	9	9	98	44	5	6	91	46	8	4
Scotland	75	58	11	8	98	49	8	6	94	57	8	4

*MA+FA: Male and Female Activity Rates   ME+FE: Male and Female unemployment rates

Source: Central Statistical Office, *Abstract of Regional Statistics,* 1973, HMSO, 1973

exploiting. There are however two resources that can and have been successfully exploited in these areas, namely forestry and mining. Unfortunately, the exploitation of these resources conflicts with both Government leglislation on conservation, and the one econ-omic success story of the remote areas in recent years—the growth of tourism. Despite these limited successes the employment problems of these areas remain intransigent and the almost total failure of Government policies to do anything other than ameliorate employ-ment problems, has led many commentators to argue for an accelerated run down of employment in these areas. There are however compelling reasons for continuing the fight to maintain and, if possible, increase rural employment.

There are a number of reasons why Government should attempt to halt the employment and other problems of regional imbalance in Britain. The first of these is that unequal standards of living and other general inequalities give rise to rifts and divisions in society (4.6). The second reason is that agricultural and other similar basic employment cannot by themselves support economically efficient communities. Thirdly, most of these areas have substantial reserves of labour which if brought into employment would not only boost the Gross National Product, but would also save Government expenditure on unemployment and other state benefits. Fourthly, a continued exodus of people and jobs from the remote to the already overcrowded urban areas would lead to a further intensification of congestion in these areas. A fifth reason is that these areas contain a good deal of social capital, which in a period of low economic growth is very expensive to replace and reconstruct in another location. A sixth is that most people living in these areas do not want to leave, and that many who have left would return given the chance. These arguments do not of course mean that all settlements in remote rural areas should be retained. Structural changes must continue to take place within the region. What these arguments do mean is that regional totals should if possible be maintained and preferably improved. Employment policies for rural areas must first of all, therefore, be regional policies, within which local policies can be evolved.

Two further reasons for the adoption of a nationally based regional policy have been defined by McCrone (4.7) as (a) political and (b) economic. Ever since the 1920s regional policies have been an important factor in the rise and fall of Governments. Today, the resurgence of Scottish and Welsh nationalism in Britain, adding to the continuing problems of Northern Ireland clearly demonstrate to politicians that they ignore the regional problem at their peril. The economic reasons are twofold. McCrone argues, first, that free market forces alone cannot be relied upon to produce the optimal location of industry without the guidance of regional policy; and secondly that economic growth requires a policy to ensure that all the country's scarce and costly resources are utilized to the maximum.

Prospects for employment

Though *agriculture* is the most extensive user of land in Britain, and is Britain's single largest industry in terms of output, it now employs directly only about 2% of the population. The worker on the land is however supported by a much larger number of urban based workers involved in the production of machinery, fertilizers, etc, so much so that the real agricultural labour force must be about 10% of Britain's working population. Ironically, the low percentage of workers now employed on the land is not the result of a run down of the agricultural industry. On the contrary, it is the result of an impressive improvement in agricultural productivity, which has taken place largely because of the machinery given to Government by the Agriculture Act, 1947. The price for the expansion of agriculture has been a much reduced labour force and generally over the years, reduced returns for farmers. The nation has benefited at the expense of the agricultural community. The decline in the numbers employed in agriculture has been caused by both the 1947 Act and the technical and structural changes that have occured within agriculture since the war. The most important of these changes has been the replacement of first human and then animal motive power by machinery. Allied to this trend, farms have become bigger and more specialized, allowing labour supplies to be more accurately matched to work demands, with consequent economies of scale. Seasonal demands for labour have also been much reduced by the utilization of new machinery, particularly harvesting machinery, with serious consequences for the amount of part time female employment available. In terms of regional change, a study (4.8) made of the period 1945-65 found that the biggest losses of 50% and over had occurred in North and South Wales, the South-East and parts of the Midlands. All areas had lost at least 35%. No end to the loss, now running at about 4% a year, can be foreseen. Indeed, it may even increase, as contract labour, often town based, allows farmers to achieve even greater economies of scale.

The actual processes underlying the declining numbers of agricultural workers is less clear however. Earnings in agriculture are lower than in almost any employment sector, but this has to be offset against the advantages of a tied house with either no rent or only a minimal rent payable, and the fringe benefits that most agricultural workers receive, such as free milk. Various studies have however suggested (4.9) that pull factors are more important than push factors. About two-thirds of farmworkers who leave the land do so of their own accord. The losses occur when farmers fail to replace workers, rather than from a distinct decision to make a worker redundant.

A notable feature of the decline in agricultural employment is that until the early 1960s the numbers of farmers had remained remarkably constant. The number of holdings for example had remained the same at around 450,000 for a long period. But by the early 1960s the total had been reduced to around 400,000 and by the mid-1970s to around 250,000. The long resistance of farmers to leave agriculture can easily be explained. While farmworkers lose little status and often in fact gain esteem by moving to urban employment, farmers lose the status of being self-employed. In addition farmers have little training for any other occupation of similar managerial status.

Farmers will generally only leave the land when no other alternative is possible. There is thus a considerable difference between the reasons for farmers and workers leaving the land (4.10) but in both cases the availability of work in the neighbourhood and the difficulties of finding alternative accommodation to the tied cottage or the farmhouse (4.11) are the most significant factors in the decision to leave the land.

Largely because of these reasons, the structure of the agricultural labour force has also been markedly changing in recent years (4.12). Three types of person are now commonly employed in agriculture. First, the ever decreasing numbers of workers of middle age who were recruited into agriculture in their early teens. Second, teenagers who see the farm as a short term employer, and who are seen by the farmer as cheap labour. The importance of this group is clearly illustrated by Table 4.4. Third, and the only growing group of the

Table 4.4   Age Distribution of Male Farmers and Farmworkers in England and Wales 1970

Age Group	Farmers	Farmworkers
15-24	4.7	27.0
25-34	16.4	20.2
35-44	23.8	18.5
45-54	26.0	16.8
55-64	20.5	14.9
65 and over	8.7	2.7

Source: National Economic Development Office, *Agricultural manpower in England and Wales*, HMSO, 1972

three, is the specially trained worker. This worker more often than not will have been born in a town and will have made the conscious decision to seek agricultural employment. Increasingly however, especially in the remoter rural areas, farms employ no labour at all— the farmer and his family running the farm by themselves. In upland hill farming areas it is now usual in fact for farmers to considerably outnumber other workers.

For all these reasons agriculture can now no longer be seen as a major employer of rural labour, nor indeed can any long term change be realistically foreseen. It is probable in fact that EEC policies will force further redundancies particularly in the hill farming areas that characterize many of the remote rural areas. Some 30% of Britain's agricultural land is covered by hill farming, which by its very nature cannot give a high return on investment per acre. Government subsidies have in most cases been needed to keep hill farming in existence and in many cases provide at least half, if not all the farmer's income. The products of hill farms being mainly of an intermediate character, such as store cattle or sheep, makes hill farming particularly vulnerable to low prices and poor returns. It is, however, in the nation's interest to continue production in these areas because they provide the hard core of our sheep and cattle herds. Production in these areas will only continue however if the population can be retained in sufficient numbers to provide the basis of a viable social and economic community. But hill farming can only be profitable (4.13) if more workers and farmers are shed.

To counter these two conflicting trends it is essential that more non-agricultural employment be found in these areas. *Forestry* is one alternative. Over most of the upland areas of rural Britain it has long been thought that forestry represented a more intensive user of such land than agriculture. Not only does forestry employ more people per thousand hectares, but once the forests begin to mature, about four to five people for each forester are employed in secondary industries, processing the timber. According to this traditional theory then, forestry should not only provide an alternative to agriculture, but it should also provide employment expansion. For over 50 years, since the formation of the Forestry Commission in 1919, these theories about the employment effects of forestry have been generally accepted (4.15).

In the early 1970s, however, a Government based study, using cost-benefit methods of analysis concluded that there no longer appeared to be any strategic reasons on either defence or commercial grounds for continuing new afforestation (4.16). Extending the argument, the study found that new planting compared unfavourably with the hill farming it replaces, both in economic resources and in exchequer costs per acre (Table 4.5). The study did find, however, that forestry produces slightly more local employment, albeit at a higher cost per job in resource and exchequer terms. Accordingly, the study suggested that new planting should depend on the relative weight given to the three factors of job creation, resource cost and exchequer cost, while at the same time pointing out that the very high costs per job in providing employment by forestry made it likely that more effective means of supporting employment could be found. The Government accepted these findings in 1974, so that in future, new forestry planting will be limited to replacement of existing forests when they mature, or where amenity or tourism potential will be increased by new planting.

Fishing is a hunting operation, and the British industry therefore

Table 4.5   Costs Involved in Transferring Land Use and Employment from Hill Farming to Forestry

Type of Land Use	Costs Involved and Labour Employed by Area								
£000 per 1000 acres	Net Resource Benefit/loss			Local labour employed			Exchequer costs		
	1	2	3	1	2	3	1	2	3
Areas 1-3									
Hill farming	0	0	0	2.7	1.4	0.3	26	10½	4
Forestry	—62	—28½	—38½	6.7	2.8	3.7	109½	64	64½
Change from hill farming to forestry	—62	—28½	—38½	4.0	1.4	3.4	83½	53½	60½

Area 1: North Wales Conservancy Area 2: South Scotland Conservancy Area 3: North Scotland Conservancy

Source: Treasury, H.M., *Forestry in Great Britain*, HMSO, 1971

depends on nature for its sources of supplies, and operates for the most part in international waters in competition with the fishing fleets of many other nations. The extension of territorial limits because of international pressures has increasingly confined the British industry to fishing only inside its own 12 mile limit. In addition, the development of bigger and more technologically sophisticated trawlers has much reduced the deep sea fishing fleet and consequently employment. In combination, these two factors have caused a marked loss of employment in the fishing settlements of the South-West, West Wales, and the North-West and North-East coasts of Scotland.

Three recent developments may however reverse this long term trend of decline. The first development is the growth of demand for shellfish, particularly scampi and prawns. These high cost products can support more employment than the more traditional fishing products of herring and cod. The second development is the potential demonstrated by experimental fish farms, which in a small area can breed large stocks of fish very quickly. By concentrating on high cost products such as salmon, trout and shellfish these fish farms can provide considerable local employment along the coast, rivers or reservoirs. The third development concerns new Government incentives to persuade individuals to start their own fishing business. Such incentive schemes have been particularly successful in the Highlands and Islands of Scotland region.

Like fishing, *mining and quarrying* must be concentrated at those points where economically exploitable resources occur. Because the remote rural areas of Britain generally correspond with the oldest and most geologically disturbed rocks in Britain, they are rich in minerals. Unfortunately, most of the pure and easily exploitable resources have long since been worked out, leaving only fragmented and complex deposits, generally of a low grade. New techniques of separating out even low grade and complex ores, allied to rising world prices for many minerals, has however allowed new exploitation to take place in certain areas. A notable example is the modest revival of the Cornish tin mining industry. But world commodity price trends are however extremely volatile, and it needs a good deal of confidence in their stability before investment can take place in the very heavy cost of exploiting the remaining low grade minerals on rocks (4.17).

A further problem is that mining resources usually occur in National Parks and other areas of protected landscape. Their proposed exploitation is thus more often than not bitterly opposed. The case of potash mining in the North York Moors National Park illustrates this point all too well. In the mid-1960s a world shortage of potash, a basic ingredient in fertilizer, forced Britain's chemical industry to explore the possibilities of exploiting local rather than international resources. The best resources in terms of cost and location to existing plant were found to occur in the North York Moors. Because the extraction of this potash involved considerable alteration to the landscape of the National Park, the proposal was strongly opposed. Eventually, the chemical industry won the right to exploit potash, but only after a long and costly fight (4.18). In addition costly and stringent conditions were attached. By the time the whole process had been completed, the world price for potash had fallen, and the chemical industry no longer wished to exploit the resource.

For the country as a whole, *manufacturing industry* provides about 40% of all employment. In the remote rural areas it rarely provides more than 20% and often provides as little as 10%. The reasons for this are mainly historical. At the start of the industrial revolution the remote rural areas already had a smaller share of the population, and thus less economic potential anyway. But more importantly, once water power gave way to steam power they lost access to the means of production. What water based industry there had been, declined because it could not compete with coal powered industry. Because of their economic stagnation the remote rural areas were not provided with the new transport facilities of first canals and then railways. Ironically when the railway did come to the remote rural areas later in the nineteenth century it was instrumental in hastening economic decline. Faced with continued decline the population of the remote rural areas began to migrate to the still growing towns of the industrial regions of Britain. By the end of the nineteenth century all the symptoms and causes of the vicious circle of decline in remote rural areas had become well established. Once such a trend is established it is very difficult to reverse.

The continued failure of manufacturing industry to become established in remote rural areas, in spite of Government efforts since the 1930s, can be blamed on other factors as well as historical ones. The most important of these is often overlooked: the lack of an entrepreneurial base in these areas. In London, for example it is easy to start an enterprise, for finance, premises, skilled labour and all the other factors of production are near at hand. Most important of all, the successful example of others is there to be followed. Nothing inspires like success. Nothing dampens initiative more than decay and failure.

Moseley (4.19) has concluded that the advantages of agglomeration accrue most importantly to firms in terms of labour availability. This advantage of a wide and skilled labour force allied to industrial linkage makes rural locations even less attractive. Therefore the early adoption of most entrepreneurial innovation depends largely upon urban size, location and growth rate. The policy implication of these facts is that channeling as much development as possible to a region's largest centre(s) seems justified. If Moseley's conclusions are correct, and they represent the distillation of many similar findings, industrial economic growth will not be stimulated in remote rural areas until the conditions of the larger cities of Britain can be recreated in them. Clearly this is impossible in present conditions, and if it were the areas would no longer be remote and rural. Two positive conclusions do however emerge. First, manufacturing industry cannot alone solve the employment problems of the remote rural areas. Government policies that have attempted to solve the problem by encouraging industry to relocate have thus been doomed to failure by starting with a false hypothesis. Second, some manufacturing industry can profitably be located in remote rural areas, but its chances of success are immeasurably improved if it is concentrated in key areas of the remote rural region.

The initial effort must therefore involve the transfer of jobs to the key growth areas of the region, until they cross the threshold of self-generating growth and no longer need Government aid. Such efforts face a number of problems. First, little industry is truly mobile, and so the amount of job creation that can be provided in any one year by direct transfer is strictly limited. A 1975 White Paper (4.20) on regional employment policy examined figures drawn from a Government study of industrial mobility between 1966 and 1971. In this period 865 new openings took place outside the Economic Planning Region in which they originated. 811 of these survived to 1971, and employed 103,000 people. Out of this total 86,000 jobs were created in Scotland, Wales, Northern Ireland, and the Northern North-West and South-West regions of England. During the same time 2000 new openings were recorded within their region of origin giving rise to 175,000 jobs by 1971. Even when an industry wishes to expand, and the expansion could be achieved by transfer, few industrialists want to leave their base area where both business and personal relationships are well established. In addition, the disadvantages of the remote area will loom large; remoteness, untrained labour, poor social and economic facilities, poor transport, and often chaotic traffic congestion in the holiday months are seen as the main

Table 4.6   Factors Considered by Employers when Moving to the South-West of England

Plus Factors[1]	Percentage+	Percentage*	Minus Factors[2]
Attractive area	29	17	Roads
Availability of labour supply	22	16	Distance from raw materials
Promimity to other factories and other regions	12	11	Air line transport
Access to local market and raw materials	9	11	Workers transport
Other	6	10	Labour availability
Unknown	6	8	Distance from maor marks
Available premises or site	4	7	Railways
Local authority cooperation	4	6	Labour turnover
Board of Trade influence	3	6	Other
Other labour advantages	3	4	Port facilities

+ Percentage of factories where factor was the main factor in locational decision
* Percentage of total complaints mentioned by all respondents

Sources: 1. SPOONER, D.J.,'Industrial movement and the rural periphery: The case of Devon and Cornwall', *Regional Studies*, 6, 1972, pp. 197-215.
    2.NEWBY, P., 'Attitudes to a business environment: The case of the assisted areas of the South-West', In *Exeter Essays in Geography*, RAVENHILL, W.L.D. and GREGORY, K.G. (Eds.), Exeter University Press, 1971.

disadvantages (Table 4.6). In spite of these difficulties many firms have been able to move all or some of their plant to remote rural areas often with a good deal of success (4.21) (Table 4.6). The environmental quality of life is often a crucial factor in persuading management; other advantages are low labour costs and generally fewer labour disputes in traditionally non-unionized areas.

Second, the sort of manufacturing that can succeed in rural areas is limited by type. The most suitable industries are those involved in craft or design based industries. Good examples are provided by Caithness glass in Scotland and Dartington glass in Devon. There is a limit however to the market penetration that such high cost products can achieve. The only other industries that can be expected to do well are large scale products based on a local resource. Good examples are provided by the Fort William pulp mill based on Scottish forestry plantations of the Forestry Commission, aluminium smelters based on hydro-electricity and deep water for importing the raw alumina, and recently of course the advent, also in Scotland, of North Sea oil. In between these two extremes of craft

Table 4.7   Size of Manufacturing Establishments in the United Kingdom 1971

Type of Establishment   Analysis by Number of Employees per Establishment

	11-19	20-24	25-99	100-199	Above 200	Total
++Food, drink and tobacco	1240	620	1626	532	923	4941
Coal and petroleum products	47	16	51	71	—	185
Chemicals and allied industries	475	247	617	250	438	2027
Metal manufacture	476	272	689	295	473	2205
+Mechanical engineering	2688	1313	2278	710	1001	7990
++Instrument engineering	361	164	353	127	168	1173
++Electrical engineering	750	385	830	368	705	3038
+Shipbuilding and marine engineering	188	107	209	59	115	678
Vehicles	494	239	541	254	471	1999
+Metal goods not elsewhere specified	2474	1124	2344	560	534	7036
++Textiles	859	530	1607	768	769	4533
++Leather, leather goods, fur	283	102	323	99	—	807
++Clothing and footwear	1509	778	2282	688	462	5719
+Bricks, pottery, glass, cement etc	546	301	926	263	322	2538
++Timber, furniture	1631	625	1728	342	191	4517
++Paper, printing and publishing	1763	656	2125	533	635	5712
+Other manufacturing industries	833	380	1020	302	344	2879

++Very suitable for rural areas   +Suitable for rural areas
Source: Central Statistical Office, *Annual Abstract of Statistics*, 1974, HMSO, 1975.

based on large scale resource based industries, there exists a good deal of normal industrial potential capable of providing employment. Table 4.7 clearly demonstrates how much employment is still concentrated in plant employing fewer than 25 operatives. It is however just this sector of employment that remote rural areas have failed to attract in sufficient numbers to make industrial employment in the area self generating.

In most rural areas, *service industry* employs about 60% of the population. This high figure, some 10% above the national norm, is due to both the scattered nature of the population and to the absence of other employment. Apart from the Midlands every region has a greater percentage in service employment than in manufacturing. But it is only in the remote rural areas that there are four or more jobs in the service sector for every one job in the manufacturing sector (4.6). Over the rest of the country the ratio is normally about two service jobs for every manufacturing job. In terms of overall percentages only the South-East region exceeds the 60% figure for service employment found in the remote rural areas. It can and has been argued that a good deal of this employment could profitably be transferred from the South-East to the remoter rural areas, the most favourable for transfer being the office and scientific sectors.

In the case of the office sector a number of factors make rural locations attractive. First, rents and rates are considerably lower than in the overcrowded urban areas. Second, if firms are going to decentralize, key staff will be more willing to move to an attractive rural area than say a Northern industrial town. Third, most rural areas have a large pool of unemployed female labour suitable for clerical work. Fourth, the Government is now beginning to transfer its employment policies towards the office sector, partly because it has been shown that it is cheaper to increase employment by attracting office employment rather than manufacturing employment (4.23). Fifth, the disadvantages of rural locations commonly cited as remoteness, loss of contact of staff with business and fashion trends are now being eroded. The development of the highly manoeuverable light aeroplane, able to land almost anywhere, has brought almost all locations within one hour's flight of central London. In addition, modern telecommunications and computer terminal access make the precise physical location of many offices irrelevant. Finally, most office work is increasingly centred on routine data processing which again is largely independent of location. In spite of this, many firms are extremely reluctant to leave their prestigious city centre sites. But Central Government has set a good example, and is encouraging private firms to follow suit so that a growing trend has been established. Once firmly established it is hard to see it being reversed.

A second likely growth area concerns scientific research and manufacture. Such employment is often sparked off by the introduction of higher education into rural areas. Since the war many universities, polytechnics, and further education colleges have been established in rural areas. Examples include Exeter, Lancaster, Lampeter and Norwich. In most cases these have not only proved to be potent growth centres in their own right but have lead to the setting up of small firms using the education centre as a source of expertise and advice. Even where such centres have not been established, remote rural areas make excellent sites for science based service industry.

These two growth sectors must, however, offset declines in the other sectors of service industry, particularly in the *distributive and transport sectors*. These two sectors have only gone into decline in recent years for between 1921 and 1951 (4.24) they grew in importance as rural services such as the blacksmith, corn merchant, the brewer, the shopkeeper, the doctor, the publican, the policeman, the schoolmaster, the rector and the postmistress were transferred from the village to the town. Distribution and transport facilities were thus in greater demand to distribute these services now centrally located in towns. This demand was increased by the fact that over much of remote rural Britain the typical settlement is not the nucleated village but the isolated farmstead. Now however improved transportation facilities, particularly mass car ownership has reduced the demand. Furthermore, planning policies are increasingly seeking the concentration of people and services into fewer but larger rural settlements (4.25).

On some counts *tourism* is the world's largest single industry. It is without doubt an industry with a phenomenal growth record in recent years, and one that is capable of yet further growth. The number of British people taking a holiday has risen from 25 million in the early 1950s to 35 million in the mid 1970s. Their expenditure rose from £300 million to £800 million. Holidays are however one of the first items to feel the cold blast of economic recession, and thus an employment strategy based on tourism is the one most likely to suffer if economic growth slows down. Further disadvantages of tourism are that it (a) creates an unbalanced employment situation, heavily biased towards unskilled, seasonal female labour; (b) congestion; and (c) produces a low return on capital invested. Nonetheless tourism must rank alongside service industries as the one most likely to produce genuine employment growth in a remote rural area. Three types of tourist development can be defined:

1. Unspoilt countryside holidays can usefully subsidize the local economy by providing supplementary income. For example, in unspoilt areas farmers can add to their incomes by taking in tourists or allowing them to camp or caravan in their fields (4.26). In such areas tourism plays a minor but crucial role. In spite of this, many farmers resent the tourist and their dependence on his income, even though without it, hill farming would no longer be practicable for many.

2. Resource based holidays depend on making a conscious effort to develop a local resource. In such a case tourism becomes more than a supplement to income, it becomes the main income. The Swiss Alps provide eloquent testimony to the degree to which such resources can be exploited. By providing a wide enough range of facilities, even the seasonal problem can be overcome. For example, the Aviemore centre in the Scottish Highlands is utilized the whole year round.

3. Seaside resorts remain the most popular destination of most tourists. In the remote rural areas traditional villages or small towns, particularly if they have special character, can be successfully developed as summer tourist resorts. If these settlements can retain their character by limiting the growth of tourism so much the better. Where tourism takes over a town, however, the result may be worse than the initial problem. In the South-West of England this has happened to a number of small towns, and the result is winter unemployment rates of between 15 and 20%. But tourism has such a hold in the South-West that it does in fact provide about 10% of the region's income (4.27).

Whichever mode of tourism is to be developed a number of aids to development may be employed. Firstly, the Countryside Commissions can give grant aid to approved schemes for up to 75% of the cost of the work; in addition they can give grant aid towards running costs. Secondly, new hotels and similar facilities can be financed by two methods:

1. The Development of Tourism Act, 1969 which allows the payment of grants or loans. This act superseded the Local Employment Acts 1960-66 which included provision for tourism development.

2. Council for Small Industries in Rural Areas (CoSIRA) (See p. 154) can give loans for small scale tourism enterprises, for example chalet type developments.

In spite of these grants few hotels have been provided in remote rural areas in recent years. This is mainly because self catering holidays have grown in popularity at the expense of hotel and boarding house accommodation. Such holidays create all the disadvantages of traditional holidays to the local area without providing any of the benefits of traditional holidays to the local economy. Archer (4.28), for example, has calculated that for every £10 spent by a tourist, £3 is retained by the local economy. But this general average conceals a difference between £7.70 retained from expenditure by tourists based in bed and breakfast accommodation, to £3 retained from hostel and chalet based tourists, to only £2 retained from camping and caravan based tourists. The continued spread of self catering holidays could thus have a serious effect on tourist based employment.

Rural employment planning

It has only been since the 1930s that Governments have accepted a responsibility for the maintenance and distribution of employment. The Government's new role was first fully spelt out in the wartime Barlow and Scott reports (4.29). The Barlow report on the distribution of the industrial population pointed out that strategic and urban congestion reasons argued against allowing employment to further congregate in the already overcrowded South-East and Midlands of Britain. To counter this trend the report recommended the decentralization and relocation of employment, into either garden cities, new towns, expanded rural towns or trading estates. The Scott report on the utilisation of land in rural areas recommended that industry should be located in the countryside wherever possible, as long as it did not conflict with agriculture. Barlow in particular laid the foundations for post war policy, and in the mid 1960s when the impetus of the post war economic boom began to slow down some of the Barlow ideas were resurrected in the 1965 National Plan (4.30).

Though the National Plan was later abandoned, its ideas were carried forward in regional planning policies. A further continuation of its ideas can also be seen in a 1971 inter-departmental study concerning the long term population distribution of Great Britain (4.31). This study could, however, only see limited scope for employment redistribution, and thus predicted a pattern of employment in

2001 remarkably similar to the present pattern. Nonetheless attempts to speed up change were provided by the Industry Act, 1972 and the subsequent Industry Act, 1975. This latter Act set up the National Enterprise Board (NEB) whose powers to invest in many forms of economic activity and to influence the investment decisions of major companies; it could mark a turning point in attitudes towards national employment planning from an indirect to a more direct approach (4.31). Further evidence of a return to the attitudes of the National Plan was provided by the setting up of both the Welsh Development Agency and the Scottish Development Agency in 1975 (4.32). Both Agencies are involved in the promotion of further economic development, industrial efficiency, international competitiveness and the provision, maintenance and safeguarding of employment. In addition, the Scottish Development Agency took over the functions, staff and property of both the Scottish Industrial Estates Corporation, and the Small Industries Council for Rural Areas in Scotland (SICRAS), while the Welsh Development Agency took over the functions, staff and property of the Welsh Industrial Estates Corporation, and any land held under the Distribution of Industry Acts, 1945 to 1958 and the Local Employment Acts, 1960, 1971 and 1972.

The regional employment problem first emerged in the inter-war years (4.33). Throughout the 1920s unemployment had run consistently at about one million, but in the 1930s it rose to over 3 million. This rise was not however uniform across the country. In the worst areas it rose to between 25 and 35% of the working population, while in the South-East it only rose to about 15%. In order to rectify such large differences in unemployment rates two types of solution could be applied: either workers must move to jobs, or jobs must be taken to the workers.

Both types of solution were in fact applied, but before long the latter policy began to assume greater importance. These were set out before the War in three Acts of Parliament which between them set up four Special Areas for economic aid. These Areas were all mainly urban and generally located around declining coal fields. Within these Areas four types of policy operated:

1. Government grants and loans to help industry invest
2. The building of industrial estates
3. The levying of a lower rate of taxation in the case of certain taxes
4. The removal of Government work into the Special Areas

Before the effectiveness of the policies could be assessed however, the war and a gradual return to full employment intervened. Importantly however the main types of policy to be used in the post war period had already been set in motion.

At the end of the war the Government set out to aim for the maintenance of full employment. Central to this aim were subsidiary plans for the introduction of an effective regional planning system, schemes for influencing the location of new industries, the provision of retraining facilities, and plans to encourage labour mobility. In order to achieve these aims the Government introduced a number of legislative measures. The first of these was the Distribution of Industry Act, 1945. This remained the basis of Government policy till 1960. The Act extended the Special Areas of the 1930s and renamed them Development Areas. By 1953 South Wales, Industrial Lancashire, Cumbria, the North-East of England, Central Scotland, and Tayside had all received this designation. The only rural area to be made a Development Area was that to the north-west of Inverness. The Areas were administered by the Board of Trade which had five powers:

1. Acquisition of land (compulsorily if necessary) and construction of advance factories
2. Granting of loans to industrial (trading) estate companies
3. Improvement of local services such as transport, power, housing and health
4. Reclamation of derelict land
5. Grants or loans to assist industrial firms, given on the advice of a special Treasury committee (DATAC)

These policies followed the pre-war model, but a new weapon was introduced in the Town and Country Planning Act, 1947, the Industrial Development Certificate (IDC). Under this Act all factories or factory extensions involving more than 5000 square feet had to obtain an IDC from the Board of Trade before the local planning authority could give planning permission.

In the immediate post-war years both the policy of grant aid (the carrot) and of IDC control (the stick) worked well, and the Development Areas took a major share of new development. In the late 1940s however Britain entered the first of her many post-war balance of payments crises, and export potential began to be more important than regional policy. In the 1950s therefore it became easy for industrialists to argue that a refusal of an IDC would seriously affect their chances of gaining exports. Throughout the 1950s therefore regional policy was relaxed and IDC control exercised less strongly.

In the early 1960s regional policy underwent a major change of emphasis when the Distribution of Industry Act, 1945 was replaced by the Local Employment Act, 1960. This legislation moved away from the concept of an ideal pattern of industrial distribution, to one of dealing with local troublespots as they arose, believing that concentrated doses of expenditure in key areas were preferable to the diffusion of aid throughout the Development Areas. Accordingly the Development Areas were replaced by Development Districts. These were markedly rural in comparison with the Areas that they replaced. They included parts of the South-West of England, Coastal Lincolnshire, West and North Wales, the Northern Pennines, the Cumbrian coast, the North-East coast of England, Central Scotland, and most of Scotland north of the central valley but excluding the Grampians. The Districts were based on local employment exchange boundaries, and were normally defined by a rate of unemployment in excess of 4.5%. Previous powers given to the Board of Trade in Development Areas were retained. Extra powers were given by the setting up of three Industrial Estates Management Corporations, one each for England, Wales and Scotland, to replace the individual companies that had operated in the former Development Areas.

Further grants were provided by the Local Employment Act, 1963 but the essentials of the policy remained unaltered until 1966. By this time it had become clear that the 1960 approach had a number of serious drawbacks. The most important of these was that the Development Districts were based on existing unemployment. Not only did this mean that the boundaries of the Districts were subject to frequent amendment and did not thus offer a sufficient guarantee of continued aid to incoming firms, but also that the Districts were based not on potential for future growth, but on past failure. Some of the Districts, for example rural mining villages, clearly had little potential for growth; on the other hand neighbouring villages with greater potential for growth could not be considered for aid because their lower unemployment disqualified them from receiving aid.

Consequently, the mid-1960s saw a return to regional policies based on wider areas than the Development Districts, but with key development centres or 'growth poles' being retained within the framework of the new Development Areas (4.34). The Industrial Development Act, 1966 marked the introduction of this new policy and made the following changes:

1. Development Districts were replaced by Development Areas. These areas covering 40% of Britain's land surface and 20% of her population, included all the remote rural areas for the first time.

2. Cash payments were made to all firms undertaking investment. In the Development Areas the rate was doubled to 45%.

3. Derelict land could be reclaimed with the aid of an 85% grant as long as the land was to be used for industrial development.

In addition to these changes, IDC applications were more strictly scrutinized and the exemption limit was lowered. Controls in a new field, office development, were initiated by the Control of Office and Industrial Development Act, 1965. To supervise this new policy a new body, the Location of Offices Bureau (LOB), was formed with the duty to encourage the decentralization of office space, and employment.

Further measures were provided by Industrial Retraining Schemes, and the regional subsidization of labour costs by regional variations in the rates of both Selective Employment Tax (SET) and the Regional Employment Premium (REP), introduced in 1966 and 1967 respectively. The policy was further refined by the introduction of Special Development Areas in 1967, for areas of very high unemployment. For areas near to the Development Areas, and thought to be suffering from the competitive edge given to firms able to use Development Area grants, a new type of area (Intermediate Area) was introduced in 1970 following the recommendations of the 1969 Hunt Report (4.35).

The 1960s also saw the introduction of a system of advisory regional planning, concerned with both the environmental and economic life of regions. These two aspects of a region's life are examined by Regional Economic Planning Councils. These Councils were set up following investigations into the regional problems of the North-East Region and the successful precedent of the Scottish Development Department. England is divided into 8 regions (Table 4.3) with both Wales and Scotland being treated as single units. In their first eleven years of operation (1965-1976) the Councils have confined their work to the production of regional reports and surveys, advisory plans and programmes of expenditure priorities for Central Government (4.36). Their role has recently been criticized as being too divisive, with each Council bidding for more than its fair share of national economic growth. The 1974 Kilbrandon Report (4.37) recommended more powerful regional bodies, and though moves have been made towards devolution of power to Wales and Scotland, no action has yet been taken to give any real executive or financial power to the English regions.

By the end of the 1960s industrialists were expressing increasing concern about the volatility and complexity of Government actions

147

Table 4.8   Grants Paid Out for Regional Development by Development
Area 1966-71

Development Area	Local Employment Acts Grants	Industrial Development Act Grant
North	49.4	228.0
Merseyside	24.9	188.5
South-West	3.6	14.5
Wales	20.8	128.5
Scotland	42.2	232.5
Total in £000,000	140.9	792.0

* Though these Acts were superseded by the Industrial Development Act, grants were still paid out under the Local Employment Acts for a number of years.

Source: CHISHOLM, M., 'Regional Policies for the 1970s', *Geographical Journal,* 140, 1974, pp. 215-44.

over regional policy (Tables 4.8 and 4.9). The Conservative Government elected in 1970, set out to rationalize and stabilize the pattern, but like its predecessor it eventually found itself overtaken by events. The new Government's first measures were to replace investment grants with tax allowances (4.38), to alter the exemption limits for IDC and office control, to increase the number and size of Special Development Areas, and to change the level and type of grant payable for new investment in plant and infrastructure.

In 1971 however, rising unemployment forced the Government to introduce further measures for regional development (4.39), which were eventually passed in the Industry Act, 1972. In a bid to promote confidence the Government promised that these measures would remain unchanged until at least 1978. The main changes introduced by the Act were:

1. 100% depreciation throughout the country on all investment in plant and machinery, for both service and manufacturing industry. An initial allowance of 40% on new industrial buildings.

2. A new system of cash grants restricted to the manufacturing sector, with different rates depending on the status of the assisted area.

3. Higher exemption limits for IDC control, and the phasing out of REP from 1974.

4. Improved training schemes to encourage job mobility between employment sectors and between regions.

Overall the new policy marked a major change in emphasis away from one of attracting industry to the assisted areas, to one of promoting the expansion of existing employment in the assisted areas. Disappointingly, office developments were not made a major

Table 4.9   Timetable of Principal Measures used in RegionalPolicy 1934-75

Date Legislation	Area Schedules	Special Assistance	Standard Grants Buildings	Plant Machinery	Tax Incentives	Controls	Other
1934 Special Areas Act	Special Areas	Commissioners' Fund	—	—	—	—	—
1936 Special Areas Reconstruction (Agreement) Act	—	SARA loans —	—	—	—	—	Trading estates —
1937 Special Areas (Amendment) Act	—	SALAC loans	—	—	Minor tax concessions	—	—
1945 Distribution of Industry Act	Development Areas	DATAC loans grants				Building licences	Advance factories till 1948
1947 Town and Country Planning Act	—	—	—	—	—	IDC control	—
1958 Distribution of Industry (Industrial Finance) Act	Development Areas and other places	DATAC aid extended to all trades	—	—	—	—	Advance factories restarted
1960 Local Employment Act	Development Districts replace Development Areas	BOTAC loans and grants replace DATAC	Cost/ value grant up to 85%	—	—	IDC control	Industrial estates reorgan- ized
1963 Local Employment Act, Finance Act	—	—	25% cost grant	10% cost grant	Accelerated depreciation	—	Advance factory programme stepped up
1965 Control of Office and Industrial Development Act						IDC limit lowered ODP controls started	—

149

Table 4.9 Continued

Date Legislation	Area Schedules	Special Assistance	Standard Grants Buildings	Standard Grants Plant Machinery	Tax Incentives	Controls	Other
1966 Industrial Development Act	New Development Areas (DA) replace Development Districts	Increased assistance for clearing derelict land	Up to 35%	40% in DAs 20% elsewhere	Discontinued	—	—
1967	Special Development Areas added SDA	Grants towards operating costs	35% as against 25% in DAs	Raised to 45% 25% elsewhere	REP started SET rebate	—	Rent free period in advance factories
1970 Local Employment Acts	Intermediate Areas (IA)	—	25% grant	—	—	—	Advance factories
1970-71	Number and size of SDAs increased More IAs	—	Raised from 25% to 35% in DAs and from 35% to 45% in SDAs	—	Tax allowances replace investment grants	IDC and ODP control relaxed	—
1972 Industry Act	IAs extended	—	Restricted to manufacturing 22% in SDA 20% in DA 20% in IA	22% in SDA 20% in DA none in IA	Tax allowances on new investment phased out	IDC control relaxed	Increased retraining and migration incentives to labour
1974	SDAs DAs and IAs extended	—	—	—	REP continued and doubled	IDC tightened	—
1975 Industry Act, EEC Regional Fund	—	—	1972 grants to continue indefinitely	1972 grants to continue indefinitely	—	—	National Enterprise Board and planning agreements

SARA: Special Areas Reconstruction Association
SALAC: Special Areas Loans Committee   REP: Regional Employment Premium
DATAC: Development Areas Treasury Advisory Committee   SET: Selective Employment Tax
Conservative Government 1951-64, 1970-74. Labour Government 1945-51, 1964-70, 1974-

theme of the new policy (4.40). The hoped for stability in economic affairs did not however materialize, and the oil crisis of 1973-4, and the subsequent recession quickly outdated the assumptions of the early 1970s. In addition, the Government was replaced in 1974 by a Labour administration committed to a programme of major economic reform. The regional vote remained of crucial importance (4.41), and further regional measures were inevitable.

Though recognizing the importance of regional policy the new administration found its room for legislative manoeuvre severely limited by economic constraints. This was particularly spelt out in a 1974 report from the Expenditure Committee of the House of Commons on 'Regional Development Incentives', and in a 1975 White Paper (4.20). In spite of this the Government did manage to make a number of changes between 1974 and 1975:

1. REP was not phased out as planned, but retained and the rate doubled.

2. The areas of Special Development Areas, Development Areas, and Intermediate Areas were further extended.

3. IDC control was further strengthened.

4. Extra powers to control regional development were provided by the setting up of the National Enterprise Board, following the passing of the Industry Act, 1975. Planning agreements were to include regional proposals (4.42).

5. The Welsh and Scottish Development Agencies were set up in 1975, giving further impetus to development proposals in their two countries.

A further constraint was Britain's entry into the EEC as from 1st January 1972. So far this has been to the benefit of the remote rural regions in straight terms of aid for employment, for since January 1st 1975 the EEC has operated a Regional Development Fund. In the first three years, 1975-77, Britain's share amounts to 28% of a total of £540 million. This works out at an annual total of £50 million compared to the £500 million already spent by Britain on regional policy. To qualify for this relatively small bonus, a region must satisfy three main criteria:

1. The gross domestic product must be below the average for the EEC.

2. The percentage employment in agriculture must be above the EEC average (10%), or the percentage employment in industry must be below the average (44%).

3. There must be a heavy dependence on employment in declining industries.

Using these and a number of other factors, among which is a population minimum of 100,000 and a size minimum of 500 km², the EEC has picked out all of Scotland and Wales, most of Northern England north of the Wash-Mersey line, and most of Devon and Cornwall, for aid.

Regional planning policies for employment (Table 4.9) have so far only achieved partial success. In some areas, employment has grown, but in most cases regional policies have only slowed the decline in employment. In the Northern Planning Region of England for example, 170,000 jobs were lost between 1959 and 1974, but only 129,000 jobs were gained. There are a number of reasons for the limited success of these policies. First, Government departments have too frequently acted in a contradictory manner; for example, an area may be outlined for special environmental protection by the Department of the Environment, but may at the same time be earmarked for industrial expansion by the Department of Trade and Industry. Second, political factors have too often been allowed to influence the choice of areas for assistance. Third, short term factors have often been allowed to overrule longer term aims and objectives.

The major reason however is that no one has been able to agree on the real nature of the problem, and thus over the way to treat the illness. If the patient's malady cannot be diagnosed, we can hardly expect to cure him. McCrone (4.7) suggests that two explanations may be accepted for explaining differential rates of regional economic growth, the explanation lying either with structural disadvantage or locational disadvantage. One solution is to accept that both are in some part to blame and thus to adopt policies for improving employment structure so that by making a region more structurally balanced the effects of locational disadvantage are to some extent automatically minimized.

Continuing this thesis, Richardson (4.43) has suggested that investment in infrastructure, and measures to stimulate urbanization and other agglomeration economies are more likely to pay off than straight investment incentives and subsidies. If correct, this means that most rural areas have little chance of effectively solving their employment problems (4.19). Chisholm (4.41) however has pointed out that the regional problem is only a microcosm of the national problem, namely the failure of industry to invest sufficient sums in new plant and machinery. Chisholm, nonetheless agrees that investment even if increased must be concentrated. The Government for its part proudly points to the massive increases in the amount of aid that it has invested in the regions (Table 4.8), though

Chisholm calmly points out that a regional policy which now covers nearly half the country has become a national policy, equivalent of robbing Peter to pay Paul.

From the first 40 years of regional policy three broad conclusions do however emerge:

1. Regional incentives are most likely to be given weight in decision making when industry is confident that they will not be frequently changed.

2. Regional policy is most effective when economic activity in the country as a whole is at a high level,

3. Basing an effective regional policy on incentives alone is too costly to the exchequer, while basing it on direct Government controls is too costly for the firm. In the past, regional policy aids have tended to favour capital intensive rather than labour intensive industry; only REP has favoured labour intensive firms. Taken together these two conclusions suggest that a combination of Government incentives and controls are the most effective sort of policy, as long as the incentives are linked to manpower requirements as far as possible.

But the formulation of regional policy is one matter, its implementation at the local scale another. We must conclude this section by considering the role and performance of the Agencies in rural employment planning. In the local context two types of body are involved in promoting rural employment, the County/District Councils and *ad hoc* groupings of businessmen. The more effective action has usually been taken by County Councils. The County Development Plans prepared between 1947 and 1970 under the Town and Country Planning Act, 1947 and the County Structure Plans now being prepared following the gradual implementation of the Town and Country Planning Act, 1968 contain employment policies for their areas. As part of these plans, housing programmes and the construction of industrial estates have frequently been used by County Councils in an attempt to encourage the growth of employment in their area. These policies are now usually geared to concentrating investment at proven growth points, and they encourage a redistribution of population within the County. In the early post-war years however attempts were made to provide employment for each settlement, and as part of this policy many small Council housing estates were constructed in small villages (4.44). These estates now present a problem, because as rural employment has contracted, commuting has become a necessity for their residents.

In addition to the work of the Local Authorities, most Counties have groups of businessmen who attempt to promote the growth of employment in the county. Chambers of Trade are good examples of such bodies, and they frequently work in close liaison with the County Council. Their main function is to make the first contact. After this has been made it is essential that the Local Council can then offer the industrialist a first class industrial site with good services, access and transport links with the rest of the country.

The Development Commission is a coordinator of local action. When established by the Development and Road Improvement Funds Act, 1909 and 1910 it was the only body dealing with rural employment. The primary objective of the Commission was to provide a source of Government funds, through the Development Fund, for the development of agriculture, rural industries, forestry, harbours, rural roads, inland waterways and fisheries. Since 1909 however most of these activities have been covered by specific legislation, a good example being the aid given to agriculture since 1947 following the passing of the Agriculture Act, 1947. In spite of this the Commission still has a role to play in helping along any scheme which may be calculated to benefit the rural economy as long as no other statutory fund exists. This role can be divided into six types:

1. A nationwide service of advice, intelligence, instruction and limited credit for small rural manufacturing and service industries.

2. The development of factory premises where increased or more diversified employment is needed to check or prevent rural depopulation.

3. The support of experimental or pioneering schemes until they either become self sustaining or incapable of further support.

4. The encouragement of voluntary bodies which enrich social and intellectual life for rural people, such as the National Councils of Social Service.

5. The promotion of miscellaneous marketing or cooperative schemes designed to strengthen agricultural or fishing communities.

6. The carrying out of surveys or research into the rural economy.

The Commission, formerly controlled by the Treasury, is now the Ministerial responsibility of the Secretary of State for the Environment. Two smaller bodies exist inside the Commission. The first of these is the Council for Small Industries in Rural Areas (CoSIRA) which covers England and Wales; the second body is the Small

Industries Council for the Rural Areas of Scotland (SICRAS). These two bodies also administer the Tourism Loan Fund, which exists to promote the development of small hotels, guest houses and other facilities to make rural areas more attractive to visitors (see p. 142). The Commission has further attempted to devolve its work by dividing the country up into Special Investment Areas, and other rural areas.

The Special Investment Areas are those parts of the country which have had a consistent record of population decline. In these areas, since 1965, the Commission has employed an experimental policy of concentrating investment in a limited number of 'trigger areas' centred around growth points where a nucleus of small industries might be developed. The idea behind the policy is to retain the population in the area as a whole by providing more varied employment, but in fewer locations. Thus the population is retained but concentrated into fewer settlements. The main policy instrument is financial aid for the construction of industrial estates, often in close collaboration with the various Estates Corporations or the local County Councils. An important subsidiary policy is the giving of grants to help the development of local social life. By 1973, 35 factory projects had been completed and 49 authorized.

Table 4.10 shows how limited the funds available to the Commission are. This means that not all demands can be met, particularly

Table 4.10   Annual Gross Expenditure from the Development Fund 1969-73

Type of Expenditure	£000,000			
A. Small Industries	1969-70	1970-71	1971-72	1972-73
Advisory, instruction, administration	655	778	951	999
Credit services (Industrial)	543	808	1,224	1,323
Credit services (Tourism)	627	658	801	362
B. Factories				
Department of Trade and Industry	124	112	330	257
CoSIRA	—	—	27	60
C. Social Provision				
Rural Community Councils and Councils of Social Service	261	298	339	402
Women's organizations	18	21	19	20
Other social	—	—	—	2
D. Other Development				
Industrial development agencies	10	30	22	34
Housing guarantees	—	—	—	2

Source: Development Commissioners, *33rd Report*, HMSO, 1974

after priority has been given to the Special Investment Areas. In the remaining areas priority is given to:

   (a) Firms providing increased opportunities for employment
   (b) Firms likely to benefit the balance of payments
   (c) Firms providing a service to the agricultural industry
   (d) Firms holding the promise of significant development

   To assess the effectiveness of the Commission's work a survey of 2212 small Scottish firms was conducted by SICRAS between 1971 and 1972 (4.45). These firms had experienced a 6% growth in employment compared to 4% decline for Scotland as a whole. Within the overall growth pattern however, a number of failures emerged. These failures tended to lie within the traditional industries, such as clothing and blacksmiths. The successful industries tended to lie within the high technology field, such as electronics, plastics, electrical engineering and food processing. The growth of small firms aided by SICRAS was a marked feature of the survey.

   The net gain of jobs produced by these small firms was 1495, and though at first sight this may seem a small total there are two reasons why it does in fact represent a success. First, in rural areas, even a small increase can have a profound effect on confidence. Second, small firms are an essential part of economic growth, simply because the owner or manager of a small firm is deeply committed to its success. This factor was further enhanced by a second survey which found that the chief motives for establishing small industries in rural areas were better financial and environmental prospects, plus greater independence. The survey concluded that there were bright prospects for any enterprising person wishing to establish a business in rural Scotland, and that the Development Commission would continue to play a vital and successful role.

Case study 1 : Mid-Wales

   Mid-Wales exhibits all the problems of the remote rural areas. Its hill farms are mainly too small to support economic holdings, and the loss of employment from agriculture has been severe. Earnings are about 20% below the national average. The population has declined for over a century, and is overbalanced by old people. The Local Authorities are poor and cannot provide good services or attract outside employment by themselves. The population is scattered and transport is slow and inefficient so that a normal catchment area for employment is a mere 14 miles (22 km) (4.46). The paradox of the problem is that if the area is to attract industry on the scale required to boost its growth, it needs more people (4.47). Mass population transfer is in fact one of the few solutions that have not been attempted by the bodies set up to alleviate the problems of the area.

The establishment of a policy specifically for Mid-Wales was first achieved by the setting up of the Mid-Wales Industrial Development Association consisting of the five counties of Brecon, Radnor, Merioneth, Montgomery and Cardigan in 1957. The aim of the Association was twofold. First, to act as an intermediary between industrialists and Central and Local Government bodies. Second, to promote Mid-Wales by advertisement and publicity. The Development Commission's help was also enlisted. The need for the Association soon became apparent, for in its initial research it was revealed that only 6 acres (15 ha) of land were allocated for industry throughout its entire area, and even this was restricted to two locations (4.48). Accordingly one of the first actions of the Association was to persuade the Development Commission to finance factories and factory extensions for specific companies and to allow them to be let at well below current rates as an experiment. This was so successful that in 1963 the Commission agreed to finance further developments in advance of need. A target of 200 jobs per year was adopted in 1965, but this has never in fact been quite reached (4.49). In 1966 a further policy instrument was added when the whole of Mid-Wales was made a Development Area. This meant that the Board of Trade (from 1971 the Department of Trade and Industry) took over most of the financing of the purpose built factories. Advance factories however remained the responsibility of the Development Commission. Further policy instruments were created by the establishment of the Mid-Wales Industrial Development Corporation in 1967, as an office within the Association to develop new factories in Newtown and Montgomeryshire.

This new idea of concentrating efforts on particular sites developed in part from the 1964 report of the Beacham Committee (4.50). By 1969 it had become a formal part of policy with growth being restricted to Aberystwyth, Bala, Brecon, Llandrindod Wells, Newtown, Rhyader and Welshpool. By March 1973, 20 factories built by the Development Commission, were occupied and employed 1540 people (4.49). In addition to this programme CoSIRA and its predecessors had also helped by the provision of advisory services, and loans for working capital. The Tourism Loan Fund was used for 58 loans totalling about £377,000 between 1968 and 1973. Between 1971 and 1973 CoSIRA also made loans totalling £65,000 for buildings, equipment and working capital. In addition, the activities of the Welsh Economic Council set up in 1965, and replaced by the Welsh Council in 1968, have had an effect, particularly in obtaining Development Area Status and the designation of Newtown as a New Town (4.52).

Since 1957, therefore, five bodies have become involved in the development of Mid-Wales. The Mid-Wales Industrial Development Association, the Development Commission, the Department of Trade and Industry, the Mid-Wales Newtown Development Corporation and the Welsh Industrial Estates Corporation, replaced in 1975 by the Welsh Development Agency (4.52). Between 1957 and 1970, 3000 additional jobs were provided by light manufacturing firms. Out of this total 60% were the result of action by one of these five bodies (4.53).

The main difficulties encountered by firms moving to the area arose from attracting a suitable labour supply. Skilled labour for engineering firms did not exist and training took longer than expected. In addition, unskilled female labour could only be obtained by recruiting from up to a 25 mile (40 km) radius, which normally meant the provision of a special bus because of the poor public transport facilities. A further problem was the transition of local workers into the different rhythms and routines of factory working. The fear of factory work also kept many people away, even though the wages were higher than paid elsewhere in the area. Key workers brought in from outside were found to be the best solution. The relative isolation of the area from other manufacturing industry also caused initial problems. Odd jobs could no longer be contracted out to the works down the road, a problem ultimately solved by making the local factory more self sufficient, and less dependent on outside supplies and services. Most firms were able to overcome these difficulties, and indeed no factory has been forced to close, though some have changed hands. As early as 1951 in fact a survey had found that few firms had suffered long term effects from remoteness, although large towns were found to suffer far less than small towns (4.54).

Since the foundation of the Association in 1957 a major effort has clearly been made to break into the vicious circle of crippling stigma engendered by continued economic failure and population decline. In terms of population some degree of success can be claimed. Between 1951 and 1961 the population fell by 7000 or 4%, an accelaration of the trend of the previous 90 years. Between 1961 and 1966 the trend continued to accelerate, with a further 6000 people being lost. Between 1966 and 1971 however the trend of a whole century of decline was reversed and the population actually grew by 1600 or 1%. (Within a 100 years however the region has still lost 100,000 people or about 40%.) It is interesting to note that between 1966 and 1971 the population continued to decline in all areas except for the selected key growth centres. Regression analysis has also estimated that the provision of new factories has prevented the outmigration of 3000 people since 1957. This means that the overall reduction in population from 1957 was only 2.7% compared to the 4.3% it would have been without aid. Perhaps most important of all, the saving has been achieved in the younger age groups, a vital factor in halting future declines.

By 1970 it could be estimated that 700 men and 800 women were directly employed by financially aided factories (Table 4.11). In

Table 4.11   New Industries attracted to Mid-Wales 1957-69

Industry Type	Total	Industry Type	Total
Clothing	9	Plastics	2
Engineering	15	Office equipment	2
Packaging	2	Others	18

Total 48

Source: GARBETT-EDWARDS, D.P., 'The establishment of new industries', In *The Remoter Rural Areas of Britain*, ASHTON, J. and LONG, W.H., (Eds.), Oliver and Boyd, 1972

addition, a further 450 people were employed in servicing the factories and their employees. Furthermore about 50 people were employed in the continuing programme of factory construction. In spite of this, employment in Mid-Wales still fell by 7%, though without aid, the fall would probably have been nearer 12%. In addition, the aid programme has managed to diversify employment away from the declining extractive industries of mining and agriculture. The agricultural problem should not be exaggerated, however, since even in 1951 there were fourteen farms to every ten farm workers (4.55). The real problem is finding employment for the children of farmers when they reach adulthood, for there is little prospect of them being able to continue in farming.

The outdated settlement pattern of Mid-Wales (4.56) is a substantial deterrent to economic growth. Policies for attracting growth

G

have taken this into account by channelling growth into only the larger and more centrally located towns. This policy has hastened the concentration of the settlement pattern. Between 1961 and 1969 for example, urban areas increased their populations by an annual rate of 0.4%; while rural districts lost their populations at an annual rate of 0.4%.

In addition to concentrating industrial development in key locations, policy measures have also attempted to concentrate social provision into the same locations. Unfortunately housing is the responsibility of the Local Authorities who are unwilling to embark on expensive projects to satisfy some future hypothetical demand. Much of the success of Newtown seems to be due to the fact that the Mid-Wales New Town Development Corporation is responsible for the provision of both factory sites and buildings plus the provision of advance housing (4.49). Many have argued that the provision of new housing should be a vital part of policy throughout Mid-Wales for two reasons. First, it would attract key workers, who are so essential in the transformation of a community from one of decline to one of vigour and growth. Second, it would accelerate the depopulation of the remoter areas and thus hasten the process of agglomeration. It has been argued that this would have two benefits. First, social problems and the provision of social services can only be solved by concentration. Second, the houses thus vacated could be used for second homes or holiday cottages (4.57). On the other hand it has been argued that commuting can let the population have the best of both worlds, by concentrating employment in key centres, yet at the same time retaining the population throughout the region (4.58).

The Development Association has always taken the view that there were too few people in Mid-Wales and that these few were too evenly spread (4.48). As far back as 1959 the Association had advocated the formation of a New Town to help settlement rationalization. Between 1953 and 1966 when Newtown was designated with a target population for the 1980s of 11,000 compared to the initial 5500, it attracted 27 factories, 250 houses were occupied, 1200 people moved in and a 50,000 square foot office block was completed. Newtown has been successful in attracting people from outside the region, indeed 70% had come from outside Mid-Wales and over 50% had come from outside Wales itself (4.59).

Most of the studies made of Mid-Wales have concluded that the policy measures taken have generally been successful. The rate of decline in the population has been slowed by about 30%, and in employment by about 40%. Industrialists unable to expand in their original location, have by coming to Mid-Wales increased the gross national product of the whole country. In turn it has been estimated that the annual rate of return to the Exchequer of a Development Commission factory is about 23% and may reach as high as 30% (4.49). The success of industrial investment has also led people to believe that encouragement has been given to too narrow a range of developments and thus that, in future, office developments and tourism should be given equal weight (4.60). Indeed one survey went so far as to suggest that future developments should be based very largely on non-manufacturing industries (4.61).

It is tempting in light of the success of Mid-Wales, in first slowing decline, and then in the 1970s of actually reversing it in some areas, to advocate similar policies for other areas (4.62). But Mid-Wales possesses certain advantages not found in all other rural areas; it is near to the industrial centres of the West Midlands and South Wales, and it has an attractive environment in which to live. It has also to be borne in mind that the amount of truly mobile industry is extremely limited, and thus that if the policies adopted in Mid-Wales were to be adopted elsewhere that the available jam would be spread too thinly to do any one region enough good. The major lesson of Mid-Wales that could be applied elsewhere however, is that concentration of resources is a vital prerequisite of any policy (4.63). Accordingly it could be argued that regional aid should be concentrated in only a few rural regions and within these selected regions it should be concentrated in a few localities. It would be dangerous, however, to base final conclusions on only one case study, further areas must be studied before such a conclusion could be reached.

Case study 2 : The Highlands and Islands Development Board

Like Mid-Wales, the Highlands and Islands of Scotland exhibit all the properties of a problem region (4.64). The population is sparse, the economy is structurally unbalanced and there is only a limited range of employment opportunity (Table 4.12). Income is lower than elsewhere in Scotland and Great Britain. These problems stem from a lack of resources, the region's severe isolation located as it is at the periphery of both the British Isles and Europe, poor regional transport facilities, and the past misuse of resources and manpower (4.65). In recent years however the long period of decline

Table 4.12   Employment in the Highlands and Islands of Scotland 1938-1962

Type of Employment   Number Employed Each Year *(thousands)*

	1938	1950	1959	1962
Farming	16	15	10	11
Farmers+	7	7	4	4
Fishing	2	2	2	2
Forestry	1	2	3	3
Extractive	1	1	1	1
Manufacturing	11	10	8	9
Construction	15	13	13	14
Service	42	35	40	43
Administration, defence	6	8	7	8
Total	94	86	84	89

+Self employed farmers, not employees
Numbers may not sum to total due to rounding

Source: OPENSHAW, K., *The Remoter Rural Areas*, Fabian Society, 1966.

and defeat has been halted and indeed in some parts of the region dramatically reversed. This major transformation has been mainly due to two factors: the foundation of the Highlands and Islands Development Board and the exploitation of North Sea oil.

The purpose of the Board which was established by the Highlands and Islands Development (Scotland) Act, 1965 is to enable the Highlands of Scotland to play a more effective part in the economic and social development of the nation (4.65). The Board's powers are normally limited to the Crofting Counties (first recognized for aid in the 1880s), but they can be extended to include other adjacent areas if necessary. The Board consists of a Chairman and not more than six other members appointed by the Secretary of State for Scotland. The Secretary of State may give effective directions to the Board, and a Highland Development Consultative Council may advise the Board on the exercise of its functions, but normally the Board is left to its own devices. The duties of the Board are to submit proposals for Highland development to the Secretary of State, after consultation with Local Authorities and other bodies, and if these are approved, to implement them, either through the various agencies available or by themselves.

To implement proposals the Board has a wide range of powers. The Board can acquire land, by compulsion if necessary, and can hold and manage it. In addition the Board can erect buildings, carry out works and provide equipment, and acquire or set up and carry out any business or undertaking. It can also provide a variety of technical services and may also make grants and assistance available. For the longer term the Board can also carry out or commission enquiries, investigations or researches into the future of the region.

Sir Robert Grieve, the first chairman of the Board, described the Board as a sort of New Town Corporation (4.67); while a later chairman described it as a merchant bank with a social purpose (4.68). These two descriptions clearly illustrate why the Board is such a unique body in British regional planning. First, the Board has more freedom to dispose of its funds than any other similar body. It can spend up to £50,000 without consultation and up to £100,000 after agreement from the Secretary of State for Scotland. Second, it is expected to indulge in the sort of risk taking investments that even banks and finance houses would not normally consider, let alone Government bodies. If the Board did not have this freedom, there would of course have been little point in setting it up. In practice the Board has proved to be a successful and innovative entrepreneur. Out of the 661 projects it funded between 1965 and 1971 only 52 failed.

The work of the Board is not limited to industrial development, the weakness of similar bodies elsewhere. Indeed, the Board has involved itself in a wide range of activities, investing for example in agricultural, industrial, tourist, fishing and social projects. In addition, the Board has carried out a number of surveys and feasibility studies throughout the region. It has built a number of hotels and indeed promotes package holidays for the region. And finally in an area notorious for its poor transport facilities it has produced integrated timetables for bus, train, boat and air services, as well as a comprehensive booking and ticket system.

In 1974 (4.68) the Board gave grant and loan aid to the Highland economy to the tune of £5 million. This total was matched by £5.2 millions of private investment. Between 1965 and 1974 the Board advanced nearly £22 million which financed 10,700 jobs. Most of these jobs were created in Invernessshire, Argyll and Ross, reflecting the Board's policy of concentrating investment wherever possible, especially in the areas bordering the Moray Firth, the Wick-Thurso area, and the Fort William-Lochaber area. Out of the total aid paid out between 1965 and 1974, tourism received £6.5 million, fishing £5.1 million, manufacturing £5.8 million, and agriculture £1.8 million. Other grants totalled £2.2 million, with a final category, 'non economic grants' coming to £0.5 million. These 'non economic grants' are a vital part of the Board's total strategy: they are used to provide sorely missed amenities in the remoter areas and by improving the psychological infrastructure of the area they help to retain the population (4.69). The number of jobs created by this aid between 1965 and 1974 divides into manufacturing 5000, tourism 2300, fishing 1400, others 1400 and agriculture 250.

The success of the Board's work can also be judged by a number of other parameters, most of which show the same trend. First, population decline has been not only halted but actually reversed over a large part of the region. Between 1971 and 1974 the population in the Moray Firth area grew by between 4 and 12%. This rapid growth is the culmination of a trend started in the 1960s, when for the region as a whole the population rose from 278,000 to 283,000, a growth of 2%, between 1961 and 1971. Second, unemployment which throughout the 1960s had been about 8% had fallen to 4% by 1974. Third, regional incomes which had been only 65% of the British average in 1960 had risen to 90% by 1973. It is of course difficult to disentangle the effect of North Sea Oil on this success story, but undoubtedly this has been a major spur to the region's remarkable progress in the 1970s. It clearly demonstrates that physical resources are still a very important factor in the development of a region, despite the apparent freedom of much modern employment from such resources. North Sea Oil is however a double edged weapon, and unless the opportunity is taken to restructure the Highland economy in a time of boom, there is an all too real danger that North Sea Oil will represent yet another period of economic exploitation of the Highlands, similar to the clearances of the nineteenth century. Already the people of the region have come to appreciate that a number of unpleasant prices have to be paid now that the longed for economic revival has occurred.

Case study 3 : North Pennines Rural Development Board

A third, but short lived approach at solving rural employment problems by Government agency was attempted by the foundation of the North Pennines Rural Development Board in 1969. The Board was founded using powers provided by the Agriculture Act, 1967. The Board was however wound up in 1971 following the change of Government in 1970. The new administration claimed that the Board's approach was counter to Conservative philosophy and that there was a need to cut public spending (4.70). Because the Board only existed for two years it is impossible to judge the degree of success that its policies might have achieved. It is useful however to examine its aims.

The aims of the Board were to reverse the trend of depopulation and under employment in the remote hill and upland country of the North Pennines. To achieve these aims the Board was given the duty of supervising all transfers of land involving four or more hectares (10 acres) within its region, an area stretching from Skipton in the south to the Scottish Border in the north. The purpose of this supervision was first to ensure that land when transferred passed into the enterprise most likely to maximize employment, and second to reconcile the conflicts in the area between the agricultural and forestry industries (4.71). The Board also had powers to give grant aid to develop both communications and services and farm and forest based tourism (4.72). Before the 1970 change of administration, the outgoing Labour Government had been planning to set up a similar Board in Central Wales, but this Board like the North Pennines Board became a victim of political change. Probably the powers of the Board over land transfer were ahead of their time, and this underlines the lesson that Government agencies if they are to succeed must have the support of the local population. Because of the powers of land transfer the Board could never have enrolled the support of the local farming community and thus could never have succeeded.

Conclusions

This Chapter has considered the problems of rural employment under three main headings; a description of employment sectors in rural areas, an analysis of the historical evolution of nationally coordinated regional policies for employment, and a number of case studies of regionally based employment policies and plans. Various conclusions can be drawn from each of these sections.

In the employment section the conclusion was drawn that extractive industries were unlikely to employ any more people in the near future. Possible growth in fish farming or mining for example is almost certain to be offset by further losses in the agricultural sector. Forestry once seen as the panacea for rural employment can no longer be looked upon in this light because of the 1970s changes in Government policy. Manufacturing industry is also unlikely to significantly provide new jobs on any scale, since most of the obvious possibilities, such as craft industry, clothing and light engineering have already been fully exploited. Manufacturing industry could provide significant growth however when either a new natural resource, such as North Sea Oil is exploited, or where the population is agglomerated into a much larger unit. In the latter case it is doubtful, however, if the area could still be considered truly rural. The two most likely growth areas are office employment and tourism. These allow the area to remain rural, and if sensibly combined they can provide a balanced employment structure.

With regard to regional policies the conclusions were that they had been overconcerned with industrial growth and that the extension of regional benefits to about half the country by 1975 made the policy no longer a regional policy but a national one. In future it could be more advantageous if regional policies were more selective in their choice of area for aid, but less selective in their choice of employment for aid. In other words, aid should be more concentrated, not necessarily in those areas with the highest unemployment but in the areas with the greatest potential for growth outside the congested urban regions of Britain. To help in the development of potential growth sites, public investment in new roads, reservoirs and energy resources for example should be concentrated into growth areas, not into the areas already suffering from overuse of these resources. It has often been advocated for example that the M1 Motorway should have been built at right angles to its present line, in an attempt to provide a new growth axis, rather than to perpetuate an old one. In addition, regional planning policies should aim to make employment more mobile by making it easier for people to move house, particularly those people anchored to their present location and job by a tied cottage or Council house.

In the section on regionally based employment plans, the conclusions were that population concentration was a vital part of any policy and that public bodies should be able to indulge in entrepreneurial risk taking if the cycle of decline and defeat was to be ever broken. But it is obvious that such policies can only be successful if they are applied only in a few selected areas. Once they became universally applied, the jam, which is scarce, would be spread too thinly.

The overall conclusion of this Chapter is thus that over large areas of rural Britain, employment will continue to decline. Within the rural regions as a whole, however, employment could be made to grow quite markedly by vigorously pursuing the type of approach employed by the Highlands and Islands Development Board, and by concentrating investment in key centres and in particular employment sectors, especially office employment and tourism.

References

4.1   GASKIN, M., 'The remoter areas in the National context', in *The Remoter Rural Areas of Britain*, ASHTON, J. and LONG, W.H., (Eds.), Oliver and Boyd, 1972.
4.2   OPENSHAW, K., *The Remoter Rural Areas*, Fabian Society, 1966.
4.3   CHISHOLM, M., and OEPPEN, J., *The Changing Pattern of Employment*, Croom Helm, 1973: ROBERTSON, I.M.L., 'The Occupational Structure and Distribution of Rural Population in England and Wales', *Scottish Geographical Magazine*, 77, 1961, pp. 165-79; and VINCE, S.W.E.., 'Reflections on the Structure and Distribution of Rural Population in England and Wales 1921-31', *Transactions of the Institute of British Geographers*, 18, 1952, pp. 53-76.
4.4   DEANE, P. and COLE, W.A., *British Economic Growth 1688-1958: Trends and Structure*, Cambridge University Press, 1962; and DEPARTMENT OF EMPLOYMENT, *British Labour Statistics: Historical Abstract 1886-1968*, HMSO, 1971.
4.5   The amount of unemployment and the poor range of jobs available in rural areas can be examined in more detail in: CENTRAL STATISTICAL OFFICE, *Abstract of Regional Statistics*, HMSO, Annually; and in DEPARTMENT OF EMPLOYMENT, *Department of Employment Gazette*, HMSO, Monthly. Methods of analyzing regional employment problems are discussed in CHISHOLM, M. and OEPPEN, J. *op. cit.*
4.6   The amount of regional inequality is outlined in COATES, B.E. and RAWSTRON, E.M., *Regional Variations in Britain*, Batsford, 1971.
4.7   McCRONE, G., *Regional Policy in Britain*, George Allen & Unwin, 1969.
4.8   MINISTRY OF AGRICULTURE, FISHERIES AND FOOD, *The Changing Structure of the Agricultural Labour Force, 1945-65*, HMSO, 1967.
4.9   TYLER, G.J., 'The Mobility, Replacement and Wage Rates of Farm Workers—A note', *Oxford Agrarian Studies*, 3, 1974, pp. 151-3; and WAGSTAFF, H.R., 'The Mobility, Replacement and Wage Rates of Farm Workers', *Oxford Agrarian Studies*, 3, 1974, pp. 140-53.
4.10   GASSON, R., *The Mobility of Farm Workers*, Department of Land Economy, University of Cambridge, 1974.
4.11   GASSON, R., *Provision of Tied Cottages*, Department of Land Economy, University of Cambridge, 1975; IRVING, B. and HILGENDORF, L., *Tied Cottages in British agriculture*, Tavistock Institute of Human Relations, 1975; and JONES, A., *Rural Housing: The Agricultural Tied Cottage*, George Bell, 1975.
4.12   NATIONAL ECONOMIC DEVELOPMENT OFFICE, *Agricultural Manpower in England and Wales*, HMSO, 1972.
4.13   RAEBURN, J.R., 'The Economics of Upland Farming', in *The Remoter Rural Areas of Britain, op. cit.*
4.14   Further reading regarding agricultural employment can be found in EDWARDS, A. and ROGERS, A. (Eds.), *Agricultural Resources: An Introduction to the Farming Industry of the United Kingdom*, Faber & Faber, 1974. Up to date information regarding agricultural employment can be found in MINISTRY OF AGRICULTURE, FISHERIES AND FOOD, *Agricultural Statistics*, HMSO, Annually.
4.15   MATTHEWS, J.D., PHILIP, M.S. and CUMMING, D.G., 'Forestry and Forest Industries', in *The Remoter Rural Areas of Britain, op. cit.* The Forestry Commission was initially founded in 1919 to plant up a strategic reserve of timber to be used

in the event of a Second World War. Since then its role has widened to include employment and social provision as well as recreation.

4.16 H.M. TREASURY, *Forestry in Great Britain: An Inter-Departmental Cost/Benefit Study*, HMSO, 1972.

4.17 BLUNDEN, J., *The Mineral Resources of Britain: A Study in Exploitation and Planning*, Hutchinson, 1975.

4.18 Further examples are provided in GREGORY, R., *The Price of Amenity*, Macmillan, 1971.

4.19 MOSELEY, M.J., *Growth Centres in Spatial Planning*, Pergammon, 1974.

4.20 Cmnd 6058, *Department of Industry, Regional Development Incentives*, HMSO, 1975.

4.21 BEACHAM, A. and OSBORN, W.T., 'The Movement of Manufacturing Industry', *Regional Studies*, 4, 1970, pp. 41-7.

4.22 BRACEY, H.E., *Industry and the Countryside*, Acton Society Trust, 1963 examines the impact of such large scale industries on the countryside.

4.23 RHODES, J. and KHAN, A., *Office Dispersal and Regional Policy*, Department of Applied Economics, University of Cambridge, 1971.

4.24 WILLATTS, G.C. and NEWSOM, M.G., 'The Geographical Pattern of Population Changes in England and Wales 1921-51', *Geographical Journal*, **119**, 1953, pp. 431-54.

4.25 EDWARDS, J.A., 'The Viability of Lower Size-Order Settlements in Rural Settlements in Rural Areas: The Case of N.E. England', *Sociologia Ruralis*, **11**, 1971, pp. 247-75; and THOMAS, J.G., 'Population Changes and the Provision of Services', in *The Remoter Rural Areas of Britain, op. cit.*

4.26 DAVIES, E.T., *Farm Tourism in Devon and Cornwall*, Agricultural Economics Unit, University of Exeter, 1971.

4.27 LEWES, F.M.M., CULYER, A.J. and BRADY, G.A., *The Holiday Industry of Devon and Cornwall*, HMSO, 1970; BURTON, T.L., *Outdoor Recreation in Problem Rural Areas*, Wye College, 1967.

4.28 ARCHER, B., *The Impact of Domestic Tourism*, University of Wales Press, 1973.

4.29 Cmd 6153, *Report of the Royal Commission on the Distribution of the Industrial Population: The Barlow Report*, HMSO, 1940 and Cmd 6378. *Report of the Committee on Land Utilisation in Rural Areas: The Scott Report*, HMSO, 1942.

4.30 Cmnd 2764, *The National Plan*, HMSO, 1965.

4.31 DEPARTMENT OF ENVIRONMENT, *Long Term Population Distribution in Great Britain*, HMSO, 1971.

4.32 *Scottish Development Agency Act, 1975* and *Welsh Development Agency Act, 1975.*

4.33 Summaries of regional policy from 1930 to the 1970s are provided by CENTRAL OFFICE OF INFORMATION, *Regional Development in Britain*, HMSO, 1974; RANDALL, P., 'The History of British Regional Policy', in *Regional Policy For Ever?*, by HALLETT, G., RANDALL, P. and WEST, E.G., Institute of Economic Affairs, 1973; and McCRONE, G., *Regional Policy in Britain, op. cit.*

4.34 Cmnd 2874, *Investment Incentives*, HMSO, 1966.

4.35 Cmnd 3998, *The Intermediate Areas: The Hunt Report*, HMSO, 1969.

4.36 The reader is referred to the plans made for his own region. In England this will be referenced under the title of the Regional Economic Planning Council, for example East Anglia Economic Planning Council. In Wales it will be the Welsh Office and in Scotland the Scottish Development Department.

4.37 Cmnd 5460, *Commission on the Constitution: The Kilbrandon Report*, HMSO, 1973.

4.38 Cmnd 4516, *Investment Incentives*, HMSO, 1970.

4.39   Cmnd 4942, *Industrial and Regional Development*, HMSO, 1972.

4.40   KEEBLE, D., 'Regional Policy after Davies', *Area*, 4, 1972, pp. 132-6.

4.41   CHISHOLM, M., 'Regional Policies for the 1970s', *Geographical Journal*, 140, 1974, pp. 215-44.

4.42   Cmnd 5710, *Regeneration of British Industry*, HMSO, 1974.

4.43   RICHARDSON, H.W., *Regional Growth Theory*, Macmillan, 1973.

4.44   DRUDY, P.J. and WALLACE, D.B., 'Towards a Development Programme for Remote Rural Areas: A Case Study in North Norfolk', *Regional Studies*, 5, 1971, pp. 281-8.

4.45   DEVELOPMENT COMMISSION, *33rd Report*, HMSO, 1974.

4.46   MOUNFIELD, P.R. and WATTS, H.D., 'Mid-Wales: Prospects and Policies for a Problem Area', in *Geography at Aberystwyth*, BOWEN, E.G., (Ed.), University of Wales Press, 1968.

4.47   GARBETT-EDWARDS, D.P., 'The Means and Pattern of Growth', *Journal of Agricultural Economics*, 20, 1969, pp. 63-7.

4.48   GARBETT-EDWARDS, D.P., 'Development in Mid-Wales, 1957-63', *Town and Country Planning*, 42, 1974, pp. 378-82.

4.49   DEVELOPMENT COMMISSION, *Mid-Wales: An Assessment of the Impact of the Development Commission Factory Programme*, HMSO, 1972.

4.50   MINISTRY OF HOUSING AND LOCAL GOVERNMENT, *Depopulation in Mid-Wales: Report of the Committee*, HMSO, 1964.

4.51   REGIONAL STUDIES ASSOCIATION, *Regional Planning in Wales*, The Association, 1971.

4.52   Welsh Industrial Estates Corporation, *Action for Growth in Wales*, The Corporation, 1973.

4.53   GARBETT-EDWARDS, D.P., 'The Establishment of New Industries', in *The Remoter Rural Areas of Britain, op. cit.*

4.54   BEACHAM, A., *Industries in Welsh Country Towns*, Oxford University Press, 1951.

4.55   THOMAS, B., (Ed.), *The Welsh Economy: Studies in Expansion*, University of Wales Press, 1961.

4.56   ROWLEY, G., 'Central Places in Rural Wales', *Tijdschrift voor Economische en Sociale Geografie*, 61, 1970, pp. 32-40.

4.57   DAVIES, M.L., 'The Rural Community in Central Wales', in *Geography at Aberystwyth, op. cit.*

4.58   LEWIS, G.J., 'Commuting and the Village in Mid-Wales', *Geography*, 52, 1967, pp. 294-304.

4.59   GARBETT-EDWARDS, D.P., 'The Development of Mid-Wales: A New Phase', *Town and Country Planning*, 35, 1967, pp. 349-52; and JONES, H.R., *Newtown: A Case Study of Migration to a Growth Point in Mid-Wales*, University of Dundee, Department of Geography, 1973.

4.60   CLOUT, H.D., *Rural Geography*, Pergammon, 1972.

4.61   WELSH ECONOMIC STUDIES, *Industry in Rural Wales*, University of Wales Press, 1966.

4.62   HOWES, R.S. and LAW, D., 'The Success of the Policy of Introducing Light Manufacturing Industry into Rural Areas: The Case of Mid-Wales', *Journal of the Royal Town Planning Institute*, 59, 1970, pp. 406-10.

4.63   WELSH COUNCIL, *A Strategy For Rural Wales*, HMSO 1971.

4.64   TURNOCK, D., *Scotland's Highlands and Islands*, Oxford University Press, 1974.

4.65   TURNOCK, D., 'Regional Development in the Crofting Counties', *Transactions of the Institute of British Geographers*, 48, 1969, pp. 189-204.

4.66   O'DELL, A.C., 'Highlands and Islands Development', *Scottish Geographical Magazine*, 82, 1966, pp. 8-16.

4.67 GRIEVE, R., 'Scotland: Highland Experience of Regional Government', *Town and Country Planning*, 41, 1973, pp. 172-6.

4.68 HIGHLANDS AND ISLANDS DEVELOPMENT BOARD, *Ninth Annual Report, 1974*, HMSO, 1975.

4.69 GRIEVE, R., 'Problems and Objectives in the Highlands and Islands Development Board', in *The Remoter Rural Areas of Britain, op. cit.*

4.70 CLOUT, H.D., 'End of the Road for the North Pennines Rural Development Board', *Geographical Magazine*, 43, 1971, pp. 443.

4.71 MORGAN-JONES, J., 'Problems and Objectives in Rural Development Board Areas', in *The Remoter Rural Areas of Britain, op. cit.*

4.72 NORTH PENNINES RURAL DEVELOPMENT BOARD, *Annual Report*, HMSO, 1970.

Further Reading

ASHTON, J., and LONG, W.H., *The Remoter Rural Areas of Britain*, Oliver and Boyd, 1972.

CENTRAL OFFICE OF INFORMATION, *Regional Development in Britain*, HMSO, 1974.

CHISHOLM, M., and OEPPEN, J., *The Changing Pattern of Employment*, Croom Helm, 1973.

HALLETT, G., RANDALL, P., and WEST, E.G., *Regional Policy for Ever?* Institute of Economic Affairs, 1973.

HIGHLANDS AND ISLANDS DEVELOPMENT BOARD, *Ninth Annual Report, 1974*, HMSO, 1975.

McCRONE, G., *Regional Policy in Britain*, George Allen & Unwin, 1969.

RICHARDSON, H.W., *Regional Growth Theory*, Macmillan, 1973.

WELSH COUNCIL, *A Strategy for Rural Wales*, HMSO, 1971.

CHAPTER FIVE

Rural Landscape

David G. Robinson

It is likely that many people would rank the rural landscape as one of the most priceless aspects of Britain's heritage. There are many, too, who would urge that the qualities of this landscape are threatened by erosive influences to a greater degree today than ever before. Understandably, the more obvious and dramatic changes excite the greatest debate and protest, as instanced by the controversy over the proposal to build oil rigs at Drumbuie. It is only latterly, however, that the cumulative effects of more widespread and general influences, such as changes in farming practices, have become the subject of public concern. To those who have thought of the countryside as a touchstone of unchanging values the gathering pace of landscape change is unnerving. It is no longer possible to suggest, as Dower did in his seminal report on National Parks in 1945 (5.1), that the characteristic appearance of a landscape will be preserved as long as effective (i.e. economic) farming use of the area is maintained. Farming practices are changing rapidly in response to social and economic pressures and developments in technology, and as farming changes so does the landscape that it produces.

The countryside scene reflects both natural conditions and the effects of human activities. For the most part, of course, British landscapes are modified very considerably by man. None are entirely natural in the sense of resulting only from the interaction of climate, land surface, vegetation and animal life. When man's land use is much constrained by natural factors, however, there is an apparent 'naturalness' in the landscape which is produced. A landscape 'built' by hand with a spatial scale determined by walking pace has a humanized, yet still semi-natural, quality which to many may be more attractive and satisfying than wilderness. As countryside land uses are enabled to make more use of machinery and chemical aids, draw on national power supplies and supply national or regional rather than local markets, so the scale of their activities changes. There is an increasing possibility that land use may be at odds with nature rather than bounded by it. Farming, forestry, quarrying and mining, the 'traditional' countryside industries providing urban populations with food supplies and raw materials, have all shared in these trends. Thus we find concern about the ecological effects of some aspects of their activities joined with unease about the changes in the visual scene.

Other urban demands on the countryside have also grown in scale and impact. A full list of the more obviously alien visitations would be too long to catalogue. It is clear, however, that the countryside landscape does not easily assimilate motorways, power stations, oil tank farms, reservoirs, the electricity super grid, new houses for commuters seeking the country life, and the weekend and Bank Holiday tidal wave of cars bringing those in search of countryside recreation. Reaction and resistance has been such that the proponents of most major projects now ensure that their proposals include a landscape plan which seeks to show that there has been due regard to the effects of the proposed development on the local scene. Landscape impact is acknowledged to be an important part of the planning debate.

History perhaps warns that the new is not to be resisted unthinkingly. In the nineteenth century Wordsworth and Ruskin campaigned against the building of railways in mountain areas. Now railway enthusiasts and tourist boards join forces to re-establish steam services on the 'picturesque' lines which thread their way up Welsh mountain valleys or across the North York Moors. Indeed some disused railways have been adapted as landscape trails whilst elsewhere the overgrown embankments become at once an intriguing earthwork for future archaeologists and a welcome habitat for present wildlife.

Landscape change is inevitable but not all of it will be comfortably transitional and therefore easily accepted as part of a 'natural' evolution. New land uses will create new forms and features— perhaps difficult for us to recognize as compatible with more familiar scenes. There is no logical basis for attempting to fossilize the landscapes we inherit. Yet we have a responsibility to ensure that landscape change in our time is well-mannered and this requires decisions as to which changes are acceptable and which are not. It is now recognized that the approach must be one of landscape conservation rather than preservation, hence the emphasis on landscape planning and management in recent planning studies of the countryside. There is a new emphasis in the planning authorities on diagnostic landscape surveys—identifying the landscape management and development control policies required to maintain quality and character and the landscape action needed to promote them. The substitution of *Protection* for *Preservation* in the title of the principal amenity groups with an interest in rural landscape (e.g. Council for the Protection of Rural England/Rural Wales) no doubt reflects a similar realization that effective preservation entails the conservation approach of positive management. Yet from time to time there will be disagreements between planning authorities and amenity organizations on landscape policies. Often such disagreements will reflect different judgments on the quality of particular landscapes.

What criteria can be used for landscape judgements? How long-lasting are predilections for certain types of landscape? The problem is that landscape means different things to different people. For some it is a collection of physical features, for others landscape is a biological form—a total ecology. Another concept emphasizes landscape as art form—as a pictorial composition. A further group might see a landscape in terms of utility; its suitability for a particular purpose. For others it symbolizes much more abstract qualities such as heritage or nature. In reality the meaning of landscape to most people is some amalgam of these different ideas.

The Manchester University report *Landscape Evaluation* (5.2) distinguished ten concepts of landscape:

1. Landscape as a total regional environment (the town/country continuum), e.g. the 'Black Country' or the 'landscape of the Borders'.
2. Landscape as countryside.
3. Landscape as land use, e.g. a farming landscape, forestry landscape.
4. Landscape as topography or landform, e.g. downland landscape, mountain landscape.
5. Landscape as an ecosystem (the total ecological relationship realized as different types of scenery, but with visual form explained

in terms of functional analysis. The landscape is seen as the product of edaphic and climatic factors combined with the effect of man and animals—hence considerations of landscape stability and landscape health are introduced).

6. Landscape as scenery—the most familiar and least intellectually exacting concept, overall visual appearance.

7. Landscape as heritage or historical artifact, a concept concerned with historical or cultural influences, e.g. 'Constable Country', 'Bronte Country', 'The Dukeries'.

8. Landscape as a composite of physical components. Landscapes classified according to presence or absence of components such as relief, water areas, farmland, woodland, farmsteads, villages, pitheaps, etc.

9. Landscape as art form (an aesthetic/pictorial concept of landscape as a composition or unified arrangement of parts, with atmospheric qualities and emotive feeling emphasized).

10. Landscape as resource or utility feature (e.g. landscape capable of absorbing built development inconspicuously, landscape attractive to tourists, landscape suitable for picnic sites).

Research by Lowenthal and Prince (5.3) established that current public taste was for the bucolic, the picturesque (criteria derived from art), the deciduous, the tidy and the antique. Public taste is thus rather conservative in tone and likely to be unreceptive to change. As landscape planning and design looks to achieve well-mannered change, it is not surprising that there have been strenuous attempts to show that landscape aspects of planning policies are based on impartial aesthetic evaluative judgments and a knowledge of the factors controlling landscape.

Landscape evaluation

Over the last decade the increasing concern of planning authorities and countryside amenity groups over the problems of reconciling the needs for new development and land use change with protection of landscape quality has focussed attention on whether there can be a rational basis for policy decisions in this area. Landscape evaluation methods have been the subject of considerable research and experimentation (5.4). Some confusion of terminology occurs because existing studies have not always distinguished landscape classification from landscape evaluation. A landscape classification is descriptive of the character of the various landscapes in a study area. It is an inventory of landscape by type, with no judgment of quality or value imputed in the process. A landscape evaluation, on the other hand, involves assessment of either the quality (i.e. degree of excellence) or value (i.e. utility for purpose) of landscapes. Value may derive from the rarity of a landscape type; from accessibility to users or viewers; or from the suitability of a landscape for a particular purpose, such as recreation. Most landscape evaluations made by planning authorities to date have been general purpose evaluations—concerned only to assess degrees of excellence in the overall visual quality of landscapes in a county or smaller area. This information can then be related to other considerations, such as agricultural land quality, when strategic decisions are to be made on areas which will merit special protective policies, or on the location of new urban development areas and the like.

To support local and site planning more detailed landscape appraisals are necessary. These more detailed studies will be concerned with such questions as the identification of eyesores and detailed landscape rehabilitation needs, or recording individual visual attributes which make a significant contribution to the landscape character and quality of particular areas. From this information priorities for action on landscape improvement or decisions on design criteria for changes in the landscape can be derived. Such appraisals are special purpose in nature, as would be the case of a survey mounted to evaluate landscape suitability for a specific requirement (e.g. a coastal landscape evaluation concerned with the choice of sites for oil tank farms).

Landscape evaluation involves aesthetic judgements. Consideration of the basis for such judgments invokes the long-standing philosophical dispute as to whether beauty is inherent in objects or in the mind of the observer. Many people would agree with the American landscape architect, Garrett Eckbo, who concluded that the probability is that landscape quality is neither solely in the landscape nor in the minds of the people who view it, but rather in the empathic relationships established when looking at landscape and experiencing a pleasurable or distasteful response (5.5). The capacity of observers to appreciate landscape beauty depends on visual sensitivity, emotional response, the ability to comprehend order in nature, an understanding of the factors controlling landscape, historical insight, experience of different landscapes, the ability to contemplate on things seen, and, not least, on cultural factors such as prevalent landscape tastes.

An important point is that evaluative aesthetic judgments should be impartial, and akin to verdicts or findings. They should not be expressions of preference arising from personal affections and antipathies. This requirement is difficult to enforce in practice and has an important bearing on one of the most contentious aspects of a contentious process—the question of who should be the observers who make the landscape evaluation? Should they be a cross section of the general public? Or should they be drawn from one or other of a number of minority groups concerned with landscape conservation, e.g. members of the National Trust, or Council for the Protection of Rural England; ramblers and similar countryside users; landscape artists and writers; or visually-educated professionals, such as landscape architects and planners? In practice, for logistic reasons, the latter type of observer has generally been used. But, of course, there is no reason why a group of observers of another type should not also make an evaluation to explore the range of opinion and expose any differences for the guidance of those who are to use the evaluation as an aid in decision-making.

The Manchester University *Landscape Evaluation* Report (5.6) noted some 35 different existing methods for evaluation of the general visual quality of landscape, and two more are suggested in the study's recommendations. Broadly the existing methods fell into two groups:

(a) those based only on subjective judgments of landscape quality made in the field, which involved visiting all the survey units comprising a study area.
(b) those based on measurements from maps or air photographs of defined physical components of landscape (i.e. in this case components of land surface)—these components being accorded a subjective quality weight, usually defined on the basis of a sample field survey of only parts of the study area.

In some of the wholly field-based methods an element of measurement is involved although the procedures used are not arithmetically sound. Scores are accorded to both the quantity and quality of each component found in a survey unit. These scores are then arithmetically combined and the resultants for all components are aggregated to give an overall measure of landscape quality for the survey unit.

The main basis for methods using measurements of landscape

components, however, is a regression analysis of subjective quality scores for sample survey units and the measured components for those units—the aim being to determine component weights. These weights are then applied to measures of components for the survey units not visited in the field to provide general quality estimates for the unseen survey units.

All methods involve subjective assessment of landscapes in the field to at least some degree. If more than one observer is to be used (as is desirable), or if comparison of assessments made at different times by different observers is required, all observers' scores should be capable of being related to a common scale. The new methods suggested in the Manchester University Report (5.7) are the first to attempt a solution to this problem of devising a common scale.

Landscape is a continuum and the choice of survey unit for operation of a landscape evaluation method presents problems. The notionally appropriate unit would be a visually-bounded tract—but such tracts are far from easy to define on the ground and certainly have no consistency of scale. For methods dependent on measuring components the O.S. Grid Square has obvious advantages. Its use, even in wholly field-based evaluations, enables landscape quality data to be compiled on the same areal unit basis as is common for many other planning surveys and so facilitates the relation of landscape information with other factors in techniques such as potential surface analysis (5.8). Therefore the grid square has been the most favoured survey unit, despite the practical difficulty of confining assessment to the landscape within the unit and ignoring views out of the square. Evaluations undertaken on a grid square basis are often complemented by a separate survey and record of major panoramic view points—especially those accessible or potentially accessible to the public.

Landscape classifications and visual quality evaluations are both static 'snap shot' surveys. Repeat surveys after a period of years will enable some monitoring of landscape change; but as the methods record effects rather than causes it is important to supplement them with more diagnostic appraisals for areas where the landscape is changing rapidly and a decline in quality is involved.

As mentioned earlier, however, it is only lately that it has been appreciated that the beauty of the rural landscape is threatened by a variety of pressures for change; or, indeed, that it is a resource which merits recording and requires positive measures of conservation. When the post-war planning system was established a very different view prevailed. There was to be almost 20 years of gathering change in the countryside before the planning system was again reshaped to take fuller account of what was happening.

Planning control and the post-war system

The present-day concern that some aspects of countryside activities themselves may pose as great a threat to the qualities of the rural landscape as urban intrusions was far from the minds of planners, pressure groups and politicians when the Town and Country Planning Act of 1947 was under consideration. Apart from the recognition that mineral working could have unsightly effects the prevailing attitude had not advanced very far from that represented by Cowper's assertion that "God made the country and man made the town". Hence the main tasks of country planning were seen as keeping the town out of the countryside (or at least limiting and controlling its extension) and ensuring that new housing and industrial development to meet rural needs was fitted into existing villages and market towns. The visual amenity which the countryside represented was regarded as likely to be self-perpetuating provided it could be protected from the sprawling and sporadic encroachment of suburbia which had occurred in the 1930s. In effect the term 'natural beauty', which is used widely in the legislation and reports of the period, reflected a belief not so much that the countryside was a work of nature alone, but that it was natural that countryside activities would produce a beautiful landscape.

The Development Plan side of the new planning system placed little accent on the countryside—which often would be shown as an area for which there were no policies except that "existing uses should remain for the most part undisturbed." Areas of special landscape value could be shown, where particularly high standards of development control would apply. Except for proposals for farm or forestry dwellings or very large farm buildings, farming and forestry activities were exempt from planning control. Planning authorities were given powers to place Preservation Orders on trees—but effectively only on those outside commercial woodlands. Furthermore it was indicated that Tree Preservation Orders should not usually be made for hedgerow trees on agricultural land, whose "management can be left to the farmers even though in some cases they may have to be cleared in the interests of food production " (5.9).

John Dower's report on National Parks (5.10) was commissioned because there had been growing demands during the thirties from small but influential pressure groups for protection of the finest rural landscapes as National Parks and access to privately-owned open upland areas for rambling, climbing and caving. After a further Government Committee report the National Parks and Access to the Countryside Act was passed in 1949 (5.11).

In accordance with Dower's prescription the National Parks were to be extensive tracts of land covering the areas of national scenic importance. The object of their designation was to be the preservation and enhancement of characteristic landscape beauty and the promotion of its enjoyment by the public. The land in the Parks was expected to remain in private ownership and use. Provision was made for special administrative arrangements for the Parks—although the system adopted was somewhat different from that recommended by the National Parks Committee insofar as representatives of the Local Councils were to outnumber Ministerial nominees on the committee or board responsible for each Park. A new Central Government Agency, the National Parks Commission, was to be responsible for designating National Parks and Areas of Outstanding Natural Beauty, and establishing long distance footpaths. The Commission advised the National Park Authorities in their work, and was also responsible for advising Ministers and planning authorities generally about the effect of proposed development on the natural beauty of the countryside anywhere in England or Wales. On the recommendation of the Commission Exchequer grants were available to assist National Park Authorities to conserve landscape quality and provide for recreation, through activities such as tree planting and woodland management, clearing unsightly development, making public access agreements with landowners, and providing hostel accommodation, picnic sites, car parks, campsites, and warden services. There are now 10 National Parks, covering 9% of the land surface of England and Wales.

The National Parks Act did not apply to Scotland. Despite favourable recommendations from a Scottish National Parks Committee (5.12) in 1947, no National Parks have been established but there are special development control arrangements for the areas of highest landscape quality. In addition several of the largest National Forest Parks established by the Forestry Commission are north of the border and the largest areas of National Nature Reserves are also in Scotland.

Areas of Outstanding Natural Beauty can be designated under the

National Parks Act for the protection of other (and usually smaller) areas of national scenic importance. The National Parks Committee (England and Wales) (5.13) in recommending that there should be provision for the designation of such second tier protected areas referred to them as falling short of National Park standards on the grounds of extent, 'wildness', or the degree to which they incorporated intensive farming or forestry. These comments indicate the degree to which the immediate post-war thinking on National Parks was dominated by two major considerations; on the one hand scenic grandeur and on the other physical challenge to the minority of the population who sought active recreation in such surroundings. There are no special administrative arrangements for Areas of Outstanding Natural Beauty which remain under the control of the Local Planning Authority. The sole purpose of designation is to ensure an added degree of landscape protection. Exchequer grant assistance is limited to landscape improvement work (such as tree planting or clearance of eyesores), and the support of warden services for areas over which there are public access agreements. In distinction from National Parks there are no special powers under the Act to provide facilities for outdoor recreation in Areas of Outstanding Natural Beauty. There are now 33 A.O.N.B.s, varying in size from 22 square miles (57 km²) in the case of Dedham Vale to the 671 square miles (1740 km²) of the North Wessex Downs, and covering in all a further 9% of England and Wales.

During the 1930s, legislation had enabled the London County Council and other Local Authorities to acquire or reserve land to establish a Green Belt around the metropolis. In his 1944 advisory plan for Greater London Patrick Abercrombie recommended that future planning for the metropolitan area should include a continuous Green Belt, on average 5 miles wide, as a barrier to further peripheral growth. The Green Belt would be a protective zoning and need not necessarily be brought into public ownership as planning control could ensure that the land was not used for building purposes. All new housing and industrial development required as a consequence of the de-congestion of Central London could then be accommodated either in New Towns or the expansion of some existing towns beyond the outer edge of the Green Belt. The emphasis was on the containment role of a Green Belt. The earlier planning theorists who had advocated Green Belts, particularly Ebenezer Howard and Raymond Unwin, had thought in terms of a green backcloth to a regional web of urban settlement; with the protected green interstices providing nearby recreational opportunities and local food supplies for the inhabitants of the network of towns. In 1955 the Minister responsible for planning took up Abercrombie's containment theme and urged the County Planning Authorities to include Green Belts in their development plans; advising that this zoning should be used around all major conurbations, cities and historic towns. It was inevitable, with the accent on stopping peripheral expansion or the coalescence of urban areas that much of the land included in Green Belts on Development Plans lacked any positive scenic quality or worthwhile possibility of agricultural use—often its only qualification was that it was still more or less open in character. Indeed some of it was the grey area of under-utilized urban fringe—a landscape of farming on the verge of expiry because of pollution, trespass and the threat of urban development, of mental hospitals and coke-dumps, derelict river valleys and disused sewage works.

A study of possibilities for the future distribution of population in Britain showed that by 1970 more than 40% of the land area was subject to policies which protected it from the likelihood of large-scale urban development (5.14). The protective zonings or ownerships included in this calculation were the National Parks and Areas of Outstanding Natural Beauty; the areas notified as possible future National Parks in Scotland (where the Secretary of State has to be consulted on all proposals for development); zonings as Green Belts or Areas of Great Landscape Value in Development Plans; and land managed as National Forest Parks or National Nature Reserves. Thus there was some degree of protection for practically all the finest landscapes, most of which had none before the Second World War.

Planning control and landscape management

Protective zonings and designations have limitations in achieving landscape conservation unless the day-to-day management of land is carried on with landscape amenity in mind. Traditionally, country landowners had managed their estates with an eye to creating and maintaining landscape quality—if only as a largely private amenity. They also had a concern for maintaining the sporting amenities of the estates, and the two objectives were complementary. The estate's parklands, deciduous woodlands and game coverts combined with the hedgerows, ponds, pastures, ditches and stream

183

banks of the tenanted farmland to provide both a network of game cover and the warp and woof of the patchwork quilt landscape of the countryside. The landlord-tenant system of the country estates provided an inbuilt safeguard for many of the features which contributed to the intimate scale and diversity of appearance of the countryside. The break-up of the country estates has coincided with growth of the concept that landscape is a public resource. The desire to conserve landscape amenity has been one of the main props of the broad political consensus on the need for a planning system. The mantle of principal custodian of the rural landscape now rests on the planning authority. However, the post-war planning legislation gave the planning authorities very few of the management powers which would be necessary to implement conservation policy.

Change from one land use to another, with the important exception of agriculture to forestry, is within the scope of planning control. Changes in the methods of operation of a particular use may also be of great landscape significance. Unless they involve substantial building operations, many such changes in management are likely to be outside the planning system.

By the mid-1960s the weaknesses in planning powers in regard to landscape conservation were beginning to be all too evident. For example, a survey by the National Parks Commission (5.15) found sufficient evidence of widespread erosion of coastal landscape quality to merit recommendations for further special measures of protection and management.

A number of the National Parks and Areas of Outstanding Natural Beauty include stretches of coastline; other stretches are included in Areas of High Landscape Value in Development Plans, and all the remaining areas of coast had been subject to normal planning controls since 1948. At the time of the survey no less than 63% of the coast of England and Wales was already subject to planning policies which had been intended to serve as a protection against unsuitable development. Yet the investigation showed that post-war development had encroached on many stretches of hitherto unspoiled coast. The spread of caravan and chalet sites, in particular, was on a scale which threatened scenic attraction. The Commission recommended the designation of 34 areas as 'Heritage Coasts', where more stringent development control should be applied and policies for conservation, access and recreation should be coordinated. By 1975 18 stretches of Heritage Coast had been defined by County Planning Authorities. These designations covered 646 km and further stretches under discussion are likely to extend the length of coastline protected in this way to nearly 1300 km. Heritage Coast plans will provide a framework for coordination of coastal land use and management and will be the basis for decisions on grant support to conservation and recreation projects.

The truth was that over countryside and coast alike planning control and zoning policies were but partial proof against a number of changes which had either been unforeseen in the 1940s or woefully underestimated. The growth of car ownership had given the opportunity for large numbers of people to visit the countryside and remoter coasts for casual recreation. Most of these visitors were very different from the original lobbyists for National Parks and access to the countryside and had less understanding of country ways. They were not all active pursuit enthusiasts equipped with Ordnance Survey maps and rucksacks and looking "to refresh their minds and spirits and to exercise their bodies in a peaceful setting of natural beauty" (5.16). Most looked for nothing much more active in the way of recreation than the enjoyment of a good view from a convenient parking place, or a pleasant family picnic by a stream-side with the car parked alongside. The cars which enabled people to enjoy a drive to and through the countryside threatened both peace and natural beauty. The new mobility also meant that caravan sites and other low cost forms of holiday development could be located in hitherto relatively inaccessible coastal spots, well away from established resorts. Similarly people with the resources to buy or build a 'country cottage' could indulge their aspirations to live in a village yet work in the town, or acquire a country retreat for weekend and holiday use. In the countryside within commuting distance of large towns new building in villages has become one of the most obvious elements of landscape change. Despite the best efforts of planners in design control, villages just beyond the outer edge of the Green Belt have lost all appearance of simplicity. The unassuming evolution of the village as an integral part of the rural landscape is quickly disrupted by too great an amount of new development and the social changes which this brings in its train. In some cases so many of the existing cottages have been taken over and 'improved' by commuters or weekenders that the whole village has become a self-conscious pastiche of the rustic scenes which used to appear on chocolate-boxes; in others the original settlement is lost in a sea of suburbia.

The other changes in the nature of countryside land use which had major landscape effects were those in the productive activities. Planning was given no control at all over afforestation or the day-to-day activities of farming and forestry. Yet the scale of afforestation was now increasing to take as much land out of farming each year as urban growth. Most of the land taken for forestry was in the uplands where the bold, open grain of the landscape was at once its most telling and most sensitive characteristic. Economic constraints on the management of existing woodlands in both lowland and upland areas dictated much replacement of mature deciduous woods with conifers; indeed under the new economic conditions some traditional landscape elements such as coppice woodlands had become completely anachronistic. From the mid-1950s onwards farming had been in the throes of what amounted almost to a second agricultural revolution. The effects of widespread and radical changes in farming systems were sufficiently dramatic for the main Government agency concerned with the appearance of the countryside to commission a study of the *New Agricultural Landscapes* (5.17). There is a more detailed discussion of the landscapes of farming and other major land uses later in the Chapter. It suffices here to instance such considerations as the effect on landscape variety of the increasing specialization of agriculture and decline of mixed farming; the clearance of hedges and hedgerow trees in field enlargement; the new materials used for farm buildings and their industrial scale and appearance; and the reclamation of moorland and lowland heaths for improved grassland—all activities encouraged by Government grant support and facilitated by the new agricultural technology.

A realization of the importance of landscape management is a feature of all significant recent developments in countryside planning. The 1967 and 1968 Countryside Acts, for Scotland and England and Wales respectively, laid a duty on all public agencies in exercising their functions to "have regard to the desirability of conserving the natural beauty and amenity of the countryside". The National Parks Commission was replaced by a Countryside Commission and a similar body was established for Scotland. The Forestry Commission and water undertakings were empowered to provide for public recreation on their holdings. Local Authorities and private individuals were encouraged to set up Country Parks and picnic sites to meet the demand for open air recreational opportunities—with provision for up to 75% Exchequer grant assistance for the capital costs of approved schemes. The idea of the Country Park was to provide attractive locations, close to towns or in the less vulnerable parts of the areas of greatest landscape quality, for fairly gregarious enjoyment of informal countryside recreation. They were to be 'honey-pots' used as part of a strategy of diverting some of the weekend recreational pressures from the heartland of National Parks and lessening disturbance to the farmed countryside. Country Parks can also be seen as making a further contribution to landscape maintenance. They can provide a new function and *raison d'être* for landscapes which have outlived their original purpose; for example, the parkland of a now vanished country estate or a stretch of disused railway and its wayside halts in a pleasant part of the countryside. Again, Country Park grants can be allied to those available for the reclamation of derelict land to create entirely new landscapes which enhance the appearance of the countryside. This type of Country Park scheme can be instrumental in restoring both positive function and landscape attraction to some of the greyer areas of the Green Belts. By 1975 well over 100 Country Park schemes had been approved with about 37,000 acres (15,000 ha) of land involved.

The same theme of the involvement of public bodies in the management of the countryside for amenity purposes is reflected in the provisions of the 1968 Transport Act for the rehabilitation and recreational use of redundant canals. In the same year a new Town and Country Planning Act introduced a new suite of Development Plans. The Structure Plan which replaces the County Map is intended to embrace a wide range of strategic policies, providing for the interplay of settlement, transportation, industrial development, countryside land uses, and environmental conservation. Local Plans, to be prepared as necessary, can include District Plans for areas either of the countryside or in towns, Action Area Plans for localities in either setting where the need for immediate change is pressing, or Subject Plans for a particular function (e.g. land reclamation or coastal recreational use).

In contrast to the predominantly urban orientation of the post-war system the new Development Plans allow for a much fuller consideration of countryside issues; bringing rural employment and social trends firmly into the planning debate, as well as encouraging a more fundamental examination of recreation, landscape and environmental conservation problems. Although the new Act did not confer any wider powers of intervention in rural land use on planning authorities, it is hoped that Structure Plans will have a catalytic role—forming a long term framework for public and private short term investment and management policies and influencing their shape. The wide-ranging consultation and public participation which has characterized the preparation of Structure Plans has exposed the issues and problems of rural planning to public debate. The Reports of Survey of Structure Plans for rural counties include coverage of the structural and other changes in farming, forestry and mineral working. The effects of these changes on landscape, employment and rural settlement are examined with an attempt to anticipate future trends. Relationships with other countryside uses such as recreation and nature conservation are also explored so that alternative approaches to a countryside strategy can be established and given wide discussion. The final Structure Plan will emphasize policy areas over which planning has more direct influence such as recreation, conservation and improvement of the landscape, rural settlement, transportation and land transfer for urban expansion—but the new process of plan preparation ensures that such policies have a somewhat firmer basis in the realities and needs of countryside change.

Planning authorities have recognized the need for a systematic evaluation of the quality of rural landscape in the structure planning process and some have also carried out a survey of landscape character. There was some confusion as to which of the existing methods of landscape evaluation should be used. Doubts as to whether any one was wholly suitable led some of the first counties to prepare Structure Plans to spend much valuable time either evolving new approaches or adapting existing methods in an attempt to improve their usefulness in structure planning. This experimentation was valuable to the development of knowledge and experience but clearly wasteful of scarce staff resources. In order to be able to provide guidance to planning authorities, the Countryside Commission commissioned a study by the Centre for Urban and Regional Research at Manchester University (5.18). The improved methods recommended by the study have since been employed by a number of structure planning teams.

The concentration on preparation of the first round of Structure Plans has meant that there is little progress to date in regard to District Plans for rural areas. The official advisory Manual on Development Plans (5.19) emphasized the potential of the District Plan as a basis for negotiations with landowners, in order to demonstrate how their initiatives could fit into a comprehensive pattern. One aim would be to secure agreements on management policies which would protect landscape values whilst providing for necessary land use change. The inter-agency research study for Sherwood Forest (5.20), whilst not having statutory status, provides a prototype of the countryside management approach which will be necessary in preparing effective policies for areas of the countryside under severe pressures for change. The study's diagnostic approach to landscape appraisal, including an emphasis on evaluation of landscape change and the potential of landscapes to accommodate particular uses, can be expected to figure significantly in future district planning work.

As part of the reform of Local Government in England and Wales in April, 1974 new administrative arrangements were introduced for the National Parks. The effect has been to give them somewhat greater autonomy within the Local Government system (although this may be more apparent than real), improved staffing and more substantial Exchequer financial support. The two Planning Boards, for the Lake District and Peak District National Parks, remain as before. All the remaining Parks are also now under a single executive committee irrespective of whether they include land in two or more counties. Each Park Authority is now served by a National Parks Officer and supporting staff. Administrative expenditure, as well as expenditure on approved projects and services, is eligible for support by annual block grant from the Department of Environment. The previous arrangements were a source of considerable local irritation because all special administrative costs resulting from the designation of an area as a National Park, as well as 25% of the cost of Park projects, fell on the local rates. The effect was to curtail specialist staffing and reduce the ability of the Parks to prepare and implement projects for landscape conservation and recreational development. Under the new arrangements Local Authorities in a Park continue to make some contribution to the general Park budget. The Park Authorities are responsible for development control. Strategic planning policies on matters such as transportation, employment and settlement are dealt with in the County Structure Plans covering a Park area, but must be compatible with the purposes of National Parks and take account of the Park Authority's own policies. A further development in the management approach to conservation planning was introduced, because these policies are to be set out in a new document—the National Park Plan. (The two National Park Planning Boards, Lake District and Peak District, are responsible for both types of plan.)

Each National Park Plan has to be prepared by April 1977 and thereafter reviewed at least every 5 years. It will be primarily a means of expressing management policies. The plan will include guidelines for the conservation of resources (including landscape), the promotion of recreation, the zoning of different intensities of use and traffic management. Its preparation will involve extensive consultation with the local landowning and land-using interests as well as the participation of National Park residents, visitors and amenity groups. The Countryside Commission have defined the management functions involved as including "land acquisition, recreational development, recreation and land management, tree planting, clearance of eyesores, guidance and control of visitors including warden, interpretation and information services, and traffic management". The Commission notes that the management process will involve "both the activities of the Park Authority as landowner, developer and provider of services and facilities and, by arrangement and agreement, similar action undertaken by other owners and occupiers of land in the park" (5.21).

Many of the 'management' activities needed to provide for outdoor recreation and the conservation of landscape features are inherently unprofitable. As a consequence Local Authorities often have to take direct responsibility and acquire land in order to carry out schemes themselves. The work of the National Trust is also of great importance and public agencies with extensive countryside land holdings, such as the Forestry Commission and Regional Water Authorities, are making an increasing contribution to the amenity management effort.

But if a significant degree of protection for the appearance of the whole countryside is to be achieved, the positive cooperation of landowners and farmers is necessary. Management agreements provide a means by which private efforts can be influenced so that they contribute to the policies set out in National Park, Structure and Local Plans. Under a management agreement an owner or occupier agrees with a public authority to manage his land in a specified way in order to satisfy a particular public need; usually receiving some form of financial consideration in return for what he agrees to do, allow or give up. A management agreement is drawn up when the Forestry Commission gives grant aid to private commercial forestry under the Government's Dedication Scheme. Agreements for the conservation of flora and fauna have been reached between the Nature Conservancy Council and landowners in National Nature Reserves. Such agreements cover 60% of the total National Nature Reserve area and, of course, provide some incidental protection for valuable landscapes. There are many agreements between Local Planning Authorities and private owners to provide for public access to 'open country' (e.g. moorland, cliff-tops, heathland, rough-grazing land in hill country). Under an access agreement, besides making an annual financial contribution, the planning authority enforces bye-laws governing public behaviour and provides a warden service; in turn the owner agrees not to manage the land in ways which would prevent or reduce public access. As the undertakings include an agreement not to reclaim the land and turn it into improved farmland, this scheme also has some importance for landscape conservation.

There are general powers under the National Parks and Town and Country Planning Acts which can be construed as enabling planning authorities to enter into management agreements with landowners and farmers to secure conservation and enhancement of the landscape. But any costs incurred by planning authorities in taking initiatives under these general powers would not be eligible for Exchequer grant assistance. For some time the Countryside Commission has been urging the need for legislation to give specific powers for landscape agreements along the same lines as access agreements. The 1974 Report of the National Park Policies Review Committee (5.22) supported the Countryside Commission's arguments and the Government has now agreed to introduce legislation to provide for landscape agreements.

Planning: new initiatives

During the early 1970s there were Government-sponsored inquiries into the working of several aspects of the planning system. The National Park Policy Review Committee was set up in 1971 to review the effectiveness of the National Parks and to make recommendations for future policies. The Committee's most important general finding was that changes in circumstances since 1949 were such that the twin purposes of preserving and enhancing natural beauty and promoting the enjoyment of the Parks by the public are now in conflict in some areas. The Committee recommended that the statutory purposes of National Parks should be amended "to make it clear that their enjoyment by the public shall be in such manner and by such means as will leave their natural beauty unimpaired for the enjoyment of this and future generations," (5.23). The Committee also found that all too frequently National Park landscape values had been adversely affected by major developments—reservoirs, large scale afforestation with conifers, electricity power stations and transmission lines, mining and quarrying, and major road 'improvements' to accommodate long

K

distance traffic. With the arguments for such developments posed in terms of some pressing national economic need, expedient decisions on short term utilitarian grounds threatened the more intangible yet enduring benefits of conserving the National Park landscapes. Whilst recognizing that some of the economic resources in the Parks were vital to the national economy and important potential sources of local employment, the Committee urged that the "presumption against development which would be out of accord with Park purposes must be strong throughout the whole of the Parks; in the most beautiful parts which remain unspoiled it should amount to a prohibition to be breached only in the case of a most compelling national necessity" (5.24). The Committee were agreed that the characteristics and capacity of different areas within a Park would merit a matching variety of management objectives. The distinction between parts of Parks in the quotation above is also a partial reflection of the fact that some members of the Committee proposed that the very highest quality landscapes, whether inside or outside National Parks, should be designated 'national heritage area' and be given extra statutory protection against incongruous development.

The Government accepted that there is increasing likelihood of instances where planning and management will not be able to reconcile conflicts between the two main purposes of a National Park and agreed that where this happens Park Authorities must give priority to the conservation of natural beauty (5.25). The decisions on some of the other recommendations in the report indicate that the Government's response on the question of major intrusive developments was more guarded. The proposal for national heritage areas was not accepted. Most response to this suggestion after publication of the Committee's report had been unfavourable, on the grounds that it would have the effect of reducing the status and hence presumption of protection for the remaining areas of National Parks. A proposal that afforestation should be brought under planning control in National Parks was rejected, as was the recommendation that all applications for large new mineral workings or large extensions to existing workings should be called in by the Secretary of State for decision. On the other hand the Government agreed that investment in trunk roads should be directed to developing routes for long distance traffic which avoid National Parks. It is now Government policy to ban both the construction of new routes for such traffic in a Park and the upgrading of existing routes for the purpose, unless a compelling need cannot be met by other reasonable means. However, there was a warning that the new policy would be difficult to apply to some Parks because of their geographical location.

Many of the Committee's detailed recommendations for improvement of management and control procedures are to be included in a new National Parks Bill. The provision for management agreements for landscape conservation has been mentioned earlier. All new farm buildings will be brought under planning control in the Parks. Park Authorities will be able to assist farmers to meet the costs of any specially stringent design requirements. It will be made clear that Park Authorities can acquire land by agreement for the sole purpose of landscape conservation, although they are not to be given compulsory purchase powers. There is to be provision for advance notification of proposals to reclaim open country and convert it to improved farmland. A temporary standstill notice will be available to give time for negotiations; but with no compulsory purchase power the Park Authority will be reliant on either buying the land by agreement or persuading the owner to enter into a suitable management agreement.

One common feature of other recent inquiries into planning procedures is discussion of whether environmental impact statements should be required for proposals involving large scale or otherwise particularly intrusive developments. The idea of the impact statement comes from the United States where it is required for public agency developments (5.26). Unlike the United States, Britain has a nationwide system of planning control in which the environmental effects of all proposals are a matter of central concern. Nevertheless, inquiries such as the National Park Policies Review Committee provide evidence that environmental consequences are not always given due weight in planning decisions. A requirement for a more rigorous investigation of these consequences would provide better information for all concerned; including the applicant, the planning authority, and third parties with an interest in the proposal (such as amenity or conservation groups).

The Dobry report on the Development Control System (5.27) recommended that for specially significant development proposals planning authorities should have the power to require the developer to submit an impact study. The power was to be used selectively and sparingly, and an impact study was not appropriate if a planning authority was minded to refuse a proposal on the basis of the information already available from the usual application form. The responsibility for preparing an impact study would rest with the developer, although the planning authority and all other public

193

agencies would be under a duty to provide any relevant information in their possession. Dobry saw the impact study as being an objective assessment of the proposed development's effects on traffic and transportation, drainage, public services (e.g. school provision), landscape, pollution, employment, and subsequent development in the locality. The study might also discuss the comparative advantages of alternative sites. The Government has taken no action on this recommendation as the Department of Environment has commissioned a special study to consider whether environmental impact analysis has a role in the British planning process.

Another Dobry recommendation which would have affected rural landscape planning has also been shelved. He advised that there should be some extension of planning control in regard to farm buildings and that there was a case for grants or fiscal advantages to help farmers with the costs of providing agricultural buildings which were acceptable in the local landscape. His proposals were to apply to all areas and not only to National Parks where an extension of control has been accepted as necessary by Government.

The Report of the Stevens Committee on Planning Control over Mineral Working (5.28) takes a different line from Dobry on environmental impact, attacking the problem through an improvement of existing procedures. At the moment planning authorities do not have a special application form for minerals proposals and the range of information required on their general forms differs from authority to authority. The Committee proposes that there should be a standard application form for all mineral working proposals. This form would require the applicant to provide a scheme of working operations including restoration and after-use proposals; an economic justification for the proposed working; and full information on its likely external effects, social as well as environmental. The section on environmental effects would include information on proposals for environmental protection—such as landscaping to screen the workings during their operational life.

This is but one of a large number of recommendations in the Committee's report aimed at up-dating and improving minerals planning. As there were many parts of the country in which mining and quarrying had scarred the landscape from the Industrial Revolution onwards, mineral working was brought within the scope of the post-war planning system. Because of the long life of workings, however, there are many still in operation which were established before 1948. Even those which were given permission in the early post-war years were often accorded unnecessarily large areas, with inadequate conditions on the consent as regards restoration of the site. The result is that much mineral working is not subject to the degree of control which present-day standards require. Meantime, because of technological developments the average size of working has increased—with a consequential increase in environmental impact. Some of the planning controls are defective—particularly those which are supposed to stop operators working without planning permission or in breach of a planning condition, where the procedures for enforcement are cumbersome and the penalties derisory in relation to the prospective profits. The Committee makes important recommendations to deal with these enforcement problems; to define cessation and to limit the life of workings so that a mere semblance of activity does not have the effect of avoiding the need to restore the site; to clarify and regularize control over exploratory drilling; to allow for regular review of permissions so that control of later phases can be in line with improvements in working and restoration practice; and to encourage phasing so that there is gradual restoration as working proceeds.

Another proposal is that the National Coal Board should at last be subject to the same degree of planning control as other mineral operators in respect of its pit-head activities. One of the Committee's conclusions, however, is likely to be greeted with considerable scepticism and disappointment by planning and amenity interests. This is the view that there is insufficient evidence of mineral workings being left derelict because of bankruptcy or liquidation to justify a national scheme to ensure that operators make appropriate financial provision for the restoration of each site.

Nevertheless, planning powers to deal with the landscape problems caused by mineral working will be strengthened substantially if the suggestions of the Stevens Committee are accepted by Government. The emphasis in the Committee's report on consultation and cooperation between mineral operators and planning authorities is to be welcomed. Close liaison is a feature underlying the increasing number of schemes where disruption to the environment by working has been minimized and where, after restoration, a new landscape of at least equivalent quality to the old has been created.

Mineral workings are dramatic and potentially damaging incidents in the rural landscape. The main fabric of the countryside, however, is maintained by farming and forestry and the landscape problems arising from these activities are more pervasive. Here planning must look largely to influence in order to exercise any constructive concern, for in comparison with mineral working its powers of control over farming and forestry are but infinitesimal.

The Farming Landscape

Despite a continuing loss of land to other uses, notably urban growth and forestry, agriculture still occupies nearly 80% of the land surface of Britain (5.29). Changes in farming practices and patterns are therefore the dominant influences on rural landscape. Since the end of the Second World War, and particularly over the last twenty years, these changes have been momentous. All over the country the landscape effects are considerable and increasing, but they are most pronounced in the eastern lowlands generally and in the midland counties of England.

To understand why recent changes in the farming landscape have seemed so alien to many country lovers, it is useful to have a brief look at the historical background. In the mid-nineteenth century the growing demands of the industrial population were met by the 'high farming' boom, often described as the 'Golden Age' of British agriculture. But by 1875 the effects of overseas competition were beginning to be felt. With only a short revival in the First World War the ensuing agricultural depression was to last until 1940. The area under arable crops was steadily reduced until in 1939, for example, nearly two-thirds of the farmland (excluding rough grazings) in England and Wales was under permanent grass. The equivalent figure in 1875 had been only 45%. There had been little capital investment in new buildings during the depression years, farming techniques were still dominated by the long-established rotational systems, and mixed farming was the norm. Apart from the fact that there was more grassland in the 'patchwork-quilt' pattern originally established by the enclosures and the agricultural revolution of the eighteenth century, Britain still had a traditional farming landscape, although much of it was in decay.

In the Second World War the 'ploughing-up campaign' launched to increase home food production boosted cropland considerably and the permanent grassland proportion dropped to 40%, i.e. below the 1875 level. The first decade after the war showed something of a return to the pre-war picture as areas which had been pressed into cropping at the margin of potential for arable use reverted to permanent grass. But it was soon evident that a new agricultural revolution was under way. The price support system (introduced by the Agriculture Act of 1947) and technical developments opened up new possibilities of specialization, weakening the constraints which for so long had ensured the continuance of mixed farming and rotational cropping. Capital investment in machinery and new buildings became feasible in an industry which now had some assurance of stability through longer term Government support. The use of artificial fertilizers, herbicides and pesticides enabled more continuous cropping without break crops, promoting the growth of an almost completely new phenomenon—the arable farm without any livestock.

The emphasis was to be on increased scale of operation, intensification and specialization (with fewer farms creating Nan Fairbrother's landscape of amalgamation (5.30)). Mechanization substituted for scarce and high-cost labour but in turn the high level of capital investment had to be justified by creating maximum opportunity for the use of machinery. Against a background of rising costs and the need to service the borrowing which underpinned capital investment, the search for profitability dominated farming systems. The effect has been to also emphasize increased production—not always without adverse effects on the other values in the land. Activities of little importance in generating income, although perhaps crucial to the maintenance of traditional features of the farming landscape and therefore 'local character', tended to be neglected. Resources would be concentrated on those commodities suited to an area for which there was greatest demand or greatest encouragement through the patterns of Government price support. Regional differences have been sharpened through the creation of landscapes which reflect farming specialisms.

The changes in farming practice have been paralleled and influenced by changes in the structure of the farming industry. The scale of amalgamation of uneconomic small farms has perhaps been smaller than might have been anticipated, and appears to have been little affected by the modest Government inducements available. However, in the period 1960-1970 the number of farm holdings in the United Kingdom dropped by over one-fifth with a consequential increase in the average size of farm from 28 ha to 34 ha. A more important trend in its impact on farming practice has been the steady move from tenancy of farms to owner occupation. At the beginning of the century only about a tenth of the farms in Britain were owner-occupied, at the outbreak of the Second World War the proportion was under one-third; now nearly two-thirds of farms are wholly or mainly owned by the farmers who occupy them. The capital outlay involved in purchasing and operating the farm is a liability which demands that the farmer concentrates on those enterprises which are most profitable and for which he and his land are most suited. These constraints are again a powerful stimulus to specialization, intensification of production involving maximum use of every acre of land and the elimination of any traditional practices which are seen as creating unnecessary overheads.

Between 1950 and 1970 the volume of production of British agriculture increased by 70%, whilst the labour force of farmers and workers was declining at an average rate of 3% annually. The total labour force involved was more than halved over the two decades and continues to decline—currently at a rate of about 2% every year. The annual rate of growth of production has been about 2½% during the 1970s. The Government looks to a continuance of this performance in its White Paper on agricultural policy until 1980 (5.31), emphasizing the importance to the national economy of import saving from home production of foodstuffs. As the area of agricultural land is steadily declining under the impact of urban growth and afforestation (land uses whose growth rates have been very similar in the last decade), further intensification and mechanization will be required if this target is to be achieved. The White Paper quotes the average loss of agricultural land in the United Kingdom during the 5 years up to 1972/73 as being about 144,000 acres (58,000 ha) per annum; 75,000 acres (30,000 ha) per annum to urban, industrial and recreational uses and the rest to forest and woodland. The best quality farmland (Grades 1 and 2 of the Ministry of Agriculture's Agricultural Land Classification) (5.32) has the greatest potential to sustain further intensification of production. As a high proportion of the best quality land is to be found in the lowlands where urban growth is also likely to be concentrated and because there are limits to the extent to which further improvements in agricultural labour productivity can be anticipated, the Government's aim of greater self-sufficiency in national food production will require yet more stringent consideration of farmland quality in planning decisions about the location of urban growth.

The scenic effects of post-war intensification and specialization in farming go well beyond the impact on the rural landscape of the reduction in grassland and increase in arable area, although in some parts of the country this has been very dramatic (e.g. a quarter of the chalk downland of Dorset was ploughed up for arable cropping between 1957 and 1972). Three-fifths of British farmland (excluding rough grazings) is now under arable cultivation. In many arable areas there have been considerable changes in the cropping patterns. The accent has been on the expansion of cereals with a reduction in the root crops formerly grown for livestock fodder. Because barley is especially suited to continuous cropping and provides a substitute feed, it has become the predominant cereal; before the Second World War it was the least grown cereal crop.

Some of the more obvious changes in the farming landscape are a consequence of mechanization. Where farms are all arable, or such livestock as they have are housed in an intensive feed unit, there is no need for the hedgerows which were originally established to contain and shelter livestock during their turn in the rotational farming system. The hedgerows take up potentially productive land, they may harbour pests and weed species, and they impede the long runs necessary for easy and speedy operation of large machines. Ease of access and speed of operation are greatly valued because there may be very critical time limits to the most effective use of very expensive machinery during sowing, harvesting, spraying for weed control and the like. Hedges and ditches are also very expensive to maintain. The hedgerow trees originally planted to provide for self-sufficiency in supplies of farm timber are no longer needed for that purpose and are disliked because of their shading effects on crop growth. In the face of such considerations the hedgerow's contributions to ecological and landscape diversity are not likely to be uppermost in the farmer's mind. In any case he is likely to prefer a farming landscape which in his view is neat, tidy and functional. Fields of about 50 acres (20 ha) are regarded as optimal for machinery operations by agricultural advisers but some arable farmers have completely cleared blocks of four or five times this size. Where this has happened a prairie landscape is emerging whose only incidents are the often uncompromising and starkly industrial farm buildings.

Even in the wetter western parts of the country and the uplands where grassland and livestock farming predominate, the density of hedgerow pattern is likely to decrease. The landscape of small fields of 1-4 ha derives from successive enclosures from Celtic times onward. Stone walls, earth banks and ditches, (which together form about one-fifth of the field boundaries in England and Wales) are mingled with hedgerows. All these boundaries are expensive to maintain and the fields they enclose are often far smaller than required by present methods of stock management. Mechanical hedge-cutters, when substituted for labour-expensive hand cutting and laying, trim the hedges but do not weed out species which are weak links in the barrier nor do they allow new hedgerow trees to develop. Mechanically trimmed hedges soon require patching with wire and inevitably deteriorate over time. A gradual loss of such hedgerows in livestock farming areas is unlikely to be matched by replacement planting. With stone walls the effect is not so much gradual disappearance as dereliction. Many miles of redundant internal boundary walling on upland farms are crumbling into decay—maintenance would require lengthy commitment of labour to what in strict farming terms would be mere window dressing.

The rate of hedgerow removal varies considerably, even within predominantly arable areas, but the Council for the Protection of Rural England estimated in 1975 that 2-3000 miles (3-5000 km) are removed every year (5.33). A consultant's report for the Countryside Commission (5.34) examining seven small lowland areas in 1972 found rates of removal since 1945 ranging from just over 7% to 40%. The survey confirmed other studies in indicating that in lowland arable areas an annual loss of at least 1% of hedges can be anticipated. The survey also provided disturbing evidence of a heavy loss of hedgerow tree cover under most types of lowland farming. For example, in the Somerset study area, where hedges had survived well, there had been a 70% reduction in trees since 1947. The consultant's studies showed that the enthusiasm of Regional Water Authorities for clearing river banks and 'tidying up' the margins of natural water courses accounted for some of the tree loss. The Countryside Commission study concentrated on lowland agricultural areas but confirmation that there is also a threat to hedgerow trees in the uplands comes from a survey by the North York Moors National Park Committee. This found that a quarter of all the existing hedgerow trees in the National Park were likely to disappear over the next 10 to 15 years. As a result the Park Committee is offering trees, fencing materials and free planting advice to farmers and landlords who are willing to enter a management agreement to carry out and maintain new planting on their farms. A number of other planning authorities in both upland and lowland areas provide funds for similar schemes.

Another factor in the removal of tree cover, unconnected with farming practice, is the depredation caused by Dutch Elm Disease. In the late 1960s an extremely virulent form of this disease entered the country. The recent hot summers have encouraged the spread of the disease which has already killed between six and seven million hedgerow trees. Whilst it may be possible to contain the disease in the hitherto lightly affected areas of Northern England, Wales and

Scotland, the effects on the characteristic 'false woodland' appearance which hedgerow, roadside and parkland trees give to the landscape in Southern England, the Midlands and East Anglia will be severe.

The progressive reduction of tree and hedgerow cover on farms has meant that modern farm buildings are a more noticeable feature of the new agricultural landscape than would otherwise have been the case. In the nineteenth century and earlier, farm buildings were usually arranged as a courtyard, alongside or abutting the farmhouse, and reflecting its scale. Local building materials were used and the architecture of the farmhouse and farm buildings alike was the vernacular of the period. Often trees were planted to give shelter to the group—with the effect of further 'setting' the buildings sympathetically into the landscape. Where possible the choice of site would be a low point in the local topography, because of the advantages of access to surface water supplies. The farmsteads often had the appearance of having themselves grown naturally out of the local landscape. This was a consequence of the hand-made scale; the use of local building techniques and materials; and the need to relate comfortably to what must have been, at the time of enclosures in the lowlands or during the early agricultural settlement in the uplands, a rather inhospitable and bleak environment. Livestock farms often had a number of outlying byres and associated barns to reduce the need for transport of winter fodder produced in the more distant fields. Until the Second World War the only change on many farms was the addition to the original set of buildings of a timber and corrugated iron Dutch Barn or implement shed.

It has proved difficult to adapt the old buildings to modern requirements. There is now a need, for example, to house large machinery, to have buildings which conform to hygiene regulations for milk production and structures which allow large herds of either dairy or beef cattle to be handled with the minimum deployment of labour under radically changed routines of stock management. There are also many entirely new processes, such as silage feeding or grain drying, to be accommodated. The most efficient buildings for modern farming will be large enough to house a number of activities under cover; in effect providing shells which can be easily and cheaply adapted by alteration of internal subdivisions and access points to short term changes in the balance of the farm enterprises. The old buildings characteristically have limited utility in this regard, being too small, too low and in some senses too solidly built. Farmers have therefore been erecting new structures of a scale and shape hitherto quite foreign to our countryside. Because it is no longer economic for farm buildings to be hand-built by local craftsmen, they are bought instead as factory-made components from national concerns. Standard structural frames of steel, concrete or timber are assembled in the number of bays required and clad with standard panels of wall and roof materials appropriate to the uses for which the building is required.

The regional variety of small scale buildings is being replaced by national uniformity. Perhaps replaced is the wrong term because it is rare for all the old buildings at the farmstead to be demolished. It is not uncommon to see semi-derelict barns alongside new so-called 'factory farming' buildings. There are advantages in the retention of the original farm buildings provided they can be put to effective use and therefore maintained in good order. If new structures are sited compactly in relation to the old, careful attention to texture and colour of cladding, and choice of overall proportions and roof pitches can do much to blend the whole group satisfactorily into the local scene. If a belt or group of mature trees shelters the farmstead, careful detail siting can ensure that these screen and frame the new structures in the broader view. Where new buildings are located away from the farmstead a horizontal profile, uncluttered lines, sympathetic surface textures and colours and skilful siting to take advantage of tree cover are all important considerations in linking the buildings to the landscape. It is not without significance that every photograph of visually successful new buildings in the Government advisory booklet, *Farm Buildings and the Countryside* (5.35), shows trees behind or alongside the structures concerned.

It seems that the upshot of all the trends mentioned above is a less diverse farming landscape and it was perhaps the diversity in the small scale landscape of traditional farming that was the secret of its wide appeal. There is less and less to see if one looks over the field gate—fewer fields, fewer hedges, fewer trees, less wildlife, a smaller range of crops in any one locality, and fewer animals in the open because of the trend to inhousing stock all the year under such regimes as zero grazing. Men and machines are on the land for only short spells of intense activity, working through the night if necessary on certain arable cultivations. Large industrial-seeming buildings are exposed in a landscape which holds less and less welcome for the casual observer and which can be fully 'appreciated' through a car window at 50 miles per hour with every confidence that little of interest has been missed. In many upland areas the effects of rationalization have been to create the appearance of an even more deserted countryside. In some hill districts, like Exmoor, Dartmoor and the North York Moors, land improvement pro- grammes involving reclamation of open moor for improved grass- land have been sufficiently common to constitute a reduction in landscape amenity. The more common approach to improving the hill farming economy, however, has been amalgamation of small farms and management of the combined units on a semi-ranching basis. High valleys dotted with disused farmsteads and laced by a network of crumbling dry stone walls represent a relict landscape which is testimony to the territorial ambitions of a nineteenth century farming boom.

There are certainly no easy solutions to these problems. Land use, management and even educational difficulties abound. Farmers have to be persuaded to retain or replace vulnerable cover or structures which they see as being detrimental, or at best of no value, to the farm economy. The idea of receiving some compensation has little appeal, especially as those who have been the most active in the pursuit of 'rationalization and improvement' may have reaped the reward of comparative affluence. More particularly, farmers tend to dislike any schemes which may involve more 'paperwork'. Planning and other agencies have to be persuaded to devote scarce staff resources to detailed countryside management planning at the expense of other apparently more important tasks. This problem is compounded because a time-consuming micro-approach is needed in order to produce significant overall results.

But the task must be put in hand if widespread and irreversible damage to the quality of countryside landscapes is to be avoided. There are some starting points for the conservation planning effort. Policies for the retention of a basic network of cover should be the first priority. The basic ingredients are likely to be the network of country roads and lanes with their verges, walls and hedges; the other external boundary features of farms; streams and watercourses and their margins; the edges of villages; woodlands, coverts, heaths and commons. Changes in management practices for areas already under the care of public authorities may be required. More tree planting and retention of trees along roads is clearly important, especially if some visual interest is to be retained along traffic routes which run through lowland areas which are becoming modern agricultural 'reserves'. The concept of treating the road network as a linear conservation feature is developed by Mercer (5.36); if Water Authorities adopted a less rigid management regime for the margins of water courses, an inter-linking network of cover would be provided. By acquisition, management agreement, or other appropriate means planning authorities must ensure positive management of the remaining areas of heath, common and small deciduous woodlands for amenity, nature conservation, and where appropriate, recreational benefit.

The second major thrust of policy must include the conservation of important landscape features on farmland (including the strengthening or re-creation of cover by planting small unproductive areas) and due attention to the fit of new farm buildings in the landscape. Unfortunately, the very farming developments which create the problem of diminishing variety in the landscape also reduce the area of unproductive land on the holding. Fewer fields mean fewer awkward corners and improved drainage eliminates the wet patches. Nevertheless farmers may see some possibility of accommodating planting on the odd piece of rough land or steep slope where it is difficult to operate machinery, and on pockets of land around the farmstead or alongside the farm lane.

The schemes whereby planning authorities offer free trees and fencing materials to farmers are useful, especially where the authority maintains an estates team which can carry out the planting and subsequent management. The farmers who cooperate, however, tend to be those who are most sympathetic to conservation in the first place. Nevertheless their example may be imitated by others with less initial interest. Inevitably the location of planting will be *ad hoc* and unrelated to any overall scheme for the locality.

In at least two types of area a more concerted approach is merited. The areas concerned are those where there is still a high density and variety of landscape cover, and those where removal of cover has reached the stage of having a serious effect on landscape quality. The first group are potential farm landscape 'conservation areas' and the second surely constitute farm landscape 'action areas'.

Westmacott and Worthington in their report *New Agricultural Landscapes* (5.37) suggested methods of preparing parish landscape conservation schemes akin to those used by the Tennessee Valley Authority in their 1930s programmes of agricultural improvement. Under the aegis of the planning authority, landowners, farmers, Parish Councils and other bodies with local land holdings would be encouraged to meet with Ministry of Agriculture advisers, NFU representatives and Nature Conservancy Council officers to evolve and agree a countryside management plan which combined agricultural and landscape improvement. A new scheme of financial incentives for the creation or conservation of landscape cover would be required to underpin such projects, as it is likely that the management agreement arrangement will only be available for the protection of features of special visual or historical interest. The report canvasses the possibilities of cash grants, income tax and capital gains tax rebates, or death duty allowances. The Council for Protection of Rural England suggests that further measures of control are necessary (such as notification of plans to remove landscape features and the imposition of landscape conditions in the award of farm improvement grants), but they, too, agree that generous tax concessions are necessary if farmers are to be encouraged to manage their land in a way beneficial to landscape and wildlife conservation (5.38).

The landscape of forestry

Great Britain has about 4.6 million acres (1.9 million ha) of woodland. 53% of this woodland is coniferous high forest and 20% broadleaved high forest, the rest being largely scrub. In Britain woodland and urban areas each cover about 8% of the total land surface. In most other European countries woodland features much more extensively in the landscape, taking up an average of about 30% of the land area. Thousands of years of development have changed Britain, in Nan Fairbrother's phrase, from being "a land of trees to a land of people" (5.39). One aspect of public concern about the role of trees in the landscape relates to the effects of the last phase of this long-term trend in the lowlands. Another arises because of the recent reversal of the trend in the uplands, where afforestation programmes are a major factor in landscape change.

Home production accounts for only a small amount of total timber consumption. As forests established by the state Forestry Commission and by private timber growers come into production this proportion will rise, but is only estimated to reach 13% of total demand by the end of century.

The Forestry Commission was established in 1919 and charged with promoting the interests of forestry and developing afforestation. The Commission now owns just under 40% of the total area of woodland and the vast majority of its land is planted with commercial conifers. Since 1950 the annual planting rate has ranged between 50,000 and 70,000 acres (20,000 ha—28,000 ha). Some three-quarters of the Commission's woodlands are less than 20-30 years old and have not yet reached the first thinning stage. Until 1958 the main aim of the state forestry programme was to build up a strategic reserve of timber against the possibility of wartime blockade. The management of the programme related to commercial objectives although the social considerations of providing rural employment were taken into account. The Government has always been loth to take anything but the poorest agricultural land for state forestry. The result is that most of the planting has been done in hill country on wet upland heaths and moors and on dry lowland heaths such as Thetford Chase and Sherwood Forest. These are landscapes which provide the setting for upland and lowland recreational use. Initially the planting techniques took little account of amenity considerations. As the land concerned was only suitable for the commercial production of conifer species the Commission gained the unenviable reputation of blanketing some of our finest landscapes with alien 'black conifers'.

During the period 1958-1972 the emphasis underlying the state forestry programme changed to give an increasing weight to social rather than predominantly commercial objectives. In 1967 and 1968 the Countryside Acts laid a specific duty on the Commission to have regard to amenity in their forestry operations. For the first time the Commission engaged a landscape consultant to advise forest officers on the landscaping of new and existing forest areas and there was a rapid increase in the provision of recreational facilities in state forests.

In 1972 there were 1.9 million acres (0.8 million ha) of productive private woodlands in Britain, an area slightly larger than that of the Forestry Commission holdings. In addition there were about 0.8 million acres (0.3 million ha) of commercially unproductive and scrub woodlands in private ownership. Much of the latter is used for sporting purposes or as shelter belts for agriculture and most has considerable amenity value. In 1973 private woodlands produced 2.12 million cubic metres of timber (compared with a production of 1.5 million cubic metres from state forests). Of the productive private woodland area 45% is in hardwoods—a much higher proportion than in the state forests. Although private woodland exists in most of the areas where there are Forest Commission plantations, most private planting takes place on better quality land where it is feasible to produce commercial crops of hardwood species. In general there is much less public access to private woodlands than is now the case in state forests. Since the Second World War private forestry has been assisted by special grant and tax arrangements to encourage its contribution to the aim of creating a strategic forest reserve. The principal grant arrangement was the Dedication Scheme under which owners who undertook to manage their woodlands in accordance with a plan of operations approved by the Forestry Commission received grants towards their initial planting and annual management costs. Just over half of the productive private woodland was 'dedicated' by 1972.

As a result of a review of Forest Policy in 1972 (5.40) the Government concluded that a programme of new planting by the Forestry Commission on anything like its postwar scale could only be justified by bringing into consideration its potential contribution not only to the creation and maintenance of employment in the uplands but also to the provision of recreational opportunities. The new target for the Commission was set at a combined total for the planting of new land and replanting on felled areas of 55,000 acres (22,000 ha) per year. 10,000 acres (4000 ha) would be replanting, a proportion of the annual total which was expected to treble by the end of the century. The Government also asked the Commission to give increased attention to the part their woodlands play in the landscape, even if this meant some reduction in an already low level of profitability. Earlier plantations were to be the subject of landscape improvement schemes as soon as felling and replanting provided opportunity and public access was to be aided wherever possible by provision of car parks, footpaths and campsites.

The conclusions of the policy review on support for private forestry were that any grant aid in this sector should now be given as a supplement designed to encourage private planting to follow the wider social objectives proposed for state forestry. To qualify for a grant under the revised Dedication Scheme a private owner's planting proposals must now:

(a) be on land which is agreed by the Forestry Commission, Ministry of Agriculture, Local Planning Authority, and (where appropriate) Nature Conservancy Council, to be suitable for forestry use
(b) have management objectives which are acceptable to these various authorities from the point of view of forestry practice, amenity, agriculture, nature conservation, public access, recreation, and general planning considerations.

The owner undertakes (if requested to do so by the planning authority) to enter into discussions with a view to negotiating an Access Agreement and to providing appropriate recreational facilities. To encourage the planting of deciduous woodlands, a much higher rate of planting grant is available for hardwoods than for conifers.

Dedicated Woodlands cannot be made the subject of a Tree Preservation Order and felling does not require a licence from the Forestry Commission. Outside Dedicated Woodlands all private felling requires such a licence and where amenity issues arise the Commission consults the planning authority before making a decision. However, farmers can fell an amount of timber roughly equivalent to ten full-sized trees every quarter without requiring a licence or any notification to either body. Planning authorities can make Tree Preservation Orders for trees, groups of trees, or woodlands on land outside Dedication Schemes or state forests but must consult the Commission before doing so. Again there is a loophole in relation to hedgerow timber because of the understanding that Preservation Orders will only be placed on farmland trees in exceptional circumstances.

The Forestry Commission notifies the appropriate planning authorities of all its proposals to acquire land and also discusses details of planning and management with the planning authorities if acquisition goes ahead. For each of the National Parks there is a special voluntary agreement with the Forestry Commission, Timber Growers Association and Country Landowners Association which seeks to harmonize the interests of forestry and planning by agreeing a broad strategy on afforestation.

It is clear that landscape considerations are now important factors in the management of state forests and those private woodlands which are covered by the new Dedication Scheme. When the previous Dedication Scheme was in operation very little private afforestation was carried out without grant support. It seems certain, however, that tax concessions were the major incentive for the development of private forestry. Recent uncertainties about future tax arrangements have led to a sharp fall in private forestry planting rates. It has been estimated that in 1975 the amount of new planting will be about 40,000 acres (16,000 ha) below the levels of previous years. If the final arrangements for Capital Transfer Tax and the proposed Wealth Tax are favourable to timber growing there are some fears that the amenity restrictions in the new Dedication Scheme will make it unattractive, and that the bulk of future private afforestation will be carried out without any regulation by either the Forestry Commission or the planning authority. Such fears led the National Park Policies Review Committee to recommend that the afforestation of bare land in National Parks should be brought under planning control—despite the existence of voluntary agreements on the location of planting in Parks.

This highlights the fact that the landscape appearance of plantations depends as much on their design, including the choice and arrangement of species, as their location. Some of the important factors in location will be land use and forest economy matters, such as avoiding good agricultural land or sites which are inaccessible for timber extraction. Landscape criteria would include the avoidance of sites where planting would alter the character of a local landscape which is particularly attractive for recreation in its present form. Another important principle might be that planting should not be allowed where it would change the character of panoramic views from roads and major public access areas if those views epitomize the 'feel' of a regional landscape, e.g. the open moorland and rock tors of Dartmoor. There will be locations where planting would be desirable in order to heighten the interest of the landscape.

Design considerations are concerned with maximizing the contribution of forestry to the landscape. The ideal is that the timber grower takes the traditional country estate approach and regards his planting as 'landscaping with woods' rather than 'afforestation'. This is certainly the spirit which planning authorities will look for in their consultations with the industry.

The first priority is to look to landscape balance. The size of plantations needs to be in scale with the landform and the new landscape should have contrast of open ground and planting. Where the open areas are agricultural they should be those most useful for farming and must include an appropriate mix of types of land for the farming system in question. Alternatively the open contrast may be achieved by leaving generous and irregularly shaped firebreaks and forest access routes. In either case open land should be allowed to penetrate the forest edge in a way which is sympathetic to the modelling of the terrain.

The outline of plantations can be shaped to reflect the sweep of the contours. Wherever possible boundaries should follow natural lines, like valleys or marked breaks of slope. The relationship of forest to skyline needs careful treatment; it may be possible to carry the planting over dips or low hills without suppressing the landform but it is usually desirable to drop the planting line below peaks in the topography. The pattern of species within plantations is an important element in the landscape of forestry. Relating choice of species to variations in soil and topography satisfies both good forestry practice and landscape need because a natural appearance results. Where there are few variations in soil and ground conditions group planting of different species produces a more interesting texture than line planting. The use of very large areas of one pure species of conifer in hillside planting will lack the varied effect which is important in the distant view. Whilst hardwoods are only likely to be commercially viable in lowland plantations (and even there will usually be planted in mixture with conifers) they should be incorporated in the landscaping of upland schemes. Irregular drifts of hardwood planting inside the lower boundary of plantations will help to link new woodlands with the farmland landscape, especially if the hardwoods occasionally penetrate further into the forest area by following the lines of natural features like small side valleys. Where plantations are on hillsides the widths of firebreaks and rides should be varied and they should take an easy diagonal line across the contours rather than contradicting the terrain.

When recreational use is intended the landscape inside the forest needs attention in the planting scheme. Hardwoods have more colour and wildlife interest to visitors than softwoods and they should feature along access routes and around picnic sites, carparks and camping areas. The woodland areas used by the public should have as much natural interest as possible. Shrub and scrub species like gorse, birch and rowan should be allowed to colonize rocky outcrops and the edges of any forest breaks which are main footpath routes. Water interest should not be planted out, but maximized by allowing for streamside glades.

With a growing body of expertise in forest landscape planning available in both the Forestry Commission and planning authorities (5.41) (5.42) there is no reason why the further development of forestry should mar the upland landscape. There is already a discernible change in public opinion towards afforestation as a result of the encouragement of greater recreational use of state forests and the forest landscape improvements undertaken by the Commission. The danger exists that crude, utilitarian planting by an irresponsible minority in the private sector could negate the advances which have been achieved by the industry in general in recent years. If this proves to be the case there is no doubt that the planting of new land should be brought under planning control.

References

5.1   DOWER, J., *National Parks in England and Wales,* Ministry of Town and Country Planning, Cmd. 6628, HMSO, 1945.

5.2   LAURIE, I.C., ROBINSON, D.G., TRAILL, A.L. and WAGER, J.F., *Landscape Evaluation* (Eds.), Centre for Urban and Regional Research, University of Manchester, 1976.

5.3   LOWENTHAL, D. and PRINCE, H.C., 'English Landscape Tastes', *Geographical Review*, 55, 1965.

5.4   LAURIE, I.C., ROBINSON, D.G., TRAILL, A.L. and WAGER, J.F., (Eds.), *op. cit.*

5.5   ECKBO, G., *The Landscape We See*, McGraw-Hill, 1969.

5.6   LAURIE, I.C., ROBINSON, D.G., TRAILL, A.L. and WAGER, J.F., *op. cit.*

5.7   *Ibid.*

5.8   ZETTER, J.A. 'Application of Potential Surface Analysis to Rural Planning', *Journal of Royal Town Planning Institute*, 60, 2, February, 1974.

5.9   MINISTRY OF TOWN AND COUNTRY PLANNING, *Memorandum on the Preservation of Trees and Woodlands*, HMSO, 1949.

5.10   DOWER, J., *op. cit.*

5.11   MINISTRY OF TOWN AND COUNTRY PLANNING, *Report of the National Parks Committee (England and Wales)*, Cmd. 7121, HMSO, 1947.

5.12   SCOTTISH NATIONAL PARKS COMMITTEE, *National Parks and the Conservation of Nature in Scotland*, Department of Health for Scotland, Cmd. 7235, HMSO, 1947.

5.13   MINISTRY OF TOWN AND COUNTRY PLANNING, *Report of the National Parks Committee (England and Wales)*, *op. cit.*

5.14   DEPARTMENT OF THE ENVIRONMENT, *Long Term Population Distribution in Great Britain—A Study*, HMSO, 1971.

5.15   COUNTRYSIDE COMMISSION, *The Planning of the Coastline*, HMSO, 1970.

5.16   DOWER, J., *op. cit.*, p. 13.

5.17   WESTMACOTT, R. and WORTHINGTON, T., *New Agricultural Landscapes*, Countryside Commission, 1974.

5.18   LAURIE, I.C., ROBINSON, D.G., TRAILL, A.L. and WAGER, J.F., *op. cit.*

5.19   MINISTRY OF HOUSING AND LOCAL GOVERNMENT, *Development Plans: A Manual on Form and Content*, HMSO, 1970.

5.20   SHERWOOD FOREST STUDY GROUP, *Sherwood Forest Study*, Nottinghamshire CC, 1974.

5.21   COUNTRYSIDE COMMISSION, *Advisory Notes on National Park Plans*, CCP. 81, Countryside Commission, 1974, p. 1.

5.22   DEPARTMENT OF THE ENVIRONMENT, *Report of the National Park Policies Review Committee*, HMSO, 1974.

5.23   *Ibid.*, p. 54.

5.24   *Ibid.*, p. 11.

5.25   DEPARTMENT OF THE ENVIRONMENT, Circular 4/76, HMSO, 1976.

5.26   LEOPOLD, L.B., CLARKE, F.E., HANSHAW, B.B. and BALSLEY, J.R., *A Procedure for Evaluating Environmental Impact*, U.S. Department of Interior, Geological Survey Circular 645, 1971.

5.27   DOBRY, G., *Review of the Development Control System (Final Report)*, Department of the Environment, HMSO, 1975.

5.28   DEPARTMENT OF THE ENVIRONMENT, *Planning Control over Mineral Working*, HMSO, 1976.

5.29   BEST, R.H., 'The Changing Land-Use Structure of Britain', *Town and Country Planning*, 44, 3, March, 1976.

5.30   FAIRBROTHER, N., *New Lives, New Landscapes*, Architectural Press, 1970; Penguin Books, 1972.

5.31   MINISTRY OF AGRICULTURE, FISHERIES AND FOOD, *Food from Our Own Resources*, Cmnd. 6020, HMSO, 1975.

5.32   DENNIS, A., 'Agricultural Land Classification in England and Wales', *Journal of Royal Town Planning Institute*, 62, 2, February, 1976.

5.33 COUNCIL FOR THE PROTECTION OF RURAL ENGLAND, *Landscape—the Need for a Public Voice*, CPRE, July, 1975.

5.34 WESTMACOTT, R. and WORTHINGTON, T., *op. cit.*

5.35 MINISTRY OF HOUSING AND LOCAL GOVERNMENT, *Farm Buildings and the Countryside*, HMSO, 1969.

5.36 MERCER, I., 'The Role of Local Government in Rural Conservation' in WARREN, A. and GOLDSMITH, F.B., (Eds.). *Conservation in Practice*, Wiley, 1974.

5.37 WESTMACOTT, R. and WORTHINGTON, T., *op. cit.*, Appendix A.

5.38 COUNCIL FOR THE PROTECTION OF RURAL ENGLAND, *op. cit.*

5.39 FAIRBROTHER, N., *op. cit.*, p. 22.

5.40 MINISTRY OF AGRICULTURE, FISHERIES AND FOOD, *Forest Policy*, HMSO, 1972.

5.41 CROWE, S., *Forestry in the Landscape*, Forestry Commission Booklet No. 18, HMSO, 1966.

5.42 MILES, R., *Forestry in the English Landscape*, Faber & Faber, 1967.

Further reading

CLOUT, H.D., *Rural Geography*, Pergamon Press, 1972.

CROWE, S., *Forestry in the Landscape*, Forestry Commission Booklet No. 18, HMSO, 1966.

DEPARTMENT OF ENVIRONMENT, *Sinews for Survival—A Report on the Management of Natural Resources*, HMSO, 1972.

FAIRBROTHER, N., *New Lives, New Landscapes*, Architectural Press, 1970; Penguin Books, 1972.

GREGORY, R., *The Price of Amenity*, Macmillan, 1971.

SMITH, P.J., (Ed.), *The Politics of Physical Resources*, Penguin Books, 1975.

WARREN, A. and GOLDSMITH, F.B., (Eds.), *Conservation in Practice*, Wiley, 1974.

WELLER, J.B., *Modern Agriculture and Rural Planning*, Architectural Press, 1967.

WESTMACOTT, R. and WORTHINGTON, T., *New Agricultural Landscapes*, Countryside Commission, 1974.

CHAPTER SIX

Recreation and Tourism in the Countryside

Judy White

Introduction

Recreation and tourism are not the only demands to which the countryside is presently subjected. There are clamours from the city dweller for its use for agriculture, commercial timber production, water conservation and mineral working, and these conflicts of interest are illustrated throughout this book. This Chapter stresses time and again the indivisibility of recreation from other conflict areas, and the ever increasing need for its policies to be part of the political arena, and to be coordinated and harmonized with other rural land uses.

This Chapter aims to be problem-orientated, using the necessary factual background to illustrate the development of, and changes in, policies and problems. In the second section we trace the development of the use of the countryside as a recreational resource, and examine the influences generally held to be important in this—rising affluence, mobility, non-work time, and improved education. The most recent information available on the effects of the energy crisis on the pattern of recreation is also examined.

The third section considers whether the legislative framework has been adequate to deal with the problems which have arisen. It covers the major post-war landmarks in development planning and attempts to assess their impact on recreation planning; it also examines the relative failure of the National Parks Act of 1949, prior to discussion of the overall effects of the Countryside Acts. The 1949 Act's concern with protection rather than recreational use was not entirely overcome by the 1968 Countryside Act. In many ways, the 1968 legislation was simplistic, in terms of single purpose recreation areas. But there are some important questions to ask. Indeed, are country parks even necessary? Why are they provided? What advantages have they over urban parks? Does the user identify with them? Do they provide the variety of opportunity which some users want? Informal recreation must be a partner with other uses, sometimes primary, sometimes secondary. These wider questions should be taken up in Structure Plans, but the new system as at present used in our statutory planning processes seems to have helped little to improve overall examination of recreation problems.

Using the legislative framework as a background, the fourth section looks at the agencies of provision, their cooperation and policy-making. The major agencies are examined and an attempt made to see how far coordination occurs between them. This takes us into a review of Government Departments, Commissions, Councils and Authorities of various kinds. The very different organizational situation of Local Government is also discussed; stress is laid on the need to re-orientate recreation policy and place it on an equal footing with other policy areas.

The next part of the chapter looks at some new directions in recreation planning theory and the potential importance of behavioural work. The 'romantic', 'middle class' view of the countryside plays its part in attracting people to the countryside for their leisure, but there are problems in discovering and analyzing people's motives for seeking and using the countryside. Once again, there are some important questions to ask. Would it be useful to know how vital is the natural countryside *per se* in fulfilling needs? Or could needs be met by town based 'artificially created' countryside? Are new experiences required? Do we know how far the community visualizes the *existence* of a problem or set of problems in planning, using or managing the countryside for recreation? How do we best resolve the conflicts inherent in countryside recreation planning?

Finally, some thought is given to ways and means of improving policy and reducing conflict. The contribution of the White Paper on Sport and Recreation, August 1975, is assessed, and we consider how far it is possible to mobilize political opinion at national level as opposed to community level. It is concluded that much more work needs to be done to assess the significant areas of potential change before a new organization to coordinate and consolidate present policies is contemplated. The scale and nature of changes in recreation and its relationship to the countryside must be more deeply considered than has yet been done.

Emergent problems

Until the economic crisis of the mid 1970s, the most important influence on the growth of the use of the countryside for recreation was change in the levels of expectation of the user. The many other influences responsible for this have often been repeated but rarely adequately examined: rising affluence, mobility, and the increase in non-work time, as well as improved education giving increased awareness. They are in themselves welcome but in their environmental effects they must be considered as a mixed blessing. Clearly countryside recreation is influenced to some degree by the same factors that have led to an increase in participation in all forms of recreation activity.

On the whole there is agreement about the main socio-economic factors which have affected the growth of countryside recreation: they relate to time and money. Although the actual number of hours worked has not diminished radically, over the last 20 years, the five day week has now become standard in most jobs and holidays have increased considerably. In 1951 only 1% of manual workers had 3 weeks annual holiday; by 1971 67% enjoyed this length of time. The increasing affluence of the large majority of the population over the same period is illustrated by the fact that average earnings of manual workers in 1971 were 3½ times those of 1951, whilst retail prices only doubled in the same period.

What has actually encouraged more people to participate in a wide range of informal recreational activities is not so clear, although type of occupation and length of formal education are usually cited as two of the clearest indicators. The data for the Pilot National Recreation Survey (6.1) published in 1967 were collected in 1965: it has remained a pilot, with no full scale national survey being carried out since. These data showed that in general those who are in managerial or professional occupations, and those who have continued formal education beyond the statutory age, were more likely to have more numerous and more active pursuits with some leaning toward countryside recreation. An upward trend in the proportion of the population undergoing further and higher education is obvious, despite changes in the numbers in the relevant age groups: the number of university students almost trebled between 1951 and 1971, and the number of children undergoing full-time further education quadrupled in the same period.

Another important factor, which like others looked at here has been thoroughly discussed by Patmore (6.2), seems undoubtedly to have been the role of the media, especially television, in developing a wider awareness of the countryside in general and the opportunities it offers in particular for recreational use by the urban dweller. Television has a deep influence on the attitudes and tastes of its audience and has helped to promote an interest in a wide range of activities. This has become evident in the amazing surge in the number and variety of non-vocational adult education courses run by education authorities and *ad hoc* organizations, in specialisms such as natural history, ecology, archaeology, the study of historic buildings, and even rural planning, as well as an equivalent development in the membership of active recreation organizations. For example, membership of the National Trust rose from 25,000 in 1950 to 350,000 in 1972; the County Naturalists' Trusts had 850 members in 1950, 75,000 in 1972; whilst the Ramblers Association membership grew from 8,800 in 1950 to 25,800 by 1972. Phenomenal increases in membership in the same period have been experienced by the Camping Club (13,800 to 122,500) and Caravan Club (6400 to 121,500), and Royal Yachting Association (personal membership 1400 to 33,500, affiliated clubs 501 to 1559). One of the few active recreation clubs to suffer a reverse in trends was, significantly, the Cyclists Touring Club, whose membership fell steadily over the twenty years from 56,300 in 1950, to 18,700 in 1971, but with signs of a revival in 1972 with a rise for the first time to 19,600.

The most recent information available on recreation habits is that from the 1973 General Household Survey (6.3). Carried out annually by the Office of Population Censuses and Surveys (OPCS), in 1973 it included questions on leisure activities. Over 21,000 respondents were asked what leisure activities they had participated in during the four weeks prior to interview. Veal (6.4) has recently undertaken some analysis of these data, and he concluded: "Despite the few questions devoted to leisure in the General Household Survey it nevertheless tells us a great deal about the leisure activities of the population. The last national surveys of leisure activities, *the Pilot National Recreation Survey* and the Government Social Survey work resulting in *Planning for Leisure* (6.5) were carried out in

1965. Since then a number of regional surveys have been carried out, but very little on a national scale. As a consequence users of such survey data—Local Authority planning departments in particular—are basing plans and projections on out-of-date information. The GHS is the most up to date information base we have on national recreation patterns." The GHS gives information on overall levels of participation in different activities, and on the relationships between participation and various social, economic, demographic, and general factors. On a percentage basis, these data show that the most popular activities are home-based and dining and drinking out. 'Informal recreation' is next, including 'visits to the countryside and coast', undertaken by one-third of respondents. If analyzed in terms of number of visits per 1000 population per year, this reveals an average of only 10 per 1000, although for actual participants the frequency is higher. But whichever measure is used, social and home based activities are much more popular than any activities partly or wholly sponsored by public agencies. Within such activities, 'the arts' are less popular than sport or informal outdoor recreation.

The relative popularity of various informal recreation activities can also be deduced from the GHS. The 'visit to the countryside' is the most popular single activity, but whilst this "should not lead us to believe that on any one summer Sunday afternoon the majority of the population are driving around the countryside . . . the scale of the activity should not be underestimated".

There are an estimated 4000 trips per 1000 population per annum, or 148 million nationally; these are person trips and the actual number of vehicle trips involved depends on average car occupancy. 49 million adult (over 16) visits are made to historic houses, and 100 million visits to the coast annually. Most of these are made by families with relatively high incomes (£80 + per week, 1973 figures). Occupation affects participation quite considerably; non-manual, professional and managerial workers with above-average length of education undertake much more informal outdoor recreation than manual and unskilled workers, this often despite longer actual, as opposed to official, working hours.

The decade of the 1960s witnessed the most notable rises in affluence and private mobility. Consumer expenditure, at current prices, doubled, whilst job opportunities and incomes rose steadily. In 1961 there were 5.9 million registered cars and vans, and by 1971 this had doubled to 12 million, and they were being used 1000 miles more on average each year. In some work undertaken in 1974 for the

Countryside Commission for England and Wales, and summarized in *Recreation News Supplement,* September 1975 (6.6), Terence Bendixson postulated that the cheapness of petrol as being a more important factor in the growth of motoring than the development of a comprehensive motorway system, as the cost of petrol fell in real terms by 10% over the decade, despite nine separate price increases between 1968 and 1973.

In 1972, oil accounted for nearly half of Britain's primary energy. But as industry and home heating account for over three-quarters of the primary energy consumed in Britain, with cars and motor cycles only using 12%, it seems there is more scope for energy conservation outside the transport sector than within it. From this, the amount of fuel used for recreation motoring is likely to be a very small part of total national energy consumption. Bendixson used data from the 1972-3 National Travel Survey (6.7) to calculate that car-owning households were likely to have ventured out for recreation purposes about once a fortnight throughout the year, though only once a month at weekends, totalling 800 miles of day-tripping to all destinations over the year. This means the total trip might involve only about 30 miles of driving. If other classes, 'sports', 'personal social visits' and 'holidays and leisure trips' are included under the general heading of recreation, the travel attributable to recreation is raised threefold. Further, all this recreation by car was calculated to account for only between 0.4 and 1.3% of national energy consumption.

If the trends in car ownership and recreation established in the 1960s had continued through the 1970s and into the 1980s, it could well be expected that by 1985 recreation motoring might well account for as much as half the total motoring mileage in 1972. This accords with Elson's view that the kind of people buying cars in the future would be 'highly active' types with an urge to go motoring (6.8). But at the same time, very many people were to continue to be without cars. Between 1969 and 1972 the percentage of households without cars fell by only 2 points, from 49 to 47, and it has been forecast by Hillman (6.9) that even in 1981 6 out of 10 people would be without driving licences. Bendixson (6.10) examined the evidence for changes in travel patterns in 1974, and concluded that in general a slow down in the growth of car ownership and motoring mileages was likely, with recreation motoring being more affected than commuting and commercial driving.

The summer of 1974 therefore saw motorists driving less but making greater use of low-cost recreation facilities such as country parks. The implications of this are considerable. They present further evidence of the importance of locating informal countryside recreation facilities in more accessible areas nearer to towns and cities, where good public transport systems exist or can be reasonably easily developed. The usefulness of much green belt land in this respect has been often cited, but as yet there is little large scale development of new facilities in such areas. The Countryside Commission's experiments in Cheshire and Hertfordshire to monitor some of the advantages and problems of recreation in urban fringe areas may help Local Authorities to devise imaginative projects which are not extravagant of limited time and money. The Commission may find it necessary also to look more critically at those schemes which do not include an effective public transport system and alter its grant-aiding system to positively encourage those schemes which show a high level of accessibility within the context of a regional public transport plan.

A long term energy assessment made by the Organization for Economic Development led to the conclusion that the mid-1970s pattern of recreation traffic flows, vehicle registrations, and petrol consumption was a hiccup in well established trends rather than the beginnings of structural change. The hiccups however could continue intermittently and tend to be widespread in their effects. Thus the reductions in private traffic in National Parks may only be temporary, and measures will still need to be taken to conserve the natural environment and limit vehicular access. It may be opportune to re-examine the use of previously uneconomic railway lines within National Parks and see whether they could be made convenient and useful for residents and visitors on a much wider scale than the already popular narrow gauge railways. Bendixson's concluding remarks are apt: "The new conditions are a stimulus to provide alternatives to cars for getting into the country, an incentive to use Green Belts for recreation rather than just as barriers to development, and a further motivation to limit the ugly proliferation of cars in national parks. They are also likely to focus greater attention on the desirability of providing for informal recreation within towns. 'Tis an ill wind that blows nobody any good' ".

The changes in the use of the countryside for recreation reflect almost entirely changes within an urban based society. But the demands on the resources of the countryside also come from within the rural environment, especially from the developments in agricultural technology. Government support for upland farming continues to be essential both in economic terms and to maintain the quality of landscapes for recreation. Amalgamation of holdings and the improvement of road transport have been instrumental in accelerating the loss of working populations in upland areas, whilst there have been similar if slower trends in more intensively farmed areas.

In parallel with a decline in farming populations, there has been an increase in the numbers of visitors. It is rarely possible for any farmer to continuously supervise his farm, and this has often led to considerable wear and tear in the vicinity of popular areas, especially on parks, gates, stiles and walls. It is commonly felt that farmers have not received sufficient protection from such visitor pressures, and antagonism has too easily built up. Visitors who behave badly on dual purpose land—to which they have access by custom or agreement—are in a minority and usually do not appreciate the consequences of their actions. Improving knowledge and awareness must go some way to change the situation but other measures are also crucial, such as the development of new management techniques and warden services.

Many farmers in National Parks have for long benefited from staying visitors and tourists; a great many provide accommodation and in some parks, where such provision is traditional, the benefits of so doing are well recognized. These benefits are material and psychological: "the situation makes for improved relationships between visitors and the local communities, and there can be few better ways for urban visitors to gain an appreciation of country life than as the guests of a family who work the land" (6.11).

Nevertheless, there are several important issues involved in the development of farm accommodation. Inclination of farmers to cater for visitors at all must obviously be a matter of individual choice, but those that do want to undertake this need considerable advice and assistance. Financial assistance for accommodation is available from the English and Wales Tourist Boards and from the Council for Small Industries in Rural Areas (CoSIRA), and planning advice is also available from County Planning Departments on siting, type of accommodation, and access problems.

One of the most commonly quoted results of the increasing influence of an affluent and mobile urban society on the face of the countryside is the 'second home' syndrome. The loss of farm working and other rural industrial working population has in some instances been more than offset by an increase in those who have bought houses but do not work in the area. It has been argued that allowing outsiders to buy properties is socially detrimental to the life of the community, especially as they only live in the houses occasionally and their children do not attend local schools or use local public transport. It has also been asserted that the demand for properties by 'incomers' has driven prices beyond the reach of local people, and even that this is a cause of depopulation.

Work carried out in Denbighshire (6.12), by Wye College (6.13), and the Dartington Amenity Research Trust (DART) (6.14) has shown that the situation is not always as straightforward as these arguments may suggest. Depopulation was already well established before any large scale 'property boom' started, and in general it seems that the farmhouses, cottages, and ancillary buildings that have been bought and modernized or converted were surplus to local requirements and would very likely have become derelict had there been no external demand for them. Thus they have given a new lease of life to traditional buildings, and brought money into the area in the form of improvements and repairs, as well as consumer goods and services. Full rates are paid, even if the house is rarely occupied, and most owners tend to shop locally when they are in occupation.

The situation may now be changing as in some areas demand has outstripped supply. This is especially so in National Parks within easy travelling distance of urban centres, such as the Peak District. But, in the words of the Sandford Report, "the national parks were never envisaged to be, nor should they be seen as, places suitable for commuter development . . . We recommend the adoption by park authorities of a more restrictive policy of control over new residential development outside towns than has been applied in the past, and that statistics should be kept to monitor the effects of this policy" (6.15).

There is probably more scope for the development of tourism in the countryside generally. In environmentally fragile areas the development of new facilities and the management of existing ones should be the subject of consultation between all interested agencies—the Countryside Commissions as well as the Tourist Boards and the Development Commission, and the Regional Tourist Boards. The income from tourism is quite important in many countryside as well as coastal areas which cater extensively for holiday makers, and the industry offers good prospects of opportunities for employment. The seasonality of it is becoming less pronounced as more people take more off-peak holidays and more professional and business conferences are held in rural areas. Protection of vulnerable areas may make some developments uneconomic, but it can be argued that they should be sited near large

I

urban areas, perhaps most successfully in the urban fringe, or in easily accessible areas with less environmental impact. It would be wrong, *prima facie*, to improve access to remote areas, for example by turning tracks into metalled roads, so that they become usable by the majority, whereas it would be more logical to concentrate the expansion of facilities into an area already developed with a nucleus of facilities and readily accessible.

At the same time, the countryside has still to support an expanding agriculture and a fast developing technology which is revolutionizing some long accepted practices, commercial timber production, large water conservation schemes, and more mineral working. As Davidson points out (6.16), "the consequences of increased leisure activity . . . go beyond the more immediate observable conflicts of crowded beaches or congested traffic, to affect nearly all rural interests in many different ways".

The conflict does not just come from increasing recreational use. It is noted and discussed elsewhere in this book, that some of the multifarious activities of reservoir engineers and mineral operators, as well as foresters and farmers, can and have led to dramatic changes in scenery and loss of public access. Changes at a smaller scale can be in the long term equally damaging to landscape variety—hedgerow clearance, draining of wet areas, and felling of copses. Recreation itself can cause widespread problems, especially in fragile habitats suffering from heavy use, such as sand dunes, which can become unattractive for recreation and less valuable for ecological research unless carefully managed, preferably with the aid of an agreed overall management policy.

The legislative framework

The sepia coloured photographs in rural museums today tell us something of the countryside fifty years ago: small scale, intimate, labour intensive agriculture and *static in its outlook*. Towns were still quite compact, the road system had not yet expanded to meet the demands of the motor car, and railways and canals enjoyed acceptance and use as rural transport. Agricultural methods were still traditional and forestry was, under the Forestry Commission, only just beginning to have a visual and emotional impact on the landscape.

It was only a few years later that this position began to change. In the 1930s towns had begun to spread out along main roads, absorbing villages and converting some into dormitories for the new breed of urban commuters. The 1932 Town and Country Planning Act, inadequate though it was in encouraging Local Authorities to use the system of local planning schemes, which were clumsy and ineffectual, did save some of the countryside from the effects of sporadic building and forced up the standards of some development.

The two main planning elements which were to affect the appearance and use of the countryside after the Second World War were the 1947 Town and Country Planning Act and the 1949 National Parks Act. These were considerable achievements at the time. But the glaring weakness of both Acts showed quite quickly. The main problems of the 1947 Act in relation to countryside stemmed from the 'white land' areas which were to stay generally in their existing uses. If these uses were agriculture or forestry, they were not 'development' within the terms of the Act and so were outside planning control. But it was impossible to plan the countryside comprehensively under such a system: it was easier to develop communications and settlements in isolation and only be concerned with agricultural land when it was changing into industrial or urban use. The inadequacies of the legislation were highlighted by the status of the Ministry of Town and Country Planning at Central Government level. The Ministry, newly established, was badly placed to develop a power base whereby it could coordinate the disparate and wide ranging land use activities of other Ministries, especially Transport, Agriculture, and Trade. The most noticeable omission was the inability of the Planning Ministry to strongly influence agriculture to overcome the omissions of the statutory process, which would have helped to improve development planning, especially at local level.

The main successes of the 1947 Act must lie with the control system, where development in the wrong places was prevented, and where better development was achieved than otherwise would have been. But this did not make it a popular system, and after 1950 Local Planning Authorities who wanted to improve design detailing had to work more by persuasion. In that year, when Dalton was Minister of Local Government and Planning, a General Development Order took out of control many smaller items of development, especially related to residential building, and excluded agricultural buildings. There were increasing problems of large scale developments in the countryside. Claims were made of the importance of minerals such as opencast coal, limestone, gravel and clay to the national economy. The arguments of national need had to be weighed against potential major change and damage to landscape character. Sometimes, permission was given with very optimistic conditions for tipping, dust control, landscaping and ultimate restoration. It has been argued that if the Government had been persuaded to extend the concept of the Ironstone Restoration Fund, under the Mineral Workings Act 1951, to some other types of minerals, it could have saved many planning authorities from subsequent problems of dereliction left behind by mineral operators whose financial resources could not match their restoration responsibilities.

Major public developments—such as power stations, reservoirs, overhead lines, and defence establishments—were usually only subject to consultation with Local Authorities and received their approval from their own Ministers. This was a startling position which only exacerbated attempts to integrate them with local planning factors.

This brief analysis of the immediate post-war planning legislation has aimed to provide a framework for discussing the 1949 National Parks and Access to the Countryside Act, which, although full of good intentions, was very clumsy, both in title and length. It had 115 sections, and the 1947 Planning Act only five more. The 1947 Act did establish the idea of planning as not being solely concerned with urban problems, and tried to get a balance between social, economic and environmental interests in the countryside. But it was not primarily equipped to resolve the major issues in rural conflict and it suffered above all from an emphasis on use zoning rather than management.

From the powers to protect special parts of the countryside in the 1949 Act have come ten National Parks covering about 9% of the area of England and Wales (the proposal for an eleventh national park in Mid-Wales was rejected in July 1973); plus 33 designated Areas of Outstanding Natural Beauty, forming another 9%. If to these areas are added Areas of Great Landscape Value submitted in County Council Development Plans, and areas of approved or proposed Green Belt (not that these are often or necessarily of high quality landscape in their own right) about 40% of England and Wales has some degree of extra statutory protection in terms of its character and landscape quality. There was no equivalent legislation for National Parks in Scotland after the war. The Scottish National Parks and amenity lobbies failed to convince the Scottish Office about the desirability of new legislation and no Scottish Bill was ever introduced (6.17). However, five areas became the subject of a Secretary of State directive which required Local Planning Authorities to refer planning applications within the areas to his Department for consideration, acting in fact as a monitoring safeguard.

The position of the National Parks in England and Wales has been thoroughly examined by a variety of critics and supporters (6.18). Overall, they are rather like the curate's egg. This can only be understood by examining the way they were established and run and what powers and finance were given to them. The Government paper, the Hobhouse Report (1947), which preceded the Act, advocated a 50-50 membership between Ministers' nominees and Local Government representatives, with an independent chairman. The Act produced a ratio of two-thirds local government representation to one-third Minister's nominees, so that National Park administration from the outset was firmly embedded in the Local Government system. Only the Lake District and Peak District National Parks were given powers to precept on their constituent authorities. Thus the parks have never been 'national' in the sense either of being subject to a unified policy directive from the centre or in their land ownership, as they all remain predominately in private ownership and management.

The parks had very little money given to them to meet their dual responsibilities, 'to preserve and enhance the natural beauty of the national parks', and 'to provide their enjoyment by the public'. It has usually been assumed that these two conflicting responsibilities can be reconciled, but there is scepticism in some quarters that they ever can be satisfactorily so. To date, much more has been achieved in protection than in positive visitor management and provision. For example, provision of facilities such as picnic sites and car parks, and caravan and camping sites, developed slowly and haphazardly. Information services, which by educating the visitor may encourage him to help protect it, were also poorly developed and it took a decade to establish a comprehensive wardening service to cover the parks. Only at the end of the 1960s did the total annual expenditure on parks top £1 million.

By the late 1950s, the relatively new pressure of recreation on the countryside was being felt most keenly in the National Parks. The early enthusiasts had envisaged the parks as 'havens of peace' for walkers, ramblers and those who wanted 'to get away from it all'; but they were becoming inundated at weekends as urban dwellers jammed their roads and swarmed over their fells. The most accessible areas of coastline, urban fringes and common land were beginning to experience pressures. Anxiety was beginning to be voiced, and the mid-1960s saw the predictions of Dower's *Fourth Wave* (6.19). In the same year, some tentative ideas of the possible scale and range of activities and their impacts were articulated in the Pilot National Recreation Survey, followed by regional breakdowns in 1969.

It was difficult for planners to know how to approach these problems under the 1947 Act, which carefully defined development and did not consider land management in development plans at all. National Parks had little better guidance, with emphasis on protection still being paramount. Agricultural development was still mainly outside planning control, but there were heartening signs of improvement as some planning officers managed to negotiate voluntary consultation with farmers through the National Farmers Union to try and improve standards by screening buildings and improving their designs. There was also concern about forestry, electricity lines, advertising, and derelict land. Consultation methods were developed by some planning authorities with forestry interests to enable planners to comment on major planting activities. These arrangements varied considerably between Counties, as did their success and the opinions as to how far they went into broadening the approach towards comprehensive resource planning.

This type of debate was encouraged by developments in planning education. Immediate post-war planners had been largely stolen from other disciplines and professions and they had developed skills to deal with the urgent priorities of the time, mainly urban planning and design, zoning, density, and so on. But planners were now emerging from courses of which rural planning was a part, even if not yet a major specialization. Local Authorities were also beginning to employ other specialists in their own right to work alongside physical planners, such as sociologists, statisticians, geographers, economists and ecologists. All were using their resources to make the existing legislation work, but it was increasingly obvious that it was outworn and that some fundamental and radical changes were needed.

When eventually the new Countryside Acts, of 1967 for Scotland and 1968 for England and Wales, were passed recreational problems had multiplied enormously. The Acts were intended to help the Local Authorities alleviate the problems by providing new facilities throughout the countryside, such as country parks, picnic sites, and camping sites, and improving access with the aid of grants, which were also available to private bodies. There was also an 'amenity clause' for public bodies, 'to have regard to amenity' in their projected developments in all parts of the countryside, which most had already been doing before anyway. A completely new Countryside Commission was set up for Scotland whilst that for England and Wales developed out of the National Parks Commission of the 1949 Act.

The end of the decade began to show that although the Countryside Acts had clarified possible programmes of action in the areas outside National Parks, they had done virtually nothing to ease problems of policy and administration within them which were not solely dependent on Local Authority initiative. Local interests were not being given adequate weight in National Park planning, and there was a feeling that stringent control of development imposed costs on local residents whilst denying them increased opportunities for employment (6.20). For example, farmers were not actively encouraged to take part in recreation and tourism developments to supplement their incomes; second home owners and even commuters might adversely affect the supply of houses available to local residents. Also, park authorities have been confronted by severe administrative problems and costs. Most found it difficult to raise enough revenue, even with Exchequer help, to meet their considerable administrative costs, and contributing authorities often resent the use of local finance to meet visitors' needs. There had been little overall coordinated Central Government policy, and even less enforcement of it, whilst local park planning continued to be haphazard and very reliant on normal County Council planning staff, who serviced the parks on a part time basis (except in the Peak District).

These and other problems were examined by the Review Committee, chaired by Lord Sandford, set up in 1971 by the Government (see below). At the same time, the more urgent problems of finding new administrative arrangements were tackled in discussions by the Countryside Commission (England and Wales) and the County Councils Association as a result of separate proposals for Local Government reorganization under the 1972 Local Government Act. The administrative reforms for National Parks came into effect in April 1974. The two existing Planning Boards (for the Peak and the Lake District) remained unchanged. In the remaining eight parks, there is now a single executive committee, even when there is more than one County Council involved, and this has a considerable number of planning powers allotted to it. Each park authority has appointed a National Parks Officer to serve the committee and to prepare a plan (similar to a Structure Plan) to outline strategic policies for the conservation of resources, the zoning of different intensities of use, and traffic management within three years of the authority's establishment. This is in response to the criticisms of the inadequacies of present policies for planning and management, and it is also hoped that interpretative programmes will be developed on a much larger scale than previously.

The new arrangements for meeting the costs of administering the National Parks are part of the overall re-organization of Local Government finance. The system of cost-related specific grants payable towards certain facilities and services in National Parks has been replaced by a supplementary block grant towards all the capital and revenue expenditure involved in administering and managing them. This is to comply with a Ministerial undertaking that the 'lion's share' of national park expenditure would be met by the Exchequer, and as a result the Countryside Commission and National Park authorities have been relieved of the burden of work associated with close scrutiny of detailed costs arising from the operation of a cost-related grant scheme, thus giving more scope for developing better priorities and programmes.

The Report of the National Park Policies Review Committee, under Lord Sandford, was presented in November 1973. It examined the two original purposes of National Parks in some detail, and came to the conclusions that their first purpose as stated by John Dower and in legislation—the preservation and enhancement of natural beauty—remains entirely valid and appropriate, but that the second purpose—the promotion of public enjoyment—needs to be reinterpreted and qualified, "because it is now evident that excessive or suitable use may destroy the very qualities which attract people to the parks". Then: "We have no doubt that where the conflict between the two purposes, which has always been inherent, becomes acute, the first one must prevail in order that the beauty and ecological qualities of the national parks may be maintained" (6.21).

Some of the members of the Committee felt there was a need for a new procedure to identify and protect areas of the very highest quality of landscape in the existing National Parks and also perhaps outside them. The first and supreme objective of policy for these relatively small areas would be to conserve their environmental qualities, and public enjoyment "of a quiet and conguous nature" would be a secondary purpose. These "national heritage areas" would emphasize the obligation "to safeguard for succeeding generations the outstandingly beautiful landscapes which we ourselves inherited" (6.22). Others felt such a designation to be inapt, and were apprehensive that the consequences of devoting special attention and resources to these small areas might be to depreciate the remainder of the National Parks where the needs for protection and positive management are no less.

Facilities for the kind of recreation which less active or less 'country minded' visitors to the countryside want to see are being developed by public and private enterprise. Whether the provision of country parks under the 1968 Countryside Act will relieve pressure significantly on National Parks is open to considerable doubt. They are more likely to slow down the rate of growth of pressure than divert it altogether, but whether they are the most appropriate instrument for this also remains to be seen.

Country parks were first proposed in the 1966 White Paper 'Leisure in the Countryside' to act as attractive surroundings in a countryside setting not too far from towns. Even before this time there was considerable evidence of the shortage of such open space, although there were no statistics to indicate the extent of the shortage or what future needs might be; the Countryside in 1970 Conferences were instrumental in drawing attention to this wider problem. But there was disquiet among landowners, farmers, and naturalists about the damage being done by visitors: existing open spaces eroded and disfigured by sheer feet pressure; urban fringe farmers suffering from trespass and vandalism; and wildlife disturbed by trampling, noise and fire. There was no coherent policy at either central or local levels to help rectify these problems, nor any official body with powers to coordinate countryside recreation on a national basis.

'Leisure in the Countryside' is one of the few remaining products of the Ministry of Land and Natural Resources (1965-67). This White Paper (6.23) had three policy objectives for country parks:

(a) To make it easier for those seeking recreation to enjoy their leisure in the open without travelling too far and adding to congestion on roads.

(b) To ease the pressure on the more remote and solitary places.

(c) To reduce the risk of damage to the countryside, aesthetic as well as physical, which often comes about when people simply settle down for an hour or a day when it suits them 'somewhere in the countryside' to the inconvenience and expense of those who live and work in the locality.

These objectives mirror almost exactly the problems as iterated by the landowners, farmers, and naturalists; they are barely a positive encouragement to recreational use. The defensiveness of the initial idea was perhaps an inevitable situation, but much of country park provision has had a positive birth. Whether it has thereby intensified traffic congestion, shifted trespass from one area to another, and in a situation where supply and demand are so unbalanced, managed to protect more vulnerable areas, cannot be yet satisfactorily answered.

The 1968 Countryside Act for England and Wales stresses two aspects of the policy for country park provision: (a) "the location of the site in relation to an urban or built-up area" and (b) "the availability and adequacy of existing facilities for the enjoyment of the countryside by the public", that is, to ensure that the park is conveniently located for the people it is intended to serve, and that there must be a demonstrable need for the park.

The Countryside Commission felt that its first aim in deciding on a national policy was to define certain criteria that it would bear in mind when asked to advise the Minister on applications for grant aid under the terms of Section 2 (9) of the Countryside Act. This grant was 75% of the loan charges incurred by the Local Authority for expenditure on land acquisition, erection or repair of buildings, capital expenditure, litter collection, and wardening.

These broad headings were made more explicit in Section 7 which refers to "facilities and services for the enjoyment or convenience of the public, including meals and refreshment, parking places for vehicles, shelters and lavatory accommodation," and more generally "facilities and services for open-air recreation." The criteria for grant and recognition added to the Countryside Act definition of a country park: "a park or pleasure ground for the purpose of providing, or improving opportunities for the enjoyment of the countryside by the public" by adding "an area of land, or land and water, normally not less than 25 acres in extent, designed to offer to the public with or without charge, opportunity for recreational activities in the countryside".

Such flexible criteria were deliberate, and designed to redress the defensive outlook of the White Paper and Act and encourage creativity and variety. But these sidestepped the issue of the variety of need in different areas of the country. The 1968 Act gave the Countryside Commission power to acquire land, but it has little effective power to set up country parks in a region if it felt shortages were apparent, although it can make its views known. This issue would be faced if there was a limitation on grants such that choices between schemes could not be made by considering just *local* need and the intrinsic character of each scheme.

There has been considerable unevenness in the response of Local Government to the incentives provided by the Countryside Act. This is above all a reflection of the strength of the committee and staff organization for planning and management within Local Authorities. Counties such as Hampshire, Durham, Nottinghamshire, Lancashire and Cheshire set up special teams under the County Clerk, Land Agent or Planning Officer to develop and implement countryside recreation schemes.

None of the Commission's attempts at policy making comes anywhere near to answering the problems of the original concept of country parks: can they operate effectively as multi-purpose leisure areas, and provide the variety of opportunity which some users want? Are country parks even necessary? What advantages have they over urban parks? Does the user identify specifically with country parks *per se* or are they seen within the general umbrella of outdoor recreation opportunity?

There are other problem areas outside national and country parks which are dealt with in the 1968 Countryside Act. These are principally concerned with management, and the Countryside Commission was given powers of experimentation to look at crucial problems in a more enterprising way than was previously possible. Traffic management schemes built on the original Goyt Valley experiments (6.24) are now beginning to be a useful management tool. The Upland Management Experiment, a joint enterprise with the Lake District Planning Board, covering a third of the National Park and under the control of a full-time project officer, and the Bollin Valley project in an urban fringe area of Cheshire, are designed to test methods of helping farmers to repair damage by visitors and to find out under what conditions they would be prepared to provide more or improved access for visitors, as well as to explore the scope for joint action to enhance the appearance of the countryside. The experiment has now been extended to part of the London urban fringe in Hertfordshire.

The introduction of Structure Planning to replace the Development Plan system in the 1970s has had little immediate and tangible effect on recreation planning. Only infrequently have Local Authorities considered it a useful opportunity to consider the relationship of their recreational policies (if any) to the overall objectives of the Authority, or to reappraise their provision and use of facilities. This contrasted strongly with those key sectors such as transport where it was common for numerous surveys and alternative strategies to be investigated and, less commonly, submitted to public examination.

The mid-1960s saw the emergence of groups with single-purpose objectives each determined to follow their policies for the furtherance of their rural interests. This situation was well articulated in three conferences on the 'Countryside in 1970', held in 1963, 1965, and 1970. The sectional interests of nature conservation, water supply, forestry, agriculture, and recreation were each willing to discuss the overall problems of countryside planning and specific ones of coordination between themselves, but it was less easy to see what mechanisms existed or could be developed to alleviate them. This situation was also apparent at the 1972 Stockholm Conference on the Human Environment (6.25).

The 1970s have also seen efforts at reorganization and rationalization of rural resource agencies at national level. These have had the overall effect of either nullifying or completely superceding new 'permanent' reorganizations of the 1960s. The system of 29 River Authorities which were under the general control and advice of the Water Resources Board, created in 1963, have been replaced by 10 new Regional Water Authorities and the National Water Council, with the Water Space Amenity Commission taking over the recreation function.

The useful link of the land-based professions interested in recreation and agriculture used to come mainly from the advisory services of the Ministry of Agriculture, but these have been severely curtailed. Alongside this, the Rural Development Boards have been abolished and with them, at least for the present, the hopes for really comprehensive rural resource planning in crucial upland areas. Constant reorganization can do little to improve confidence or give long-term stability to formulate policy. In the last few years there has been a feeling of retrenchment and hardening of sectional interests.

Policy formulation

If reorganization and improved legislation have left the overall problems of integrated and workable policy virtually untouched, what else can be done? What are the roles of the agencies of provision, their attitudes and policy? How do these conflict and how does this conflict stultify progress towards real integration?

This section sets out the institutional framework for outdoor recreation and the planning problems presented by it. It considers how this framework operates and whether improvements could be made through evolution or whether revolution would provide improved policy integration.

In 1972 the House of Lords set up a Select Committee on Sport and Leisure under the chairmanship of Lord Cobham. This took evidence over seven months and produced two reports, in March and July 1973 (6.26). Essentially, it recommended that the generally established pattern of institutions should remain but with some shifts in emphasis and better coordination. National coordination could be achieved through a new Minister for Recreation, whilst at regional level there would be a strong regional organization based on the Regional Sports Councils, and at local level through statutory duties imposed on County Councils and metropolitan District Councils (in Scotland, Regional Authorities), which bodies should form district recreation committees and departments. To achieve a shift in emphasis, it was proposed to set up recreation priority areas to assist inner urban communities, and to focus, in outdoor recreation, on provision within the urban fringe and accessible to non-car owners, and in sports provision, on flexibility, cost-effectiveness, and social facilities.

In August 1975, the long delayed Government reply to this report was published as a White Paper on Sport and Recreation (6.27). The responsibility for this Paper rested with Denis Howell who, since July 1974, had been Minister of State for Sport and Recreation. This Departmental umbrella still excluded the Tourist Boards, the Forestry Commission, and the Arts Council, which remain linked to Departments other than that of the Environment. The White Paper states that the Minister will "consult regularly with Ministerial colleagues"; "hold regular meetings of chairmen and directors of relevant government agencies"; "attend meetings of the Sports Council"; "keep in close touch with" a United Kingdom Affairs Committee of the four Sports Councils; and be "willing to chair" an *ad hoc* working group of the Sports Council and the Central Council of Physical Recreation.

The regional proposals of the White Paper include "the establishment in England of a strong and unified regional machinery to consult and advise on needs and provision for sport and all forms of outdoor recreation on a region-wide basis". This would involve the replacement of Regional Sports Councils by regional councils for sport and recreation, which would advise both the Sports Council (as previously) and the Countryside Commission on broad regional priorities for grant aid. They would be able "to supply information to the Minister of State to assist him in carrying out his broad coordinating role at national level". But, amongst all this is the economic reality: there is very little capital available, and the Government "think the time is not right" to impose on Local Authorities the statutory duty, proposed by the House of Lords, to provide for recreation.

Some positive good might yet come from recognition of the present difficulties. Far from being cosily optimistic, there is a sense in which both the White Paper and the House of Lords recognize the essential need for flexibility in ideas, policy, and provision, comprehensive thinking, cost effectiveness, full use of existing resources, and especial consideration for the disadvantaged. Indeed, there is an indication that they recognize the importance of recreation in the overall quality of life: the White Paper states "when life becomes meaningful for the individual then the whole community is enriched". This would seem to be where the Government can most usefully operate coordination. If the White Paper's emphasis on the quality of life and resourcefulness can be converted into reality, then progress will indeed have been made. But it is difficult to know whether Local Authorities will have the foresight and ability to see what these opportunities are and whether they will be able to cooperate as fully with the community as will be necessary to establish "humane and resourceful *management* of a wide range of communal facilities", as Dower puts it (6.28). He stresses that many of these facilities "fall outside the fashionable programmes of big capital spending but already exist and have great potential: village halls, community centres, halls, churches, play centres, coffee bars, pubs and the like. Every town and every rural area is equipped with such inherited facilities; the need is for people—animateurs—to bring them alive to communal use".

The need for flexibility and imagination and to cut one's coat accordingly was subsequently brought home by the Sports Council in November 1975, when their Chairman outlined the austerity approach to be adopted when he presented the Council's report and accounts for the year ended March 1975. The Council is backing a low-priced sports hall produced from a design by its technical unit; Pocklington Railway Station has been converted to a sports hall at a cost of only £50,000; while conversions of disused vehicle maintenance workshops are being undertaken at South Shields, Greenwich and Southampton. Large and small Sports Council schemes are dependent on a financial injection by Local Authorities. It was the partnership which the Council created with Local Authorities which produced the rolling programme of development throughout the country, designed to meet local, regional, and national requirements. But that has now come down to a trickle and, looking beyond 1976, the Council is not very hopeful.

The wide ranging and pervasive nature of recreation is a key reason for the widely based Government interest groups. There are a number of different facets to recreation and leisure which may be interpreted as different problems by these different interest groups— the arts, sport, the countryside, adult education, youth service and so on. The most active period of consideration of needs came in the 1960s, with a whole series of reports and White Papers which heralded new legislation or increased allocation of resources: Wolfenden on Sport, Albermarle on the Youth Service, Pilkington on Broadcasting, and White Papers on the Countryside, the Arts and Tourism, and the Russell Report on Adult Education. The House of Lords Committee Report broke new ground in the 1970s with its overall concern with a policy for leisure.

Smith (6.29) points out that the issues of leisure policy have not been defined in terms of party politics and that leisure has not been a live political issue. Commercial and industrial lobbies have not been very influential, except perhaps in broadcasting. Further: "cause groups have been active on behalf of the young, client groups active in the arts, and interest groups (especially professional physical educationalists) active in sport. These groups have not aggregated into a coalition although recreational administrators have begun to do so. One important way of demonstrating the 'significant discrepancy' has been to advance research, especially to demonstrate which groups are in the most need. As yet there has been no breakthrough in developing new strategies of access to recreation—in the arts for the working classes, and in sport for the socially deprived".

Of Central Government Departments, three have a direct interest in leisure policy: the Department of Education and Science (DES), the Department of Employment (DE), and the Department of the Environment (DOE). The Department of Education has had a long connection and interest with its concern in adult education, physical education, and the youth service. It has placed great reliance on Local Authorities and voluntary organizations as far as decisions about educational content and provision are concerned, within the resource constraints set by the Department. It has indirect responsibility for the arts due to the existence of the independent Arts Council, but there is much greater involvement in setting policy in national museums and libraries. The responsibility for sport used, in the 1960s, to be associated with the Youth Service under one Minister in the DES, until it was transferred to the DOE.

The Department of Employment has become more involved in overall leisure policy with the growth of national incomes policies, as norms for pay increases have had to take account of the working week and annual holidays. Before this intervention, the character of the normal working week and the overall working year had been left to negotiations between unions and employees.

There are several other Government Departments which have an indirect interest in leisure from their primary objectives. The Ministry of Agriculture is generally concerned with the welfare of the farming and rural communities. It is responsible for the Forestry Commission, whose role in rural recreation policy and provision is discussed below. The Department of Trade defines tourism policy and the Department of Industry supports some leisure industries directly and takes a general interest in others. The Department of Health and Social Security has institutions under its control containing those (the elderly, sick, and children in need of care and protection) who have rights of access to play and recreation.

In the context of rural recreation, it is the role of the Department of the Environment and its agencies which are dominant. The functions which have been taken over from the Ministry of Housing and Local Government for rural recreation, water amenities and sport have been hived off to agencies. But the Department's own general responsibilities for control of Local Government expenditure, their influence on the structure of Local Government, and the powers given in the 1972 Local Government Act for spending on recreation in Local Authorities, despite them falling into almost total disuse in the mid-1970s economic crisis, reinforces its potential and key role in Central Government policy making. The functions derived from the previous Ministry of Transport are generally more interventionist; there are important powers affecting recreational mobility exercised through control of nationalized transport undertakings and the national road building programme.

The following paragraphs discuss in more detail the policy roles of the Countryside Commissions for England and Wales and for Scotland, the Sports Council, Water Space Amenity Commission, Forestry Commission, and the Tourist Boards.

The Countryside Commission for England and Wales is entirely separate from that for Scotland and each has developed its individual perspective and priorities. The Countryside Commission for England and Wales is charged under the 1968 Countryside Act, with keeping under review all matters relating to the conservation and enhancement of natural beauty of the countryside, and the provision and improvement of facilities for the enjoyment of the countryside. It is the principal agency concerned with recreation and landscape; its duties are similar in some respects to those of the Sports Council but there is considerable endeavour to avoid overlap, and by mutual agreement the Commission concentrates on informal recreation in the countryside whilst the Council has responsibility for physical recreation and sport in town and country—although this division is not always easy to adhere to.

The Commission's powers are mainly advisory and not executive. It undertakes its duties by "advising on the administration of national parks, by recommending the payment of Exchequer grant aid for a range of Local Authority recreational schemes and landscape protection measures, by providing information to the public about the countryside, and by carrying out a programme of research and experiments on which much of this advice is built" (6.30). In April 1973 it issued a policy statement on guidelines for priorities in work. This stated that its responsibilities for conservation and recreation are "complementary, interdependent and of equal importance".

There is a considerable amount of informal officer liaison with relevant departments and agencies as well as several more formal groups. These include the Chairmen's Policy Group and the Countryside Recreation Research Advisory Group (CRRAG). The Chairmen's Policy Group, set up in 1970, has as its members the chairmen of the British Tourist Authority, British Waterways Board, Countryside Commission, Countryside Commission for Scotland, Development Commission, English Tourist Board, Forestry Commission, Nature Conservancy Council, Scottish Tourist Board, Sports Council, Wales Tourist Board, and Water Space Amenity Commission. At its biennial meetings, it discusses policy items of mutual importance, Ministerial decisions, Countryside Commission experimental projects, and so on; it gives opinions and recommends changes or amendments but rarely initiates action unilaterally. It sponsors CRRAG in as much as decisions made there are referred to the Policy Group. CRRAG was set up by the Countryside Commission originally, in 1968, to avoid overlap between member agencies' research work, to encourage joint working on research projects, and to determine research priorities. But its role has developed into more positive attitudes, and much of its work has been attempting to influence outside research and projecting a combined view of research and statistical needs.

The Countryside Commission for Scotland is in many ways a very different organization from its English and Welsh counterpart. It was a completely new body with its own legislative framework (the Countryside (Scotland) Act 1967), which had different components from the English Act. One of the chief differences was a result of planning history—the absence of National Parks. The Commission's functions include the provision, development and improvement of facilities for the enjoyment of the Scottish countryside, and the conservation and enhancement of natural beauty and amenity. It set itself four initial priorities to help it develop its role: a positive attitude towards countryside planning, resource management, conservation education and cooperation with other bodies. The Act requires the Commission also to have due regard to the need for the development of recreational and tourist facilities and for the balanced economic and social development of the countryside in the work they do.

In the work of recreation provision, they have some important responsibilities. The Commission has to advise the Secretary of State for Scotland on the suitability, in terms of the Act, of all projects submitted for grant by Local Authorities, and advise on priorities if there are insufficient financial resources available for all potential schemes available in one year. It is also closely involved with Local Authorities to help them to plan comprehensively for recreation provision in their areas over a period of years. With Local Government reorganization in Scotland, the Commission has been concerned to ensure that recreation planning constitutes an identifiable and adequately important element in the regional structure plans and local plans.

From the outset, the Commission has established and maintained close links with other Government bodies and research agencies. By 1973 over half of the commissioned studies in which the Commission was involved were jointly sponsored: "We believe this trend will be welcomed both by Central Government and by agencies carrying out research, in that this leads to a more efficient use of monies available for research and enables larger sums to be made available for individual projects. For those responsible for managing research, a substantial benefit also results from collaborating with other organizations in a climate of discovery where demarcation problems may not be as marked as on other operational fronts" (6.31).

In 1965 the Highlands and Islands Development Board (HIDB) was set up under the Highlands and Islands Development (Scotland) Act. It is a strange fact that although the promotion of tourism is one of the Board's major activities, it is not mentioned specifically in its Act, whereas it is mentioned in that of the Commission. 1969 saw the Development of Tourism Act and the establishment of the British Tourist Authority and Tourist Boards for England, Wales, and Scotland, the latter replacing an earlier, voluntary, body also called the Scottish Tourist Board. In 1971, a charter for a Scottish Sports Council received the royal assent, and the new Council in effect absorbed the former Scottish Council of Physical Recreation. In 1974 the Government's new Forestry Policy was announced which, amongst other things, gave renewed impetus to the development of the recreational use of Forestry Commission land, and reaffirmed the desire of government that the Commission should use the powers conferred on it by sections 58 and 59 of the Countryside (Scotland) Act.

There are now five statutory bodies sharing planning for recreation and tourism, in Scotland, four national and one, the HIDB, regional. There seems to be a recognition amongst the bodies that they do have this common objective, and that corporate action is a desirable means to a better end.

The Sports Council was originally set up as an advisory body under Ministerial chairmanship. In mid-1971 it was succeeded by a Council with executive powers and an independent chairman. There are now four Sports Councils in the UK, covering England, Wales, Scotland and Northern Ireland; the following notes refer to the English Council. From 1972 one of its functions has been to grant-aid sport from central funds, replacing the grant-aid of the Department of the Environment and, before that, the Department of Education and Science. According to the 1973 Circular which explained the new set-up, "the new Council is to concern itself with sport and physical recreation in its widest context. It is establishing relationships with other bodies having direct interests in these fields such as the Countryside Commission and agreeing with them the way in which their various responsibilities can best be coordinated".

At the same time, the Regional Sports Councils' roles were changed, giving them a consultative function to the Sports Council on regional matters, and allowing the Sports Council to delegate the performance or suspension of some functions. The principle new functions of the Regional Sports Councils were:

1. To cooperate with and assist cooperation between Local Authorities and others in keeping the region's facilities for sport and physical recreation under review.

2. To collect and bring to the attention of Local Authorities and other appropriate bodies information on the need for such facilities and to advise on the type and scale of provision required and on priorities in relation to resources.

3. To cooperate with Local Authorities and others in regional planning process.

4. To be concerned with the general development of sport and physical recreation in the region, and to assist, advise and liaise with other bodies in this field.

The Regional Sports Councils, originally set up in 1966, have become well established and well respected bodies in their own right, and have given the national body a valuable relationship with local and regional sports interests.

The division of responsibility and functions of the Sports Councils and Countryside Commissions are not entirely clear. Broadly, however, the Sports Councils are directly concerned with active recreation, whether in town or country, whilst the Countryside Commissions are primarily concerned with informal countryside recreation. Tourist Boards are responsible for those aspects of both formal and informal recreation that involve holidaymakers, either from home or overseas.

The Sports Council is responsible for the allocation of grant aid to Local Authorities, other public bodies, and private organizations, to help provide sport and recreational facilities of a sub-regional and regional size. The Council itself provides national sports centres. The Council has wide discretion in the allocation of grants, and relies heavily on advice from the regions on the merits or priority of applications for capital grants.

The Council has four main aims:

1. To promote general understanding of the importance of sport and physical recreation in society.

2. To increase the provision of new sports facilities and the use of existing sports facilities to serve the needs of the community.

3. To encourage wider participation in sport and physical recreation.

4. To raise standards of performance of sport and physical recreation.

In fulfilling these general aims, the Council seeks to promote and coordinate plans for future provision; encourage a planned programme of capital investment; cooperate with Government Departments and statutory bodies by joint meetings and groups; and establish necessary procedure for consultation and collaboration in the planning, provision and use of sports facilities and the development of sport and physical recreation, by closer links with the Countryside Commission, attempting more dual use of existing facilities and joint provision of new ones, and undertaking prototype schemes, for example at professional football fields. At a regional level they are concerned to encourage regional promotion and coordination, to persuade Local Authorities to give higher priority to the encouragement of sport, and to give consideration to the special needs of various sections of the community including the disabled.

The Water Industry underwent its second major reorganization within a decade when the 1973 Water Act came into operation. This abolished the Water Resources Board and set up a National Water Council to coordinate the work of the ten Regional Water Authorities. The Act also set up, in section 23, the *Water Space Amenity Commission* (WSAC) with the duty of formulating, promoting and executing the national policy for water recreation and amenity. This came into being in April 1974. The Chairman sits on the National Water Council with the Chairmen of the Regional Water Authorities, whilst those chairmen are themselves members of WSAC. Members are also drawn from the Sports Council, the Countryside Commission, the English Tourist Board, and the County Council's Association. In the words of the Director of WSAC: "This new approach to all forms of water recreation is made much more important because both the prime responsibility and the statutory obligation for providing recreation and amenity on waters, which are under the control of the water authorities, fall on the industry itself" (6.32).

Initially, one of the Commission's priorities was to assess existing water recreation provision to enable it to formulate a programme of development, management and research. It is attempting to relate its work as closely as possible to that of the recreation staff of the water industry in the regions. Two areas of special interest in its short existence have been water parks (which range from those under the control of specially created statutory bodies (the Lea Valley Scheme) to those in private ownership or developed by New Towns Development Corporations) and rivers which in the past have not been used for recreation, due either to the multiplicity of ownership, the quality of water, the lack of funds to support recreational facilities, or the lack of statutory powers.

The British Waterways Board has a statutory duty under the 1968 Transport Act to encourage the recreational use of certain canals under its ownership. Recreation on BWB feeder reservoirs for the canals is also a policy encouraged if this does not interfere with canal operations, and at present 70% are used, primarily for fishing or boating.

Statutory water undertakings (the Regional Water Authorities) are less willing to allow recreational development on water supply reservoirs than on regulating and compensating ones, principally because of the slight health risks. More sympathetic understanding of the recreationist's viewpoint has been noticeable in new reservoirs opened in the last ten years, partly as a result of a review carried out in 1966 at the request of the then Ministry of Land and Natural Resources, which advised them to pay particular attention to the needs of recreationists in the 'Leisure in the Countryside' White Paper (6.33). Sailing and game fishing are the activities most commonly allowed, whilst coarse fishing is confined to a few reservoirs. The Countryside Act allows Local Authorities to create country parks on those reservoirs where the water undertaking wants them to do so.

The Forestry Commission has long been recognized as being an important *ad hoc* provider of recreational facilities in its forests. Some provision dates from the 1930s, with the development of Forest Parks in Scotland, but until recently conservation and recreation were a part of the Forestry Enterprise which was developed or not at the discretion of individual regions and conservancies.

The Commission has always been somewhat troubled by its dual functions—Forestry Authority and Forestry Enterprise. In July 1974 the Ministry of Agriculture, the 'responsible' Minister, set out the way in which the Commission's objectives under these two heads would be redefined. In the words of the 54th Annual Report (6.34): "The Forestry Authority activities follow from the Commission's general duty of promoting the interests of forestry—including the dissemination of forestry knowledge, the promotion of the supply of timber, the conduct of research, the administration of schemes of grant or other aid to private forestry, the protection of woodlands through planting, felling, and plant health controls. In all these functions attention is paid to the desirability of conserving the natural beauty and amenity of the countryside". Then: "The main objective of the Forestry Enterprise remains that of producing wood as economically as possible. However, in pursuit of this aim, as in the case of the Forestry Authority, attention is paid to amenity, and the Commission is required to preserve and enhance the landscape and to develop the potential of its properties for nature conservation and recreation".

Most Conservancies now have Recreation Planning Officers who have been responsible for preparing Conservancy Recreation Plans. These plans are the basic documents to be used in planning recreational development strategy. They were introduced as a means of trying to interpret Commission policy more consistently over the country than in the past and of ensuring better liaison with other planning interests.

The growth in facilities and use over the ten year period, 1964-1974, can be gauged from a few figures. In 1964 there were eight fully equipped campsites and no minimum facility ones; by 1974 there were 11 and 5 of each respectively, and the number of camper nights over the same period rose from 586,200 to 1,217,420. There were two information centres in 1964, and 24 by 1974, which indicates the importance the Commission attaches to interpretation, also reflected in forest drives (one in 1964, five in 1974) and forest trails (none in 1964, 381 in 1974), and observation towers and huts (one in 1964, 26 in 1974).

The organization of tourism was drastically changed under the 1969 Development of Tourism Act, under which the British Travel Association was replaced by an overall *British Tourist Authority* and national boards for England, Scotland and Wales. The BTA is responsible both for attracting foreign visitors to Britain and for encouraging residents to take holidays in Britain. The BTA and the national boards together are authorized to encourage the provision and improvement of tourist amenities, to which they can give financial assistance, and in general they are, or at least have been, less concerned with conservation of the resource than its development potential for tourism. Also, the Authority's concern extends over the whole of the country, although a large proportion of their and the national board's work has been attempting to assess the place of general and specialized tourism in countryside areas also popular for informal recreation, and to this end their membership of CRRAG and close liaison with conservation agencies is vital. A common problem is that of distinguishing between facilities used by tourists and those used by local residents or recreationists, especially as the one may also be the other at different times. Perhaps the key difference lies in accommodation and the more marked seasonality of tourism, although recreation shows more pronounced weekend peaking. The resident population may benefit from the provision of facilities which would not be justified for them alone or with non-staying recreationists, but they may also suffer considerable inconvenience and pressure as a result.

The Nature Conservancy Council's functions are, primarily, to maintain a nationally representative series of natural and semi-natural habitats, and secondly to provide advice to public bodies on issues that affect or are likely to affect the conservation of natural flora and fauna or features of geological or physiographic interest. But its advice has no back-up powers outside National Nature Reserves, some 26% of which are owned by the Council, the remainder being either under lease or Nature Reserve Agreements which bind the landowner to manage the land in the interest of conservation. The management plans for these reserves are primarily concerned with conservation but visitors are allowed where possible and where this does not conflict with scientific needs or clauses in reserve agreements. The Council has encouraged bodies interested in specialist pursuits, such as caving, rock climbing, skiing and wildfowling to use reserves where there is little likelihood of them harming the resource.

The National Trust for England, Wales and Northern Ireland was founded in 1895 (that for Scotland was separately constituted in 1931). They are neither private nor public bodies but occupy a key position in informal outdoor recreation. The National Trust's primary aim has always been preservation, and it now owns about 377,000 acres (152,700ha) in England, Wales and Northern Ireland, and some 200 houses of outstanding architectural or historic importance. It has also accepted covenants which protect against development a further 61,000 acres (24,700ha) of land. In 1907 Parliament conferred on the Trust the unique power to declare its land unalienable. The majority of its properties are unalienable, which means that they can never be sold or mortgaged, nor can they be compulsorily acquired without the special will of Parliament. Although this has never caused problems in the recreation field, some erosion of this right has recently occurred with the passing of the Offshore Petroleum Development (Scotland) Act in which the Government Minister concerned has the power to acquire unalienable land compulsorily in the same way as any other land, whereas before there existed a right to appeal to a joint select committee of Parliament. The matter of principle has been broken, and it is only to be hoped that this does not set a precedent for further erosion of the Trusts' ownership rights.

Much of the Trust's land is farmed and the Trust has over 1000 farm tenancies; as landlord the Trust has an obligation to preserve the countryside by controlling the design and siting of agricultural buildings and the planting or felling of trees. Subject to the requirements of farming, forestry, and the protection of nature, the public is usually given free access to all the Trust's open spaces at all times; about 4 million people a year visit the Trust's houses and gardens, although there is no record of the numbers visiting open spaces. It is experiencing similar pressures of over-use of popular properties either near large centres of population or in tourist areas to other landowners, and it is endeavouring to find management techniques to combat this in consort with government conservation agencies. It has adopted a policy of restraint and limitation in the worst affected areas, and in its guidebooks makes special mention of the properties likely to be visited by 'uncomfortably large numbers' on Bank Holidays and Sundays in summer when 'full house' notices may be posted and tickets issued for timed entry only.

Local Government are providers first, and policy makers second. The philosophy, objectives and criteria on which to base decisions are often lacking, or at least badly articulated. If Local Authorities are to be effective planners and providers, they must reconcile their overall objectives with their policies, but too often they are in competition with the views of other interested bodies. Perhaps the projected regional councils for sport and recreation could act as conciliators. The Local Authorities have to balance recreational ideas with other policy areas. As providers, they must decide what to provide and where, when and how; then have to meet democratic scrutiny, which is more effective than at Central Government level and in fact may have little direct connection, although the Local Authority may have embarked on a scheme due to legislative plus grant 'push'.

The relationships between central and local agencies should be well defined, and administratively straightforward and efficient, as well as dividing roles so that the respective power bases are not undermined. At present, some of the muddles which appear can be traced to a lack of this definition and clarity of responsibilities. The reorganization of Local Government, in 1974, seems in the short term to have exacerbated these types of problem within the sphere of recreation planning. District Councils are developing their own recreation and leisure departments to deal with responsibilities for

247

provision and management, but they now rightfully look to the metropolitan and shire Counties and central bodies for guidance on planning strategy. County Councils, with some notable exceptions, have on the whole failed as yet to develop a corpus of strategic policies in the regions which can be truthfully called comprehensive. The advent of structure planning has improved the likelihood of recreation policies being integrated with others. Work done on structure planning in the West Midlands region (6.35), however, has revealed that although priorities in objectives gave more prominence to recreation than any other statutory planning in the region, strictures of programming eventually usually resulted in work being limited to a rapid surveillance of generalized policies and their relationship to other strategic issues.

The demise of County Boroughs has weakened the strategic policy functions at district level but there is as yet insufficient will and inadequate staff to allow Counties to shoulder the complete problem. In any case, it is likely that the new Counties' interpretations of their priorities will still ensure the precedence of County or sub-regional policies over wider regional or (even) national ones.

There has been a general feeling amongst many recreation planners that with an evident stretching of manpower resources, it is imperative that such expertise as there is in recreation planning and management should be centralized—initially as a task force in the first tier authority, but subsequently into a regional unit, perhaps the new regional sports and recreation councils. The 1975 White Paper proposed that these councils should "make a balanced regional assessment of the relationships and interactions of conservation and outdoor recreation in the countryside". This and other related work is "to provide an agreed framework within which recreational proposals in structure and local plans can be developed". This proposal was not welcomed by Thorburn (6.36) as he felt: "It is not sensible for powers to be extended to include decisions upon the trade-off between recreation and environment *without regard to other uses of land and demand upon resources* (author's italics). Only authorities with concern for all these areas can make proper decisions in this field. In a democracy, such bodies must be democratically elected, and must be advised by professionals whose understanding is of the total environment". He is therefore arguing for an elected regional body with powers to undertake comprehensive planning—powers which Counties do not have. But even if this were feasible, would it improve policy planning, would it lead to more carefully considered objectives designed to clarify priority needs and methods of implementing them? The answer must be unsatisfactory, and echo problems at Central Government level: more work needs to be done, more comprehensive and detailed consultations to include all remotely relevant bodies, more investigation of overlap in present policies, and more cognisance taken of the relationship of recreation planning to the rest of social planning, before any wide-ranging changes are implemented.

Why do people use the countryside?

It has already been hinted that the 'romantic', 'middle class' view of the traditional countryside plays its part in attracting people to the countryside for their leisure. But there are problems in discovering and analyzing people's motives for seeking and using the countryside. How vital is the 'natural' countryside *per se* in fulfilling needs? Could needs be met by town-based artificially created countryside? Are new experiences required? Furthermore, it is pertinent to ponder just how far the community visualizes the *existence* of a problem or set of problems in planning, using, and managing the countryside for recreation? Moreover, how far does it differentiate between recreation in urban and rural environments? Some attempt to examine these questions, however briefly, is made in this section, which concludes with some thoughts on the opportunities for sharper thinking in a time of economic recession, which may provide an ideal moment for reappraising existing programmes and policies, some of which are patently failing to solve problems.

The interests of those statutorily and voluntarily involved in informal recreation have been overwhelmingly concentrated on the most equitable use of scarce resources of land and money to meet the demand for recreation. They have looked closely at quantity, imbalance and deficiency, but not at quality, or motivations behind those demands, or the assumptions underlying the major programmes of provision and research.

Even if it is argued that deficiency or shortfall is so great and demand so pressing that it is only sensible to provide a range of facilities which are known to satisfy demand, there is a new sense of questioning developing about the assumptions on which such statements are made. The statutory agencies have begun tentative probings about their own policies and assumptions on which they are based.

Perhaps one of the key assumptions which needs questioning is that which is inherent in much of what has been discussed in this Chapter—that informal outdoor recreation is 'good for you', that contact with natural environments is fulfilling and replaces something otherwise lost to urban man. If the evidence of the use of the coast and country parks, and visits to farms and wildlife parks is taken as supporting this view, then it is right that the providers' priorities should be more facilities which are compatible with the conservation of the countryside. But this reasoning is somewhat superficial, and it may be more beneficial to planned and planners in the long run to look at motivations more closely. How real is the need for natural countryside; are most people looking for the reality or the appearance of reality when visiting the countryside; what is their conception of the place of nature—do they want reassurance of man's supremacy or evidence of the humbleness of his relationship with other elements of nature? The answers, or partial answers, to such questions would be more practical than the questions themselves. They may point to a need for a wider variety of types of recreation experience which should not be conveniently pigeon-holed into categories. The skills of the anthropologist and sociologist, which have become increasingly evident in the past decade, should be utilized even more to complement the land-based preoccupations of the planner. This may be difficult in practice but there does seem to be a general disenchantment with the single-discipline approach which might be partially rectified by a re-learning process.

A further area begging joint investigation is the myth of recreation being a 'different' part of our lives from the rest of it. Our lives are constantly being parcelled into parts, and leisure has suffered from being considered as a 'left over' after work and personal chores. Parcels of certain times—annual holidays and weekends—are identified as leisure, as something different from everything else, and implying that the fulfilments of leisure can only be searched for in leisure time. In reality, of course, the lack of boundaries and the haziness of definition are all too common. Work and leisure continuously overlap, seemingly in different degrees for different individuals. Do-it-yourself, voluntary overtime and evening education are both leisure and work. As Dower points out, even more important is "that life is, or people wish it to be, integral. Life-satisfaction is to be gained from all parts of it, from 'work' and 'personal chores' as much as from leisure. The human need may be not for a white (leisure) patch to cancel out the black (work), but for a rich fabric with the light thread running through weft of alternating activity" (6.37).

The implications for recreation providers could be quite significant. The main emphasis now in policy is on separate leisure provision, rarely allied with other activities or land uses, and located to be used during 'leisure time'. This includes country parks as well as sports halls, caravan sites as well as golf courses. It may be that there is also a place for leisure facilities inter-mixed with other life facilities, whether urban or rural in location. It may be that this type of provision would illustrate the relative meaninglessness of the urban-rural split for many areas of life, and allow closer examination of the exact nature of the type of countryside which most people want to use and for what specific reasons. Organizational and administrative separateness must, to some degree, remain but this does not mean that it cannot encompass multiple activity and conflicting interest.

This re-orientation would be very helpful in two further areas which have been alluded to before in this Chapter: the importance of socio-economic variables in determining who uses the countryside and why, and the dangers of using total numbers of users, rather than individuals, as a criterion of successful policies. The need to use the tools of sociology is again obvious. To quote Dower again: "Administrators and planners ... know that the production of facilities is not an end in itself but rather a means to a greater end, namely the personal fulfilment or satisfaction of the populace. And this ought to provoke the question—*why* do people fish, or dance, or go on a camping holiday? The answer is not 'because they earn £2000 a year', but rather 'because they need to fulfil themselves in some way'—and this is where we look to the fields of sociology and psychology to help us. We land-oriented researchers may guess that the basic impulses and preoccupations have to do with questions of personal identity, of social reassurance, of escape or fantasy, or rootedness in natural things, of wholeness or integration in personal life—and we may believe it is important to probe these things, in order that physical provision may most closely satisfy these impulses. But we need the man-orientated researchers to bore a tunnel toward us from the other side of the hill" (6.38).

Also, concern with numbers can often be to the detriment of quality of the experience: to each recreationist the activity or event in which he is participating is something unique, even if it is unimportant to the whole overall pattern of his life. This is not to say that numbers are irrelevant to recreational planning, but there must be some perspective on their usefulness. Indeed, the perception of an experience is coloured by the presence or absence or disposition of other people, but to use numbers baldly is unhelpful to managers and users alike. Basic information and statistics on numbers and types of users, their likes and dislikes, what facilities they would like to see, do not go very far to explain leisure behaviour patterns, or what quality of experience people are seeking (or if they know!), or what real alternatives exist. Perhaps many more extended small group interview surveys, similar to those of Young and Willmott (6.39) and the Rapoports (6.40), might help in answering some of the problems.

A current study financed by the Department of the Environment and being carried out by the Institute of Family and Environmental Research (IFER) and the Dartington Amenity Research Trust (DART), entitled Leisure Provision and Human Need, is attempting to widen the behavioural scope of leisure research. It is concerned with establishing a 'fit' between the present pattern of provision of leisure facilities and the needs of the population, whilst the Department of the Environment is interested in how far existing Government policies for sport and recreation are meeting those needs. At one level, the concept of 'fit' relates to the present responsibilities and activities of the bodies who provide leisure facilities: Government agencies, Local Authorities, private landowners, and commercial companies. They have a set of implicit or explicit motives in establishing leisure facilities and in their subsequent management policy. The users also have a set of motives in using these facilities and a set of perceptions acquired through the use of them. Studies designed to identify the quality of the fit between the objectives of the providers and the needs of the consumers would benefit the providers in several ways: by helping them to understand their own purposes more clearly; by showing them the need to convey their purposes more clearly to the public so that expectations and attitudes are adjusted; or by helping them to adjust their management policies, within the framework of their statutory duties, to accord more closely to the desires of the people.

At a more fundamental level, study of the 'fit' between leisure provision and human need should probe deeper questions of human satisfaction. This may move the focus away from leisure provision as such onto the issue of how different parts of society's structure can best be combined to satisy people's deeper preoccupations. This is also designed to illuminate policy, since the different and interlocking parts of society's structure are all the subject of major public involvement and expenditure.

The end results of this research, as stated by IFER and DART, are hoped to be:

(a) a statement of the present state of knowledge in the field of leisure provision and human need, with supporting documentation, and

(b) an analysis of the relevance of the pattern of present leisure provision to the overall need of the community aiming in particular to identify, with particular reference to facilities for sport and recreation,

(i) which sections are served well,

(ii) which sections are not adequately served and how they might be better served.

This re-orientation and re-direction of physical planners towards the human element has coincided with a period of fundamental structural problems in society. It may be maintained that this is far from accidental and that it is a quest for a focus to allow a reappraisal of recreational policies in a fresh framework. The final section takes up this theme.

The future

Recreation is only one of a wide group of conflicts in rural planning, and to those not intimately concerned with its welfare, can often be trivial or unimportant. But its ramifications are major. What is the nature of potential change and how is it going to be crystallised? It is too easy to think that attempting to resolve conflict today will ensure a 'better future'. Have we the tools for improvement? Do we know what stimulates certain courses of action now? And do planners and the public see the need to develop a consensus of the problem?

It would be easy to dismiss those questions as uncomfortable and unanswerable and revert instead to a cosy optimism, with a concern to resolve present conflict rather than to anticipate the future: "To conserve any environment so that as many as possible of the demands upon it may be satisfied presupposes some vision of what the future might be. This requires a good deal more thinking than has been evident so far about the agencies and nature of potential change: the implications of the Common Agricultural Policy for Britain; the effects of inflation on land ownership and management; new industrial demands for water and minerals; social changes in the pattern of work and leisure" (6.41).

What clues exist to the possible ways in which the future may be influenced? The White Paper of August 1975, 'Sport and Leisure', indicates something of the Government's approach. Both that and the House of Lords reports see the need for comprehensive thinking, flexible provision, cost-effectiveness, full use of existing facilities, and provision for the whole community and particularly for those who are disadvantaged. They recognize that sport and recreation are vital in terms of the quality of life—"when life becomes meaningful for the individual, then the whole community is enriched". This points, perhaps uncomfortably, to the need for humane, imaginative and resourceful management of a wide range of communal facilities. It is easier, even in times of economic stringency, to carry on as before rather than to attempt fundamental reappraisal but the opportunities for sharper thinking are immense. This could help to humanize the whole process of recreation policy making at a local level, where community involvement is vital, with 'animateurs' to imaginatively utilize the heritage of neglected facilities, ranging from church halls to redundant public houses in town and village.

Humanizing the recreation system at local level will undoubtedly make it a more political part of the local government structure. To effect the same response at central level is a more difficult problem. It has always been felt that in national terms, recreation policy has been a political Cinderella, something that can be either conveniently pigeonholed or forgotten. The lack of congruence between the principles of departmental organization in Central Government and the very different basis in Local Government (especially if there is a corporate planning structure) is bound to mean that policy is nore unified at local level than it is in Central Government. But to politicize these central policies is even more problematic. The traditional approach of a land-use based ministry has not been a notable success.

It is a matter of judgement whether the attempts to change course at a local level for a more humanized approach would be enough to profoundly influence Central Government policy overall to such a degree that leisure could be seen as a part of a policy continuum, embracing work, education, and all other areas of normal life.

The White Paper does not advance very far towards helping to improve decision-making processes; it talks of coordination at national agency and regional agency level but it gives little consideration as to what the basic aims of coordination are and what improved policies and decisions could be expected to flow from it. Other parts of life are also the empire of multifarious agencies who are equally prone to individual decisions on which relevant decision makers from other agencies are not consulted. This leads in general to inefficiency, over-lap, and sometimes complete contradiction which confuses the recipient of the decision. But would a completely new organization to oversee a wide spectrum of leisure policy be able to gain political maturity? There seems little enthusiasm for a new agency and/or ministry, partly as it would remove large power bases from existing ones, and partly because no one has successfully argued that this would improve integrated policy making and consequent action or improve the overall status of leisure policy within the Government. It is a much more common view that, more fundamental than administrative inertia, why a centralized leisure policy has not emerged is that the community as a whole has not developed its consensus of the leisure problem, and that the role of politicians in articulating that consensus has to precede administrative reorganization. Perhaps more truly the community has not been asked the right questions in the right way and has not been educated to feel that it can influence the development of these areas of policy which fall outside the traditional preoccupations of politicians.

How then do we resolve the problems inherent in countryside recreation planning? The conflict of interests between different groups of the community is as intense in the countryside as in the urban environment. The key to decreasing conflict, to attempting to resolve the problems, is to determine how the power of each group can be channelled into productive cooperation and management. It is this 'how' which is causing continuous discussion and has been the background theme of this Chapter in which we have illustrated the inadequacies of the legislative, financial, and organizational measures which were developed after the war to deal with the conflicts of the seventies in a useful way.

The 1947 planning system proved to be entirely inadequate to resolve many rural planning conflicts. It had little control over many important rural land developments. It was primarily a system to define use of land rather than its management, and it is the way in which countryside is organized—what *type* of agriculture is undertaken, *how* recreation sites are run—rather than the fact of *use* for agriculture or leisure which is important. National Park legislation was designed to protect the uses of only a small proportion of the countryside and had been unable to cope with the recreational pressures developing within National Park boundaries, let along the rest of the country, especially in the urban fringes. An attempt was made in the 1968 Countryside Act to overcome some of the recreation problems which had developed but it has been unable to diminish conflict to any appreciable degree.

Each interest group in the countryside is generally concerned with the achievement of single-purpose objectives, whether it be nature conservation, forestry, agriculture, recreation or water supply. What is needed is a way in which these groups can be brought to understand the benefits of productive cooperation. The approach adopted by the Nature Conservancy in the early and mid-1960s in attempting to identify areas of conflict as well as ways of diminishing them in the Broads is instructive. It undoubtedly succeeded in showing the advantages of involving all key interests in the process of planning the alternative futures for the Broads, but it was less successful in putting forward feasible policies on suggesting how any ideas could be implemented.

The joint work undertaken in East Hampshire went further in attempting 'integrated resource planning'. Clashes of interest and the possible conflicts arising from further developments in agriculture and recreation were carefully explored. The five major resource interests were identified—agriculture, forestry, recreation, wildlife and landscape conservation—and an attempt made to assess the acceptability to each of activities such as tree felling, fencing, draining, footpaths, and country parks. This was analyzed and 'policy zones' delineated on grounds of resource quality, within which certain activites were considered to be more or less acceptable and for which policies of promotion or restriction might apply. For example, in some zones where landscape or ecological values were high, it was suggested that priority should be given to these interests; in zones of high agricultural quality, recreation activities might need to be diminished, if not wholly diverted to areas of poorer farming. In the zones where values were high for several interests and direct policy conflicts could be anticipated, more detailed studies were recommended, especially if there were suggestions of new types of management by agreement. Many of the recommendations were made more straightforward by the existing amount of background data available on the area. Later, studies in very different rural areas (the North Pennines for example) showed the importance of the politico-social issues and the greater degree of conflict between residents and visitors. This is especially true in the marginal agriculture areas of the uplands (most of the national parks) where a stable economic system is a concomitant of recreation and landscape conservation.

The type of work undertaken in East Hampshire was equivalent to the District Plans now being produced under the new planning procedures. These should afford most rural areas the opportunity of identifying conflicts and examining ways of resolving them in a much more coherent and potentially useful fashion than previously. But there are still considerable problems to be tackled. Rural planning has failed to keep pace with its urban counterpart in the development of useful and understandable techniques to form policies and then evaluate them. But quite apart from that, there is a reluctance to think problems through, and to look beyond the defence of the countryside *per se* against urban ideas and encroachment. Too rarely are the conflicts between and within rural activities examined: there is still too little research into the values of conflict resolution. Resolution could be accomplished for these types of conflict by the sensitive use of management policies.

These could range from the establishment of new habitats for wildfowl in defined areas of new reservoirs to protect them from the anglers and power-boat users who are also subject to area and time controls on their activities on the water. The resolution of the problems of how it is decided that there is a need for a reservoir at all in this case (or, in any other, of any major public or private undertaking, such as oil associated development) cannot be so smoothly handled. This area of conflict which is of deep concern to recreation policy makers needs the development of a concensus founded on rational argument which does not yet exist. The place of the physical planner in helping to develop this consensus is for him to make himself. He needs to appreciate the validity of other standpoints and to be prepared to accept the implications of effective public participation in the rural environment.

References

6.1   BRITISH TRAVEL ASSOCIATION and KEELE UNIVERSITY, *Pilot National Recreation Survey*, Volume 1, London, B.T.A, 1967.
6.2   PATMORE, J.A., *Land and Leisure*, David and Charles, 1970.
6.3   Office Of Population Censuses and Surveys carried out the relevant General Household Survey in 1973. Reports being published See: Moss., L., 'The General

Household Survey', *Social Science Research Council Newsletter*, 23, May, 1974, pp. 6-10.

6.4   VEAL, A.J., *Leisure and Recreation in England and Wales 1973*, Draft Report to the Countryside Commission and Sports Council, Centre for Urban and Regional Studies, University of Birmingham 1975.

6.5   SILLITOE, K.K., *Planning for Leisure*, Government Social Survey, HMSO, 1969.

6.6   BENDIXSON, T., 'The Effect of Changes in Fuel Supply on Transport for Countryside Recreation', *Recreation News Supplement*, 12, September, 1975.

6.7   DEPARTMENT OF THE ENVIRONMENT, (unpublished), National Travel Survey 1972-73, some unpublished tables available from the Department.

6.8   ELSON, M.J., 'Some factors affecting the incidence and distribution of weekend recreation motoring trips', *Oxford Agrarian Studies*, 11, 2, 1974.

6.9   HILLMAN, M. *et al.*, *Personal Mobility and transport policy*, Political and Economic Planning Broadsheet 542, London: P.E.P., 1973.

6.10   BENDIXSON, T., 1975,, *op. cit.*

6.11   NATIONAL PARK POLICIES REVIEW COMMITTEE (Chairman, Lord Sandford) *Report*, HMSO, 1973.

6.12   JACOBS, G.A.J., *Second Houses in Denbighshire*, Tourism and Recreation Research Report No. 3, Denbighshire County Council, 1972.

6.13   BIELCKUS, C.L., ROGERS, A.W. and WIBBERLEY, G.P., *Second Homes in England and Wales*, Studies in Rural Land Use Report No. 11, Wye College, University of London, 1972.

6.14   DOWNING, P. and DOWER, M., *Second Homes in England and Wales*, HMSO for Countryside Commission and DART, 1973.

6.15   NATIONAL PARK POLICIES REVIEW COMMITTEE (1973), *op. cit.*, para 12.22.

6.16   DAVIDSON, J.M., 'Countryside Conservation: Some National Prospectives', Ch. 24 in WARREN, A. and GOLDSMITH, F.B., (Eds.), *Conservation in Practice*, John Wiley, 1974.

6.17   CHERRY, G.E., *Environmental Planning 1939-1969, Volume II: National Parks and Recreation in the Countryside*, HMSO, 1975.

6.18   See References in Further Reading.

6.19   DOWER, M., *The Fourth Wave: the Challenge of Leisure*, The Civic Trust, 1965.

6.20   DAVIDSON, J.M., 1974, *op. cit.*

6.21   NATIONAL PARK POLICIES REVIEW COMMITTEE (1973), *op. cit.*, para 2.15.

6.22   *Ibid*, para 3.8.

6.23   MINISTRY OF LAND AND NATURAL RESOURCES, *Leisure in the Countryside*, Cmnd 2928, HMSO, 1966.

6.24   COUNTRYSIDE COMMISSION and PEAK PARK PLANNING BOARD, *Goyt Valley Traffic Experiment Interim Report*, Countryside Commission, 1971.

6.25   DEPARTMENT OF THE ENVIRONMENT, *Sinews for Survival: Report on Natural Resources for the United Nations Conference on the Human Environment, Stockholm*, HMSO, 1972.

6.26   SELECT COMMITTEE OF HOUSE OF LORDS ON SPORT AND LEISURE (Chairman, Lord Cobham), *First and Second Reports*, HMSO, March and July, 1973.

6.27   DEPARTMENT OF THE ENVIRONMENT, *Sport and Recreation*, Cmnd 6200, HMSO, 1975.

6.28   DOWER, M., 'Denis Howell's empire', *Town and Country Planning*, 43, 10, October, 1975, pp 423-26.

6.29   SMITH, C., 'The Emergence of Leisure as a Policy Issue for Central Government and the Administrative Response', Leisure Studies Association Conference, Birmingham, 1975.

6.30   DAVIDSON, J.M., 1974, *op. cit.* p 381.

6.31 COUNTRYSIDE COMMISSION FOR SCOTLAND, *Sixth Annual Report*, HMSO, 1974, p. 3.

6.32 WATER SPACE AMENITY COMMISSION, *Who Are We and What Do We do?*, W.S.A.C., 1974.

6.33 MINISTRY OF LAND AND NATURAL RESOURCES, 1966, *op. cit.*

6.34 FORESTRY COMMISSION, *54th Annual Report*, HMSO, 1974, paras. 6 and 7.

6.35 WHITE, J. and DUNN, M.C., *Countryside Recreation Planning: Problems and Prospects in the West Midlands*, Occasional Paper No. 33, Centre for Urban and Regional Studies, University of Birmingham, 1975.

6.36 THORBURN, A., 'Regional Sports Councils: too much power?' *The Planner*, 61, 8, September/October, 1975, p. 298.

6.37 DOWER, M., 'Attitudes to man and the land', Symposium on Work and Leisure, Salford, 1973, para. 20.

6.38 *Ibid*, para 10.

6.39 YOUNG, M. and WILLMOTT, P., *The Symmetrical Family*, Routledge & Kegan Paul, 1973.

6.40 RAPOPORT, R. and RAPOPORT, R.N., *Leisure and the Family Life Cycle*, London, Routledge & Kegan Paul, 1975.

6.41 DAVIDSON, J., 'A Changing Countryside', Ch. 20 in WARREN, A. and GOLDSMITH, F.B., (Eds.), *Conservation in Practice, op. cit.*

Further Reading

APPLETON, I. (Ed.), *Leisure Research and Policy*, Scottish Academic Press, 1974.

CHERRY, G.E., *Environmental Planning 1939-1969, Volume II: National Parks and Recreation in the Countryside*, HMSO, 1975.

COPPOCK, J.T. and DUFFIELD, B.S., *Recreation in the Countryside: A Spatial Analysis*, Macmillan, 1975.

PARKER, S., *The Future of Work and Leisure*, MacGibbon and Kee, 1971.

PATMORE, J.A., *Land and Leisure*, David and Charles, 1970..

RAPOPORT, R. and RAPOPORT, R.N., *Leisure and the Family Life Cycle*, Routledge & Kegan Paul, 1975.

SELECT COMMITTEE OF THE HOUSE OF LORDS ON SPORT AND LEISURE, *Second Report*, HMSO, 1973.

WARREN, A. and GOLDSMITH, F.B., (Eds.), *Conservation in Practice*, John Wiley, 1974.

WHITE, J. and DUNN, M.C., *Countryside Recreation Planning: Problems and Prospects in the West Midlands*, Occasional Paper No. 33, Centre for Urban and Regional Studies, University of Birmingham, 1975.

YOUNG, M. and WILLMOTT, P., *The Symmetrical Family*, Routledge & Kegan Paul, 1973.

CHAPTER SEVEN

Conclusions and Reflections

Gordon E. Cherry

Towards a conceptual framework

The Scott Report on Land Utilisation in Rural Areas (1942) (7.1) carefully reviewed the countryside scene as it had appeared to observers at the end of the 1930s. It looked at changes which had occurred over the past decades, noting the decline in arable farming in favour of pasture and, after World War I, the dereliction of the countryside as the general state of British agriculture became depressed. It looked too at the drift from the land and the reasons for it. In the first place there was the great disparity between rural and urban wages: in 1923 the average agricultural wage ranged from about £1.25 to about £1.60 for a 50-54 hour week, in comparison with £1.75 to £2.50 per week for an unskilled industrial labourer working between 42 and 48 hours. By 1939, the average agricultural wage had risen to a range of about £1.60 to £1.87½ and unskilled labourers to £2.15 to £3.00 for the same working hours as in 1923.

Lack of capital meant restricted opportunity for advancement on the farm. Housing conditions were poor and the worker in the tied cottage enjoyed no protection under the Rent Restrictions Acts. Standards of accommodation were low; less than 30,000 agricultural holdings out of 366,000 were served with electricity in 1938; one-seventh were without piped water, and sewerage systems were scarce. Furthermore, education facilities were much inferior to those in the town.

261

This analysis of the general state of rural communities in the late 1930s testified to a long economic history with an implied pattern of social relations. The planner in looking at today's problems is helped by an understanding of rural history, just as much as urban history, with which he is probably more familiar. He has access to a wide range of literature, dealing with such matters as the history of British agriculture, the rural labourer, landed society, the landscape and the enclosure movements. The historian, economic historian, historical geographer, and others, all provide the background in such titles as *History of British Agriculture, 1846-1914* (C.S. Orwin and E.H. Whetham, 1964), *The Village Labourer* (J.L. and B. Hammond, 1911), *The Making of the English Landscape* (W.G. Hoskins, 1957), *English Landed Society in the 19th Century* (F.M.L. Thompson, 1963), and *A New Historical Geography of England* (Ed.) H.C. Darby, 1973). The totality of this scene has recently been interpreted by Raymond Williams in *The Country and the City* (1973) in which he relates English literature to rural social change.

Williams reminds us that rural England has indeed undergone a long transformation; significantly earlier than any other country in Europe there had been an enforced dissolution of a true peasantry; it had been replaced by capitalist agriculture with its labour system based on rent and wages. In Scotland and Ireland the problem of absentee and alien landlords added nationalist dimensions. Well before the nineteenth century the capitalist order in farming had been established; even in the eighteenth century about half the cultivated land of Britian was owned by 5000 families, and nearly one-quarter by only 400 families.

At the other end of the spectrum from the large landowner, the aristocracy and the squirearchy, there were the labourers, for whom during the nineteenth century there was only little improvement to record. In the two decades after 1815, in particular, large numbers of agricultural labourers were on poor relief, wages were low and rick burning was only just one manifestation of discontent. But not solely in this period, throughout the century rural Britain was the scene of struggle: between owners and tenants and between employers and workers. Dispute centred on rents and leases, on wages and the right to form unions, on prices and the relation of domestic production to exports in a free trade economy. Sustained emigration from the countryside both to the towns and to the colonies overseas was the result, and migration rates were pronounced between the 1850s and the 1890s. In the latter part of this period, British agriculture was hit by the Great Depression, and in particular, the wheat growing counties of the east and south suffered from the import of cheap grain. The triple influences of the opening up of the North American wheatlands, railway expansion in that continent, and the development of the steamship dealt a heavy blow to Britain. By comparison, the pasture counties suffered less because of the continuing and, indeed, increasing demand for home meat and dairy produce. By the end of the turbulent nineteenth century, the numbers of people actually employed on the land had not greatly changed (indeed the figures for 1801 and 1881 were the same). But substantial changes relative to the national workforce had taken place. At the beginning of the twentieth century less than one in ten of all workers were employed in agriculture, though at the beginning of the nineteenth one in three had been so engaged. During the twentieth century this decline has continued, as we have seen (see page 132).

The Scott Report's review was therefore an illustration, a snapshot at a particular time, of the long-term consequences of agrarian capitalism as it had flourished in the nineteenth century and had become depressed in the face of changing world markets. Post-war Britain was to address itself to solutions which restored British agriculture, the conditions of labour and the standard of accommodation of the farming communities. A good deal was done in the wartime years themselves. Life was brought back to the countryside with agriculture promoted to a new strategic significance, new manpower of evacuees, prisoners of war and the land army, and new local markets from defence establishments.

The Scott Report also looked at the impact of town on country, particularly the suburban spread of the inter-war years. The Committee observed: "The agricultural depression had so intensified the weakness of the countryside to the encroachment of the town, that land considered suitable for building could be purchased readily, irrespective of its agricultural usage or quality. Far larger tracts were thus bought than were needed for immediate development and were allowed to lie idle and become derelict. So the towns spread out and sprawled over the countryside in ways that have been both terribly wasteful of agricultural land and also inimical to the development of any real community life in the suburban fringes themselves" (para. 71). Some 3,800,000 dwellings were built on agricultural land between the wars, and an articulate protest grew in volume about the desecration of the countryside. Clough Williams-Ellis in *England and the Octopus* as early as 1928 could write, "Mercifully, and perhaps just in time, there is now a small minority, even passio-

263

nately alive to our misdeeds both past and present, and determined that, so far as in them lies, England shall cease to grow less lovely year by year, but shall halt, then face about, and begin to regain order and beauty" (7.2).

But it was not just house building that attracted adverse attention; it was also the attendant ramifications of the urban invasion of the countryside. There was an increase in road traffic, a proliferation of snack bars and filling stations, and a rash of unsightly advertising; holiday settlements sprawled, the coast was despoiled, and the countryside suffered the weekend invasion of the recreation minded urbanite, the rambler and the hiker. No wonder Patrick Abercrombie asked Wordsworth's question:

> Is then no nook of English ground secure
> From rash assault? (7.3)

Abercrombie of course had been prominent in the interests of the Council for the Preservation of Rural England (CPRE). There was also a Council for Rural Wales and together they formed one of the most articulate and respected lobbies for rural amenities and landscape conservation. This was well seen in their pressure for National Parks.

All these preservation issues were prominent in planning thinking during the years of wartime reconstruction. Land planning and amenity control featured strongly in the development of post-war policy and a strictly preservationist view of the countryside took root. It is not too much to say that this theme has remained throughout the last 30 years to all intents and purposes, and has given rural planning its essential rationale. Urban sprawl was to be avoided; agriculture's revival was to be protected; rural communities were to be buttressed by assistance in jobs and social services. A relatively static, little change future was envisaged. But the assumptions soon proved faulty. Continual loss of agricultural manpower could not be matched by new employment, and out-migration in many areas has persisted. On the other hand, urban affluence and personal mobility through the motor car has encouraged a persistent attraction towards forms of rural or semi-rural living. The scene has changed sharply over 30 years: the new problems need to be identified and new policies forged. We need a conceptual framework.

By comparison, urban planning is rather more favoured. For example, an urban template is given by the growth and development of the British city during the nineteenth and twentieth centuries in terms of capitalist dynamics. Industrial capitalism created and exploited the city; particular kinds of economic and social order ensued. Post industrial capitalism has continued to feed on the city, sometimes in new ways, for example the exploitation of land values. The economic and social structure of the city is now manifested in spatial forms, changing over time with typical distributions of primary land use and areas of social advantage and disadvantage. In other words, the urban planner has a broad model of the nature of the physical, economic and social problems before him: their origins, evolution, relationships, and their likely patterns of change. He can therefore begin to consider how to fashion possible tools of intervention in order to encourage forces of change which are to community benefit and resist those which are not.

The rural planner is not nearly in such a good position. As we have observed, there has been a marked lack of interest in many rural questions, and an overall framework of understanding has not so far emerged. As a consequence, rural planning has been a patchwork of bits and pieces with fragmentation of effort being the keynote. At the very most, it has had a land-orientated fixation, which might be overplayed. So far British rural planning has never had a broad conceptual model before it, and it is small wonder that the various problems which emerge are tackled in either an uncoordinated way, or in a manner which is over-dependent on outmoded policies. We need to begin, therefore, by considering whether a coherent statement as to the nature of rural planning problems can be offered.

One way of making sense of the present scene in the context of many centuries of history is to regard the process of rural change as the progressive substitution of one dominant economic and social order over another. Over a number of centuries the feudal order was replaced by an agrarian capitalist order. Over the last 100 years we have seen how the enfeeblement of agrarian capitalism produced the twentieth century problems to which planning in its widest sense has reacted: land, poverty, insecurity of jobs, housing squalor, community disadvantage and restriction of opportunity. In the last 30 years new forms of conflict have arisen, and others have been sharpened as one dominant value system has challenged another: the urbanite earmarks rural land for recreation, urban water needs takes over rural farm land for reservoirs, the city dweller moves into rural housing.

The rural planner needs this broad contextual picture before him. The problems which the community expect him to tackle are those of conflict and clash of values; they arise when one dominant form of development challenges and perhaps supercedes another. The long recurrent thread is the economic drive of agrarian capitalism with its related social order; the more immediate source of difficulty is the economic and political power of largely urban values over countryside interests. In either case, the cost has been, and is, social displacement. The problem for today's rural planner focusses on both land and people; we have fashioned a tool, of sorts, in land use control but we have developed little understanding of the nature of the interrelated social problems.

The emergence of the capitalist landlord came early in British history. We go back to the clearance of the woodlands, the drainage of the marshlands, the recovery of waste, and the early enclosure movement needed to secure more pasture for the wool trade. By the eighteenth century a structure of tenant farmers and wage-labourers had emerged, and the parliamentary enclosure movement of the eighteenth and nineteenth centuries firmly cemented these social relationships in agrarian capitalism. From the 1750s to the 1820s, 6 million acres (2.4 million ha) of land were appropriated through nearly four thousand Acts, by, in the main, landowners with political power. This was equivalent to a quarter of all the country's cultivated land, and it set the seal on a long process of concentration of land holding. The economic system of landlord, tenant and labour was finally asserted, and many of the landless became the working class of the new industrial towns.

The enclosure of the wastes and of open arable land, together with the technological aspects of the agricultural revolution dramatically increased crop yields and home food production. Later in the nineteenth century British agriculture could not meet the competition of cheaper producers overseas and the countryside entered the twentieth century beset with problems: economic difficulties of the agriculture industry, a countryside ripe for new forms of exploitation and an inherited social structure characterized by massive disadvantages. The years of this century have seen one form after another of competing claims on rural land and facilities which the countryside has found difficult to withstand.

The first form of rural exploitation was for urban building. The twentieth century has not only needed to house an increased population, it has demanded that it be accommodated at much lower densities than ever before. Suburban space, air and sunlight has been an imperative which has transformed the physical form of the British city. Urban man has successively moved into the countryside. Ebenezer Howard's Garden City was an urban solution imposed on the countryside which did nothing to relieve rural Britain from its economic and social problems; only marginally did it offer a revivified British agriculture and a new market for local produce. Since then, either as peripheral suburbanization or as new or expanded towns set in the countryside, urban man has treated the countryside as his, as something to live in, as a resource to take over. He has not been content to live at high densities in cities of an earlier type; he had abandoned the concept of the tightly knit, medieval city surrounded by its agricultural hinterland; his own values and preferences are imposed on the countryside.

Another form of exploitation and super-imposition of dominant interests is represented by the urbanite's discovery of the countryside for recreation purposes. A new-found mobility through the flexibility of road transport, increased through ever-widening private ownership, gave the city dweller from the 1920s onwards access to the farm land, hills and dales, moor and forest of the British countryside. The 1920s and 1930s were the heyday of the hikers, ramblers, cyclists and tourists, and conflict of interest abounded. The hikers clashed with the landowners of the grouse moors and the issue of trespass was emotive. The six men convicted at Derby Assizes in 1932 for trespass on Kinderscout enter into the history of the Access to Mountains Act, 1939, and, later, the National Parks and Access to Countryside Act, 1949 (7.4). But the tidal wave of urban weekenders clashed with many established interests: the farmers, those who wished to protect the peace and tranquility of village environments, and those who sought to protect rural visual amenities from the eyesores of urban development.

The erosion of the countryside has also been effected through the piecemeal invasion of the urban resident (quite apart from the massive suburbanization process). The seventeenth and eighteenth century country house with its landscaped garden was an early example of the city dweller identifying a rural location for residential purposes. The twentieth century is different in terms of the scale of the operation, but the principle is very similar: there are preferred locations for living and the economically and politically powerful urbanite sees advantages in exercising his choice in a rural setting. In both cases, the seventeenth century town merchant with his country seat and the twentieth century middle-class representative, the result may be social dislocation for the rural community. The present day town dweller who takes over a country cottage as a second home for holiday purposes or retires into a village community is demonstrating his economic power, political articulation and set of values which may be at sharp variance from those of his new neighbour.

A whole set of urban land uses is now demanded of the country-side. Once again a conflict of interests is apparent. A proposed National Park for Central Wales came to nought because of the weight of local opposition; country parks as honeypots for urban interests may be bitterly contested among many sectional interests. Land for industry is required: Milford Haven, Trawsfynydd and Nigg may have been decided in the 'national interest' but they represented fundamentally different interests from many of those in the local community which has had to withstand the consequences of the development. Local demands for sites for sand and gravel, mineral extraction, ironstone mining, oil rig construction, quarrying or potash mining constantly throw up disputes. Land for urban water is a heavy demand; battles over Cow Green (Teesdale) or in South Devon are classic examples of confrontation which result from clashes of interest; whose requirements are the greater, and how do we adjudicate on this question?

And so we see the countryside as a scene of confrontation. There are many problems which are consequences of agrarian capitalism and its evolution over many centuries. There are other problems which are consequences of contemporary conflicts between urban and rural, social class and sectional interests which relate to land and social preferences. This is the context which the rural planner should have in mind as he is called upon to devise public policy in the name of planning. This measure of understanding should help to give a sense of direction to rural planning and a comprehensive purpose to strategies of land management, employment, community affairs and recreation. Local policies relating to housing, key settlement location, transport, service provision and land use control fit into this framework.

The rural planning system

In the light of this framework of understanding, we must now consider the adequacy of the present statutory planning system and its institutional arrangements in relation to the countryside. The early years of planning legislation were entirely urban oriented, the focus being on the preparation of town planning schemes, which were largely measures for regulating suburban expansions. Indeed, it was not until the Town and Country Planning Act, 1932, that the word 'country' entered into legislation for the first time—and it is significant that that Act began life as a Rural Amenities Bill. From the operative date of 1st April 1933, the opportunity was given for the preparation of planning schemes for rural as well as urban areas. This was not an obligatory duty, and so throughout the inter-war period, 20 years of active development in rural areas, Britain had no compulsory planning system in relation to the countryside. Regulation proceeded by locally determined 'interim development control'; it was assisted by voluntary agreements with landowners to avoid payment of compensation for the carrying out of development at very low densities, and a loose framework of regional planning carried out by Joint Planning Committees of a large number of planning authorities. The Restriction of Ribbon Development Act, 1935 only succeeded in widening the 'ribbon' and Green Belt legislation for London and the Home Counties in 1938 depended on voluntary cooperation for its implementation.

Inherent weaknesses like these were resolved in the Town and Country Planning Act, 1947, which provided the essential basis for post-war land planning. County Development Plans were required to form the basis for controlling future development over a 20 year period, particular proposals being programmed for the first 5 and the subsequent 15 years of the Plan period. Development control was exercised against the provisions of the Plan. In practice, as the County Plans came to be submitted during the 1950s, there were very few land proposals for the rural areas other than 'no change'. Detail was largely confined to the urban areas, which were covered by Town Maps; by comparison, the countryside was seen as a residual area outside the limits of urban expansion and was technically termed 'white land' which was considered unlikely to change in land use during the Plan period. Some Counties went a little further than this and dealt with such matters as rural settlement policies, design of buildings, mineral working, landscaping and restoration of derelict land. But with hindsight, we can now observe that the planning system focussed remarkably on two things: land use control in which agricultural interests were paramount (criteria of land quality were slavishly followed) and protection of landscape amenity. Questions of development came a poor third, and the planner moved into a position of freezing the countryside as a visual landscape. Social questions of village life were neatly linked to school provision in the Educational Development Plan and the provision of County facilities such as community centres, libraries

269

and health clinics. It was assumed that a healthy agriculture, such additions to employment as could be made and modernization of essential services would provide an adequate basis for village life.

The National Parks and Access to the Countryside Act, 1949, led to the designation of National Parks and Areas of Outstanding Natural Beauty and gave a further seal of landscape protection to the areas in question. Duncan Sandys' Green Belt Circular of 1955 gave encouragement to Local Authorities to give special protection to the urban fringes of the major urban areas. The Civic Amenities Act, 1967, required Local Authorities to designate as conservation areas those parts of their areas which are of special architectural or historic interest; the careful preservation of parts of country towns has benefited from this measure. The Countryside Act, 1968, (1967 for Scotland) established the Countryside Commissions and gave further powers for the conservation of natural beauty and amenity of the countryside. The Local Government Act, 1972, set up new Executive Park Authorities, provided for the appointment of National Park Officers, and required the preparation of National Park Plans.

The Town and Country Planning Act, 1968, replaced the Development Plan by the Structure Plan, a more flexible and adaptive device, not tied to a fixed time scale and subject to continuous review. Moreover, the intention is that the issues of land use and development be seen more effectively in their economic and social contexts. Public participation in the preparation of the plans is hoped to release the nature of community needs and aspirations. County Structure Plans are still mostly in the preparation stage and it is too early to say how far the Structure Plan system is capable of getting to the heart of complex economic and social problems in countryside areas.

Another planning level has been provided by the Regional Economic Planning Councils. During the later 1960s the whole country was covered by their Regional Plans. There have been other regional plans, such as for the South East and the North West, produced by joint teams of Central Government and Local Authorities. These have dealt largely with urban questions, and because they have been prepared during periods of economic growth and active building they have largely been concerned with land allocation questions. There has been no significant addition to the ideas of countryside planning through these plans.

Throughout the whole of the post-war period, development control has remained an essential feature of the planning system.

The 1947 Act indicated a number of operations which did not constitute development and which therefore did not require planning permission. One of these was "the use of any land for the purposes of agriculture or forestry (including afforestation) and the use of any of these purposes of any building occupied together with the land so used". The present situation is that a large number of farm buildings are exempt planning control; planning permission is only required for new buildings above a certain size (exceeding 465 square metres in area or 12 metres in height) or close to main roads (buildings within 25 metres of a trunk or classified road). Farm buildings have a major impact on the landscape: tall silos and factory style agricultural buildings for example require permission, but a wide range of smaller buildings do not.

Alongside this statutory planning framework there are also other elements of planning which have an important bearing on the countryside. The agriculture industry is looked after by the Ministry of Agriculture, Fisheries and Food. Liaison with Local Authorities is made through its Agricultural Development and Advisory Services and Land Services Divisions. Forestry is the responsibility of the Forestry Commission; nature reserves the responsibility of the Nature Conservancy Council. With regard to industry and employment, the Development Commission, established in 1909, occupies a special place in encouraging the development of the economic life of the countryside. Its relationship with the Council for Small Industries in Rural Areas is a close one. But responsibilities for employment planning are somewhat scattered: the tourist industry for example is the responsibility of the National Tourist Boards in England, Wales and Scotland.

Other aspects of countryside life have their own frameworks. Rural electrification to an extensive degree was a consequence of the nationalization of the electricity industry in 1947. The Rural Water Supplies and Sewerage Act, 1944, secured the extension of piped water supplies, sewerage and sewage disposal facilities. Since 1974, the new Regional Water Authorities and the Welsh National Water Development Authority have taken over responsibility for these services, with the prospect of more effective coordination with those responsible for land drainage and water pollution.

Public housing provision is a Local Authority responsibility, exercised formerly by the Rural District Councils. Sport, leisure and recreation is dealt with by the Local Authorities (in which there can be a tantalizing lack of relationship between Planning and Education) and the *ad hoc* bodies, namely the Sports Councils and the

271

Countryside Commissions. Road programmes are the responsibility of the Department of the Environment. Public transport now has a useful planning focus in the County Council's Transport Policies and Programmes (TPPs). First commenced in 1974, they are annual submissions to the Department of the Environment to justify the Council's claim on the Transport Block Grant.

The institutional framework is therefore highly fragmented. In addition to Regional Economic Planning Councils, County Councils, District Councils and Parish Councils, there is the Department of the Environment, Ministry of Agriculture and Fisheries, and Department of Trade (tourism). The other Government Departments of Education, Trade and Industry, Health and Social Security obviously have their remits. In addition there are other national organizations: the Development Commission, Sports Councils, Countryside Commissions and Nature Conservancy Councils. Voluntary bodies are well represented in the councils for the Protection of Rural England and Wales, the National Council of Social Service, the Civic Trust, the Women's Institutes and the Committee for Environmental Conservation.

Contemporary problems

We have stressed so far that the essential problems before rural Britain are in respect of competition: competing claims on land and resources from different sectional interests with economic and political power. There are different value systems within the rural communities themselves based on an inherited social order, but there are also different urban-based values which clash with rural interests. We suggest that most of the problems which the rural planner has to deal with have these origins. The main issues then are social in origin and their resolution has social consequences. The issues are complex and interrelated and can rarely be resolved without reference to other factors. As with urban planning, it is most unlikely that land oriented policies alone will adequately provide a planning strategy for the countryside.

Conflict is the keynote then, and it may be readily illustrated from a variety of settings. For example, the Editors to *Dartmoor* in the New Naturalist Series wrote in their Preface: "The competing claims of national defence, water supply, mineral working, afforestation, hill sheep-farming, public recreation and nature conservation which affect so many of the remoter parts of Britain are here all concentrated in one compact area in the heart of a single county. Should a television mast be allowed to rear its head in this domain of wild nature? Are man-made lakes a desecratation or a desideratum? Do planted conifers destroy or enhance the landscape?" (7.5). The Editors might have gone on to ask 'and who decides these questions and against what criteria?'

At a different level, a rural sociologist, Anthony Russell, captures the conflict of interests in village life, contrasting the ethos, attitudes and expectations of locally born, lower income groups with urban, expatriate, middle-class newcomers. The contrast "may be thrown into relief by the possibility of a major local development such as a new town, a motorway, an oil rig construction base or an inland airport. Assuming that the proposed development will not damage their living environment too severely, it seems that members of this group (the locally born) welcome the opportunities and amenities that such a development would bring. By contrast, the urban expatriate having moved to a village, among other reasons, for its peace and beauty, is more likely to be found providing the leadership for the local conservation, preservation or amenity group" (7.6).

The lesson to be learned from these illustrations is that it is increasingly difficult to make assumptions about the resolution of particular problems which are shared by the whole population of an affected area, village or community. The problems of housing, transport, and provision of health and welfare services bear differently on community groups. With these thoughts in mind, we can now turn to highlight the problems identified in earlier chapters; they relate to land, to people, their activities and the community services they require. Lastly, we consider the problems inherent in the planning system itself.

Land. As David Robinson reminds us in Chapter 5, the land use pattern of rural Britain is dominated by rural land uses, and in lowland England, at least, by agriculture. This remains so even in the relatively urbanized regions such as in South-East England where 36% is given over to urban land uses or in North-West England where the figure is 29%. But we know that urban growth, particularly since the 1920s, has had severe implications for the countryside: there have been demands for more building land, roads, airports, mineral working, water storage and holiday making, particularly on the coast. The provision of urban land has increased throughout the century from around 20 ha (50 acres) per thousand population at about 1900 to 34 ha (84 acres) per thousand population in 1971 through a radical lowering of densities and complementary improvement in the provision of urban living space (7.7).

The years most heavily charged with anxious speculation about the future (largely because of the unavailability of accurate data) and most marked by protest were the 1930s—a formative decade for post-war planning policies relating to land use control and country-side preservation. In the 12 years before 1939 the urbanization of rural land was proceeding at about 60,000 acres (25,000 ha) a year. This meant that more than 2% of the entire area of England changed from rural to urban in that time. The annual rate of urbanization since 1945 has only been half this. Nonetheless, with a projected population explosion from the 1960s to the end of the century there was real concern as to the preservation of agricultural land. This was nicely allayed by Edwards and Wibberley in their preparation of an agricultural land budget for Britain to the year 2000. Their conclusion was that "the overall land use position of this country should not be difficult in terms of the availability of land for all major uses . . . there should be enough land area for us to use—but, of course, we shall have the constant problem of using it wisely or unwisely" (7.8).

It is at this point that the conservation movement has so much to offer. O'Connor has usefully differentiated between a number of different aims of conservation. First, there is species conservation, a concern for the protection of rare, interesting or beautiful species. Then, there is habitat conservation, concerned with the maintenance of representative habitat types. But of greater importance for the rural planner are two other aspects of conservation: on the one hand conservation as an attitude to land use ("an input to land-use planning and management so that the demands of people upon natural systems can be balanced against their ability to support them"), and on the other, creative conservation (large-scale modification of the landscape through motorway construction, and reclamation of derelict land) (7.9). Nan Fairbrother has beautifully illustrated how conservation, landscape design and resource planning might be taken up at the present time (7.10). She thought in terms of landscape organization, landscape pattern, landscape material, and landscape texture to produce a total environment to translate land use, population densities, settlement patterns, traffic flow and local site conditions into physical reality.

People. In earlier Chapters a good deal of attention has been given to the pressure of urban population on rural areas. Michael Dunn, Ian Martin and Alan Rogers, in Chapters 1-3, have all noted this particular problem. The introduction of the urbanites and the appearance of the urbanized village is an adequately explored theme, although certainly one which can hardly be exaggerated.

Perhaps we should give more attention to the employment problems in rural areas. The transformation of British agriculture through mechanization and rationalization has reduced the national labour force working on the land to about 4% of the total. In the light of this situation, planning attitudes to the introduction of other forms of employment, particularly industry, have been cautious and ambivalent. Andrew Gilg in Chapter 4 has sketched the general background, and we might now take up these factors in relation to others, particularly land use and community attitudes.

The first part of the Development and Road Improvement Funds Act, 1909 (an Act "to promote the Economic Development of the United Kingdom and the Improvement of Roads therein") laid the early foundations of an organization for rural industries. But for a long time it was the beleaguered position of the country craftsman that attracted Government attention. In the early 1920s in the light of a rapid fall in and World prices of farm products heavy taxation including the incidence of death duties, the break up of rural estates began. The survival of rural crafts was an identifiable problem and it was realistic at that time to contemplate a measure of Government support. In 1921 the Trustees of the Rural Industries Intelligence Bureau were appointed, and in the same year the first Rural Community Councils were created. Four years later, they received grants to employ Rural Industries Organizers. By 1939 the Rural Industries Bureau had an administrative, technical and clerical staff of 20. By 1948 the figure had doubled and in 1958 the total had reached 113 (7.11).

Meanwhile the Scott Report reflected particular attitudes towards industrial development. The Report had been written in strongly preservationist terms; great anxiety had been expressed to protect the countryside from any large scale invasion of urban industry. But in a Minority Report Professor S.R. Dennison disagreed. His view was that "it is by the introduction of some industrial development that there is most hope of the improvement of the social and economic conditions in the countryside, in the future as in the past" (para. 38, p. 112). Bonham Carter writing in *The English Village* (1952) took the same line, but most early post-war County Development Plans adopted a strictly preservationist approach. The trend was set by the example of the County Plan for Herefordshire, *English County, A Planning Survey of Herefordshire*, 1946.

It is probably fair to say that a characteristic planning response would still be to fight shy of industrial development on a large scale in rural areas. Where it has occurred at all, it has generally been regarded as exceptional, necessary because of overriding pressures and therefore something to accept resignedly, as in the case of nuclear power stations, oil developments or new coalfields. Only in the Highlands of Scotland, as evidenced in the pulpmill at Fort William and new industrial development in the Moray Firth, has there been a positive planning strategy to introduce large scale industry into the countryside.

The worst employment problems occur in the marginal regions. The problem is hardest to solve, and when development does occur, with new employment gains, it is accompanied by the most extreme of social pressures. The exploration of North Sea Oil and its implications for Shetland, Orkney and certain coastal settlements in both West and East Scotland provides a classic contemporary dilemma and brings together all the aspects of confrontation and conflict that have been considered in this book. On the west coast at Drumbuie the search for an oil rig construction site led to a passionate objection on grounds of amenity; many of the local residents in the job-starved area of Kyle and Plockton perhaps saw the issue differently. In spite of the oil company's claim that Drumbuie's deep water location was the only one possible site in that area of Scotland, none the less when development at Drumbuie was refused, a site across the sea inlet at Kishorn was duly identified and approved. Development has since proceeded rapidly and it has not been without its problems. The majority of the workforce is accommodated on site in comfortable quarters and with recreation facilities, but the spill over effect in the Loch Carron area is appreciable; the introduction of a high earning, new labouring group in an area of heavy drinking could not be otherwise. Social disturbance is magnified over the question of Sunday working and observance of the Sabbath, and it is here that social value systems come into collision. This issue is even worse on Lewis where the outwardly religious codes are even more uncompromising.

Shetland has a more robust society than the North West and the Islands. Extreme forms of religious organization have not been part of social life in the past, and the local community has a more pragmatic capacity to deal with new situations. Certainly, the effect of oil at Shetland is enormous, and the way the County Council as representatives of a mere 18,000 inhabitants have stood up to the legions of the multi-national oil companies is almost a fairy tale and an allegory of David and Goliath proportions. But now there is a fair chance that oil development will exploit neither the land of the Shetlands nor its people in quite the way that unbridled opportunism might have resulted. However, storage facilities and refinery development at Sullom Voe will irredeemably affect this beautiful and wild inlet and new expanded townships will accompany this development. The landscape will undoubtedly be affected and the community structure will be hard pressed to accommodate to this change. Social processes of change will be speeded up, expectations perhaps over-released with consequent frustrations and community tensions heightened.

Judy White (Chapter 6) and Andrew Gilg (Chapter 4) both touched on another aspect of employment for rural communities: tourism. The agricultural economy of England and Wales receives between £40m—£50m from the business of providing for tourism and educational facilities. Between 10-15,000 farmers cater for tourists or recreationists through self-catering cottages, flats, camping and caravan sites, equestrian centres, fisheries, farm parks and visitor centres. But tourism provides another good example of clash of interests. If we take Cornwall as an extreme county example, at peak times half the population are holidaymakers. The powerful hotel and catering interests are confronted by local people who object to crowded roads and to the environmental damage that is inflicted. The revival of interest in the Cornish language, the rise of the political organization Mebyon Kernow (Sons of Cornwall), attempts to revive the ancient Stannary Parliament, and the stirring of public opinion in the Cornwall Conservation Forum (a group which calls for a limit on tourism) are all indications of a local determination not to erode any further the quality of Cornishness. It is not for us to say whether some of these bodies or ideas are quaint, rather to acknowledge that planning for tourism operates in this context of tension with local community values.

Services and facilities. The difficulties in maintaining adequate community services and standards of provision in rural communities have been illustrated particularly by Ian Martin in Chapter 2. There is a vicious circle out of which it is not easy to escape. A declining population means contracting services, which reinforces the trend to leave the countryside; key settlement policies might halt

277

the trend in selected areas, but abandoned districts become all the more isolated. Two examples may be stressed in this final Chapter which illustrate the complexities of the situation and how one aspect of rural planning may be interrelated with another; one has been touched on before (rural transport), another (ecclesiastical organization) has not.

For nearly 20 years various considerations have been given to the question of rural transport. In 1959 a Government Committee was set up under Professor D.T. Jack to study rural bus services. Its Report was published in 1961 under the title *Rural Bus Services.* Community hardship and inconvenience was acknowledged and various solutions were advocated. These included the carrying of fare-paying passengers on school buses and postal buses, an extended use of mini-buses, and a combined carriage of goods and passengers. The Jack Report's major recommendation, however, was a measure of financial aid to support rural bus services, the first time indeed that subsidies had been officially considered.

Six rural areas were selected in 1963 by the then Minister of Transport, Ernest Marples, in order that detailed studies might be undertaken. The areas were in the following Counties: Devon, west of Crediton; Montgomeryshire, west of Welshpool; Lincolnshire, north of Horncastle; Westmorland, north of Kirby Stephen; Kirk-cudbrightshire, north of Dumfries; and Banffshire, around Tomint-oul. Six hundred people were interviewed and 39,000 journeys recorded. The findings were published in *Rural Bus Services: Report of Preliminary Results,* 1963.

Further local enquiries were mounted in 1964 in four case studies: in Lincolnshire, Westmorland and Montgomeryshire (as above) and Northamptonshire. This time there were a number of practical experiments. These included such tests as the operation of new routes, extra timings for work people, fare paying passengers on school buses, market day services, evening journeys and additions to Sunday time-tables.

The subsidy nettle was grasped in the 1968 Transport Act. Both railway and bus companies benefited through grants for capital improvement and subsidies for unremunerative services which were considered necessary on social grounds. County and District Councils were enabled to grant-aid loss making rural services, and the Minister could make 50% grants to bus operators for investment in approved new vehicles. By 1970 the National Bus Company was admitting that its principle of cross subsidization had failed to provide for a large part of the community and in that year it instructed its subsidiary operators to abandon or drastically reduce its loss making services unless Local Authorities were prepared to provide grants under the terms of the 1968 Act.

And so the problem remains, unresolved and showing all the symptoms of getting worse. In 1972, the Local Government Act established the duty of the County Council in preparing coordinated transport plans, and since 1974 the device of the TPP (Transport Policies and Programmes) submitted annually to the Minister at least allows for yearly reviews of policy. The TPPs will perhaps focus attention on the underlying questions. In the first instance, there is the matter of needs and access. What are the needs of the different social, income and age groups in the rural communities? How can these needs be measured? What are the facilities to which access is most demanded? What are the social consequences of access being denied? Second, there are some action research questions to follow up. Actual events, such as the inauguration of a new service or the withdrawal of another needs to be followed through. Exactly how do people respond to these new arrangements? Third, there are institutional matters to consider. What really is the scope for integration? What level of support and subsidies is appropriate and who bears the cost? Questions like these are being examined in a study of rural transport and accessibility at the Centre of East Anglian Studies, University of East Anglia.

A very different kind of service in the countryside is that of the Ministry through churches of various denominations. In a period of steady contraction in the number of parochial clergy and non-conformist ministers there are at least two particular problems to which we can draw attention. One concerns the close social relationship which exists between a village community and its church(es). Declining church attendance does not necessarily imply disregard for the future of the church building: as Russell has written, "threat of structural collapse or closure will reveal an extent of feeling for the church which will go far beyond the worshipping congregation". He suggests that in some villages the church becomes a 'surrogate' village: "As other organizations and foci for the self-identification of the community have closed or dwindled through lack of support . . . so often the church is left, almost in spite of itself, as the only available symbol of village sentiment" (7.12).

A second point concerns the re-use of church buildings. What is to become of redundant churches? The Diocese of Norwich has 700 medieval buildings alone. Most certainly the problem of maintaining and probably re-using church buildings in the countryside is a real one. Dioceses such as St. Edmondsbury and Ipswich and Bath and Wells, which have produced manpower plans in order to optimize the level of pastoral care that can reasonably be given, clearly indicate the need for, and indeed inevitability of, shared or collaborative ministries. In this situation individual buildings, most of architectural quality, may be hard to maintain. Their future is likely to be at the centre of conflicting community interests. The Redundant Churches and Other Religious Buildings Act, 1969, which provides for grants for the preservation of selected buildings which are no longer used as places of worship is unlikely to answer all the problems arising.

Previous Chapters together with this concluding overview have suggested a framework within which rural planning problems might be considered. The keynote must be that the countryside needs a viable economic base in order that its communities might survive. Over most of lowland England that base is present, but sometimes only just, as is evident by sustained out-migration rates. Over most of upland Britain, and particularly in the remoter regions, communities only exist with substantial public support to services and a tacit acceptance of high unemployment figures. Unemployment rates reaching 22% have been recorded in the Western Isles during the winter of 1976.

Given that a viable economic base will emerge for at least parts of the countryside, based on the land, tourism, service industry, distributive trades and probably an increase in manufacturing industry of an acceptable kind, the next challenge is to evolve a rationalized settlement plan based on something akin to the key village or growth centre concept. No one will pretend this is easy: a planner's dream for tidy logic is readily challenged by contradictory preferences of the general public.

In the meantime, villages and small towns have to be serviced by a variety of public, private and voluntary agencies ranging from education to health, housing, transport, shops, social services, libraries, sport, and entertainment. Some small communities are already clearly at risk because population levels have fallen below normal thresholds of service provision. It is inescapable that the public sector will have to shoulder a large and expensive burden because this in the twentieth century is where the challenge of disadvantage comes to rest. Buttresses of social support will continue to be needed for the foreseeable future.

But rural planning does not deal with a static situation. Rural

Britain is in dynamic change and critical aspects of environmental development are subject to conflicting interests: land use, landscape protection, resource conservation, housing, transport and communications and the whole amalgam of countryside amenity. Many locally born rural communities must feel they are being either exploited or swamped by urban demands. Day to day planning decisions will be taken in the context of this tension.

In some other countries this range of rural planning considerations would be the concern of a Ministry of Countryside Affairs. There is little likelihood of that in Britain, and the challenge therefore is to harness the array of Governmental Departments and institutional bodies that at present have responsibilities for rural questions. It must be the hope that the Department of the Environment, as the most likely coordinating body, would take rather more initiative in this direction. It is astonishing that the Scott Report of 1942 was the last Government sponsored review of countryside matters. It is high time that the fundamental problems and patterns of change in rural Britain were considered comprehensively and in depth in order to assist in a series of policy reviews.

In actual fact a Department of the Environment Committee has begun to study the state of the countryside and its first Report, *The Countryside—Problems and Policies* was published in August 1976. It acknowledges that the countryside is in trouble. The need to grow food and timber is increasing, while at the same time people both want to visit the country for pleasure and to preserve traditional landscapes. Village life no longer centres on farms and farmwork. There are amenity conflicts from roads, pylons, army training grounds and power stations. This sort of contemporary review is a useful new start, because it implies that changes in attitudes towards the countryside are necessary. New approaches to planning seem necessary: rural planning is not to be thought of as something tacked on to urban oriented questions; conservation should not mean opposition to change; and new planning methods should be looked at, such as area management schemes. The Report argues well for further examinations.

Meanwhile, we ought to take a hard look at our Local Government agencies. It may be that in Scotland the newly formed Regional Councils will prove to be effective bodies, but in England and Wales there must be concern for the appropriateness of the District Council/County Council system. It may be argued that now that District Councils are of an adequate size for most purposes, County Councils might become increasingly redundant, particularly because they are not large enough to take a strategic view of things. If County Councils were to be abandoned in favour of Regional Authorities (perhaps three or four counties in extent) it might be expected that these authorities would be large enough geographically and in terms of rateable value to effectively undertake strategic rural planning. This leaves us with the question of the remoter regions. The success of the Highlands and Islands Development Board suggests that this additional administrative input is necessary to give power and direction to the solution of local problems. Do we then consider Wales, the Pennines (again) and the Southern Uplands as necessary overlays to the Local Authority structure? In England and Wales at least, the conclusion must be that an additional layer of responsibility would be unwelcome and an administrative burden.

But whatever decisions we come to on these matters we should have as our base the myriad hopes and fears of countless rural communities and their planning problems to which we respond. From the Women's Institute scrapbook of Askrigg we read via Paul Jennings:

"Many of us hope that a light industry will be set up in our area, so that our young people may be able to stay here. Others fear that Askrigg may become a village of country cottage weekenders and retired people. It is hoped that Askrigg may continue as a working village.

I fear that ranch farming may result in the disappearance of our beautiful flowery meadows, because all the fields may be pastures, and that all walls except farm boundary walls may be removed, and that barns, already going out of use may be demolished.

I fear afforestation in Wensleydale.

I hope that public conveniences may be built in Askrigg.

I fear that Dales hospitality and entertaining in the home may disappear, and be replaced by inviting people to drinks and then going to a hotel for a meal.

It is hoped that parents will do their best to influence their children to attend church and chapel services." (7.13).

These are the things that provide an agenda for rural planning in Britain.

References

7.1 *Report of the Committee on Land Utilisation in Rural Areas,* Cmd. 6378, HMSO, 1942.

7.2 WILLIAMS-ELLIS, C., *England and the Octopus,* 1928, reissued by Blackie and Son, 1975.

7.3 ABERCROMBIE, P., *Town and Country Planning,* Oxford University Press, 1933.

7.4 CHERRY, G.E., *Environmental Planning, Vol. II, National Parks and Recreation in the Countryside,* HMSO, 1975.

7.5 HARVEY, L.A., St. LEGER-GORDON, D., *Dartmoor,* Collins, 1953.

7.6 RUSSELL, A.J., *The Village in Myth and Reality,* Chester House Publications, 1975.

7.7 BEST, R.H., 'The Extent and Growth of Urban Land', *The Planner,* **62,** 1, 1976.

7.8 EDWARDS, A.M. and WIBBERLEY, G.P., *An Agricultural Land Budget for Britain 1965-2000,* Studies in Rural Land Use, No. 10, Wye College, 1971.

7.9 O'CONNOR, F.B., 'The Ecological Basis for Conservation', in *Conservation in Practice,* WARREN A. and GOLDSMITH, F.B., (Eds.), Wiley, 1974.

7.10 FAIRBROTHER, N., *New Lives, New Landscapes,* The Architectural Press, 1970.

7.11 WILLIAMS, W.M., *The Country Craftsman,* Routledge and Kegan Paul, 1958.

7.12 RUSSELL, A.J, *op. cit.*

7.13 JENNINGS, P., *The Living Village,* Hodder and Stoughton, 1968.

Main Subject Index

References are given at the end of each chapter. The names of authors and the titles of sources will be found on pages 11; 44-46; 81-83; 119-22; 167-70; 210-12; 257-59; and 282-83.